Teaching Literature in
Grades Seven Through Nine

DATE DUE

FEB 20 1984			
APR 2 2 1985			
GAYLORD			

D1057614

Published for the
Indiana University English Curriculum Study Center
EDWARD B. JENKINSON, *Director*

Teaching Literature in Grades Seven Through Nine

EDITED BY

EDWARD B. JENKINSON

Director, Indiana University
English Curriculum Study Center

and

JANE STOUDER HAWLEY

Formerly *Assistant Director*,
Indiana University English
Curriculum Study Center

BLOOMINGTON *Indiana University Press* LONDON

FIFTH PRINTING 1973

Copyright © 1967 by Indiana University Press

All rights reserved

No part of this book may be reproduced or utilized in any form or by any means, electronic or mechanical, including photocopying and recording, or by any information storage and retrieval system, without permission in writing from the publisher. The Association of American University Presses' Resolution on Permissions constitutes the only exception to this prohibition.

Library of Congress catalog card number: 67-63019

Manufactured in the United States of America

cl. ISBN 0-253-35750-0   *pa. ISBN 0-253-35751-9*

PS
49
.I5
T4
1967

CONTENTS

Curric (Buck)

1030893

v

ACKNOWLEDGMENTS

The portion of the project of the Indiana University English Curriculum Study Center reported herein was supported through the Cooperative Research Program of the Office of Education, U.S. Department of Health, Education, and Welfare.

The IU Center received additional financial support from the Cummins Engine Foundation, which awarded Indiana University a grant that provided funds for meetings and equipment that could not be financed by the grant from the U.S. Office of Education.

The staff of the Indiana University English Curriculum Study Center wishes to thank William E. Wilson, former State Superintendent of Public Instruction, and Edgar B. Smith, former assistant Superintendent of Public Instruction, for launching this project in 1962 by appointing teachers to committees to help develop the courses of study and by appointing Edward B. Jenkinson, Coordinator for School English Language Arts at Indiana University, chairman of the committees. The staff further wishes to thank the State Department of Public Instruction, under the direction of Richard D. Wells, Superintendent, for distributing this volume to all junior high school teachers of English in Indiana's public schools.

Many teachers played important roles in shaping this volume by contributing ideas, by making suggestions for revisions of various units, and by experimenting with the materials in their classrooms. They painstakingly helped to eliminate errors from the various drafts; the staff of the English Curriculum Study Center accepts responsibility for the errors that remain.

Members of the state-appointed Committee on Literature that helped formulate plans for this volume include:

Dr. Dorothy Bucks, Professor of English, Hanover College

Mrs. Margaret Elam, Chairman of the English Department, Central High School, Corydon

Dr. Gary Graham, Head of the English Department, Butler University

Mrs. Ruth Herin, Chairman of the English Department, Broad Ripple High School, Indianapolis

Miss Catharine Howard, Chairman of the English Department, Mt. Vernon High School, Mt. Vernon

Mrs. Norma Kelley, Teacher of English, Oliver P. Morton High School, Hammond

Mrs. Helen Lee, Teacher of English, Central High School, Fort Wayne

Dr. Terence Martin, Professor of English, Indiana University

Mrs. Katheryn Offutt, Chairman of the English Department, Noblesville High School, Noblesville

Dr. Josephine Spear, Chairman of the English Department, University High School, Bloomington

Miss Ruth Sinks, formerly Chairman of the English Department, West Lafayette High School, West Lafayette

Thomas Walker, Teacher of English, Culver Military Academy, Culver

The following teachers who were appointed to the Committee on English for Slow-learning Students also helped to plan this volume:

Dr. Eugene A. Campanale, formerly Director of Secondary Education, Marion Public Schools, Marion

Mrs. Ethel Campbell, formerly Chairman of the English Department, Central High School, South Bend

Sister Francis de Sales, C.S.C., Teacher of English, Bishop Noll Institute, Hammond

Mrs. Susie Dewey, Supervisor of English, Terre Haute Public Schools

Mrs. Furniss Holloway, Teacher of English, Crispus Attucks High School, Indianapolis

Mrs. Annette Houston, Teacher of English, Seymour High School, Seymour

Mrs. Dorothy Lewis, Teacher of English, Clarksville High School, Clarksville

Miss Muriel Ryall, Teacher of English, New Albany High School, New Albany

The staff of the English Curriculum Study Center also wishes to thank these teachers for their invaluable suggestions after they had taught the units in their classes:

Charles Billiard, English Supervisor, Fort Wayne Community Schools, Fort Wayne

Melvin Bruns, Teacher of English, Tipton High School, Tipton

Miss Blanche Burget, Teacher of English, Tipton Junior High School, Tipton

Mrs. Emma J. Cagle, Chairman of the English Department, Brazil Senior High School, Brazil

Miss Judi Chael, Teacher of English, Aylesworth Junior High School, Portage

Mrs. Catherine Cowan, Teacher of English, Franklin Community Junior High School, Franklin

Mrs. Martha Cundiff, Teacher of English, Wilson Junior High School, Terre Haute

James Daugherty, formerly Teacher of English, Central Junior-Senior High School, South Bend

Mrs. Frances M. Davis, Teacher of English, Storer Junior High School, Muncie

Mrs. Marilyn Dearing, Teacher of English, Broad Ripple High School, Indianapolis

Mrs. Margaret S. Dillard, Teacher of English, Franklin Community High School, Franklin

Mrs. Mary Dold, Chairman of the English Department, Portage High School, Portage

Miss Sandra Sue Dragoo, Teacher of English, Lakeside Junior High School, Fort Wayne

William Eaton, Chairman of the English Department, Perry Central Junior High School, Indianapolis

Mrs. Marjorie Foster, Teacher of English, Northside Junior High School, Columbus

Mrs. Florence Fox, formerly Teacher of English, Franklin Community High School, Franklin

Miss Fay Hadley, formerly Teacher of English, River Forest Junior High School, Hobart

Mrs. Mildred Hall, Chairman of the English Department, Central Junior High School, Columbus

Mrs. Jean M. Hawley, Teacher of English, Mt. Vernon Junior High School, Mt. Vernon

Mrs. Jean Henry, Teacher of English, Wilson Junior High School, Terre Haute

Mrs. Gloria Hjerpe, Teacher of English, William A. Wirt School, Gary

Mrs. Ruth Homko, formerly Teacher of English, River Forest High School, Hobart

Wayne Huffman, Teacher of English, Lloyd D. Jones Junior High School, Marion

Mrs. Ernestine Humphreys, Chairman of the English Department, Glenn Junior High School, Terre Haute

Miss Mabel Hunter, Chairman of the English Department, Oliver P. Morton High School, Hammond

Mrs. Henrietta Isaacs, Teacher of English, Sarah Scott Junior High School, Terre Haute

Mrs. Irene Johnson, Teacher of English, Central Junior High School, Columbus

Malcolm Julian, Supervisor of English and Foreign Languages, Muncie Public Schools

Tom Keller, Chairman of the English Department, Wilson Junior High School, Terre Haute

Mrs. Margaret Klippel, formerly Teacher of English, Perry Central Junior High School, Indianapolis

Mrs. Jamie Kroft, Teacher of English, Aylesworth Junior High School, Portage

Mrs. Evelyn Lindsey, formerly Teacher of English, River Forest Junior High School, Hobart

Mrs. Evelyn M. Lovelace, Teacher of English, Perry Central Junior High School, Indianapolis

Mrs. Imogene Mander, Teacher of English, Portage High School, Portage

Miss Marian McCort, Teacher of English, Hammond Technical-Vocational School, Hammond

Mrs. Judy McKinney, formerly Teacher of English, Tipton High School, Tipton

Louis F. Meek III, Teacher of English, Northside Junior High School, Columbus

Miss Arlene Miller, formerly Teacher of English, River Forest High School, Hobart

Mrs. Isabelle Morris, Teacher of English, Noblesville Junior High School, Noblesville

Mrs. Daphene Morrison, Teacher of English, Joseph P. Tuttle Junior High School, Crawfordsville

Mrs. Neva Mount, Teacher of English, Tipton Junior High School, Tipton

Mrs. Adrian Neptune, Teacher of English, Northside Junior High School, Columbus

Nick O'Neill, Teacher of English, Perry Central Junior High School, Indianapolis

Mrs. Doris Jean Phillips, Teacher of English, Mt. Vernon Junior High School, Mt. Vernon

Paul Perkins, Teacher of English, Central Junior High School, Columbus

Mrs. Marilyn Peyton, formerly Teacher of English, Franklin Community Junior High School, Franklin

David Purvis, Teacher of English, Noblesville Junior High School, Noblesville

Charles E. Reisert, Jr., formerly Teacher of English, Northside Junior High School, Columbus

Webb Salmon, Director of Freshman Composition, Florida State University, Tallahassee, Florida

Miss Agnes Scott, Teacher of English, Marion High School, Marion

Mrs. Beverly Silvasi, Teacher of English, Oliver P. Morton High School, Hammond

Donald M. Sink, Teacher of English, Storer Junior High School, Muncie

Mrs. Betty M. Smith, Teacher of English, Penn High School, Mishawaka

Mrs. Mary Tunmer, Teacher of English, Tipton High School, Tipton

Mrs. Margaret Walker, Coordinator of Language Arts and Reading, Hammond

Mrs. Elizabeth Weddle, formerly Teacher of English, Franklin Community High School, Franklin

Mrs. Carol Wheeler, formerly Teacher of English, Aylesworth Junior High School, Portage

Mrs. Annie Wilkerson, Teacher of English, Beckman Junior High School, Gary

Mrs. Marguerite Williamson, Teacher of English, Oliver P. Morton High School, Hammond

Mrs. Barbara Winters, Teacher of English, Noblesville Junior High School, Noblesville

Fred E. Wolfe, Teacher of English, Wilson Junior High School, Muncie

Mrs. Juanita Young, Chairman of the English Department, Huntington

The staff of the English Curriculum Study Center is especially grateful to Professor Philip B. Daghlian, Department of English, Indiana University, and Professor William H. Wiatt, Department of English, Indiana University, who spent many hours discussing the volume with the staff, helping with the editing, and, in the case of some units, helping with the writing.

The units in this volume have undergone many revisions, each of which had to be typed, mimeographed, and mailed to pilot-school teachers. Two secretaries—Mrs. Robert Spencer and Mrs. James Louden—cheerfully accepted the tasks of retyping the many revisions and of proofreading the final volume.

Teaching Literature in
Grades Seven Through Nine

Introduction

JANE STOUDER HAWLEY

This course of study in literature for grades seven through nine is part of the English Curriculum Study Series developed in the Indiana University English Curriculum Study Center. The two companion volumes—*On Teaching Literature: Essays for Secondary School Teachers* and *Teaching Literature in Grades Ten Through Twelve*—and similar volumes on language and composition represent the efforts of a team of school and college teachers, consultants, writers, and editors. From its inception, the Indiana English curriculum program has been a cooperative project of the U. S. Office of Education, the Indiana State Department of Public Instruction, Indiana University, and more than fifty schools in Indiana. In 1962, the Indiana State Department of Public Instruction appointed committees of teachers to initiate the preparation of courses of study in English, and in 1963, the U. S. Office of Education funded the Indiana program as the eighth "Project English" center for English curriculum development. The finished courses of study are being published by the Indiana University Press for the Indiana State Department of Public Instruction and the Indiana University English Curriculum Study Center, and the Indiana State Department of Public Instruction is distributing copies of the volumes to junior and senior high school teachers of English in Indiana's public schools.

The state-appointed teacher committees, under the chairmanship of Professor Edward B. Jenkinson, Coordinator for School

3

English Language Arts at Indiana University and Director of the English Curriculum Study Center, met in December, 1962, and May, 1963, to establish guidelines for the courses of study. The program has evolved since, of course, but the basic assumptions and many of the controlling ideas came out of those initial meetings. After a general plan had been established, teachers and English Curriculum Study Center staff members developed units within that plan and volunteer teachers in pilot schools throughout the state taught the units. On the basis of pilot-teacher evaluations and the suggestions of college consultants, the courses were revised for publication by the Indiana University Press.

Underlying all aspects of the Indiana English curriculum program are some basic assumptions about learning. Members of the Center staff and teachers who contributed to the project agree generally that a comprehensive instructional program, if it is to be the most thorough means to student development in that area, must be sequential. That is, it must present concepts in progressively more complex forms so that present learning reflects past experience and leads toward the next level of accomplishment. Further, members of the Center staff and teachers connected with the project believe that the concepts around which learning episodes are ordered should be determined, not by the external forces of society or the necessities of personal adjustment, but by the intrinsic nature of the subject. The development of school curricula becomes a critical task, then, as well as a technical one, requiring the combined efforts of subject specialists, learning theorists, and classroom teachers.

The writers of this program are particularly indebted to Jerome S. Bruner's *The Process of Education*,[1] in which the author reports the conclusions of the conference on new educational methods which he directed in 1959 at Woods Hole, Massachusetts. Dominating discussion in this momentous little book and implicating itself in all areas of curriculum design is Bruner's concept of basic structures or principles: each discipline, he says, is characterized by a complex of ideas, attitudes, and relationships which shape it

[1] *The Process of Education* (Cambridge: Harvard University Press, 1960).

and give it power. Mastery of a subject involves an understanding of these basic structures, then, and good teaching is that which enables students to grasp, through specific instances, the general structure or principle.

Bruner discusses in his book the implications of structure theory to curriculum planning. He would have curriculum writers begin by identifying the nature of the subject at hand—the body of knowledge, technique, and attitude by which it is characterized. With the basic subject structures in mind, then, he would have courses designed which present the structures in forms which are appropriate to students at each level. "There is no reason to believe," says Bruner, "that any subject cannot be taught to any child at virtually any age in some form" (p. 47). And to those who would approach a subject from fundamentally different positions for the varying ability groups, he suggests a greater continuity: "Good teaching that emphasizes the structure of a subject is probably even more valuable for the less able student than for the gifted one," he says, "for it is the former rather than the latter who is most easily thrown off the track by poor teaching" (p. 9). Clearly, teachers of English are just beginning to see the ramifications in their own area of the theories which Bruner has expressed. Ideas which he offers as working hypotheses are still only that, however, until they have been embodied in courses and taught with success in the classrooms for which they have been formulated.

Generally, the Indiana program owes much to the work of Bruner and his Woods Hole colleagues in bringing together current methodological theories. The junior high school literature program, for example, attempts the sort of introduction to the general through the specific which Bruner recommends for all areas of study. Assuming only that students who are entering junior high school have been reading and listening to stories for many years, the program acquaints them during the three years with the basic literary structures they will meet later in more complex forms. Units in the volume are sequential in that knowledge builds on knowledge, and the suggested methods of instruction are, for the most part, inductive. That is, students are led, by the order of the material presented and the questions asked of that material, to form their own critical generalizations. Of course, students may also learn about literature through non-sequential programs. But it is reasonable to assume that progress from more random instruction will be slower and less likely to end in critical awareness of the subject.

The teacher should be aware of the pitfalls as well as the strengths of sequential curriculum, however. He should not gear instruction to the few basic principles and ignore the aspects of each selection which are not accounted for in the sequential schema. He must realize that literature is qualitative not quantitative, and that expedient divisions, important as they may be in the early instructional program, are only a means to an end. Finally, members of the Center staff must acknowledge the forces which work against the accomplishment, even on paper, of a truly sequential instructional program. "Many curricula are originally planned with a guiding idea much like the one set forth here," said Bruner in his discussion of an ordered structure approach. "But as curricula are actually executed, as they grow and change, they often lose their original form and suffer a relapse into a certain shapelessness" (p. 54). The writers of this program hope that the units which follow suffer less from that certain shapelessness than some of the programs which have been available to teachers before.

Included here are instructional sequences in poetry, drama, and the novel—beginning in each case with grade seven and ending in grade nine. The unit "Action and Narration," which introduces students through comparative study to both drama and short fiction, also offers the teacher a model for teaching short stories. Though the sequences differ in format, emphasis in each is on critical examination of the way the specific novel, play, or poem works. Each unit contains critical generalizations and specific teaching suggestions. Also included in the program are two units designed to acquaint students with major sources of literary symbol and allusion: a unit in classical mythology is recommended for students in grade eight and *The Odyssey* is recommended for grade nine. Both mythology and epic are taught for their intrinsic value and for their importance as literary source.

It has not been the purpose of this program to offer detailed day-by-day lesson plans for the teacher. Rather, writers of the program have attempted to present a critical and pedagogical basis for the development of units of instruction. The role of the teacher in forming the materials for his own class is crucial. The aims of sound courses of study can be realized only by qualified teachers in their classes.

Part I
BASIC POETRY SEQUENCE

JANE STOUDER HAWLEY

The sequence which follows is more a plan for teaching poetry than a "unit" on poetry. It consists of more than thirty poems—ballads and lyrics—arranged for presentation to students in grades seven through nine. It assumes that youngsters must care for poetry before they will want to understand intricacies of style and that junior high school teachers can best spend their time by helping students to enjoy and to respond to many individual poems. On a more theoretical level, the plan assumes that poetic experience is not primarily intellectual and that much poetic "meaning" —in terms of sound, story, picture, and metaphor—can be made accessible to nonacademic students.[1]

Activities are arranged according to difficulty—from the simple and concrete to the more abstract—so that the same sequence may be presented, with appropriate modifications, to slow-learning, average, and academically talented students. The program is cumulative in that emphasis, which is first on sound and beat, moves to include story, idea, picture, metaphor, and tone. Throughout, the student is directed toward the consciousness within the poem, the "person" who lives there.[2]

Structured sequential assignments should be presented at some time during each year. In this plan, sound and story are dominant elements in grade seven, image or picture in grade eight, and metaphor and tone in grade nine. But the teacher should feel free to divide and adapt the material for his own situation. And he should consider this an approach to poetry, not a complete program. Students should hear many more poems in grades seven through nine than are discussed or listed here.[3]

Certain ideas about poetry, the junior high school student, and the learning process itself are implicit in the following plan. So that the teacher may be guided in adapting the material for his students, the basic assumptions are translated here into specific teaching suggestions:

1. *The teacher should read poems, not poetry.* The teacher should control theories of poetry and ideas of how poems should be taught, but these need not be explicit and certainly they should not be presented as generalizations to junior high school students. He should introduce a single poem by having the students hear and read it; then he should help them to see how this particular poem "means."[4]

He should have students formulate definitions and general characteristics only after they have experienced the form, concept, or technique in question. The teacher should not begin by saying, for example, "Today we will read a sonnet. A sonnet is a lyric poem having fourteen lines of rhymed iambic pentameter." For many students such an introduction will end the learning process before it has begun, and for those who really want to know the poem, the definition will be insufficient. It tells them nothing of how sound, idea, and metaphor work within this structure in this particular poem. The teacher should begin with the individual poem and move with the students toward workable definitions.

2. *The teacher should remember that poetry is sound.* Students should hear each poem before it is studied closely, and the teacher should conclude each session with a final reading. The teacher should acquire interpretive reading skill or provide re-

cordings and tapes for classroom use. He should encourage students to read the poems aloud, too—in private or, if they wish, to the class.

3. *The teacher should not insert his own personality between the student and the poem.* The teacher should let the poem speak for itself. Total objectivity is impossible, of course, and probably not desirable. But the teacher should remember that his task is to help the student to develop his own taste.

4. *The teacher should pace the assignments carefully.* Though students will hear and read many poems throughout the year, they should not attempt a detailed study of more than one poem per class period. The teacher should arrange supplementary activities for those days when the class is unable to concentrate on one poem for an entire period. Then he should return to another poem the following day.

5. *The teacher should assign writing which follows logically from the poems.* He may want to assign composition and/or poetry writing in connection with the poetry study. When the composition problem involves a particular poem, however, he should be sure the assignment proceeds logically from the poem without distorting its original intention.

6. *The teacher should encourage students to make connections between the poems and their own experience.* Particularly in the junior high years, youngsters understand in terms of themselves. The teacher's task is to help them to identify and expand their meaningful experience. Students might also be encouraged to compare poems. How does this poem compare in sound, theme, image, or "person" with the one read last week? Such exercises in judgment introduce students to critical comparative study.

7. *The teacher should minimize the importance of grades during this sequence.* Specific evaluation of the student's work with poems is difficult, because there are no exact tools for measuring understanding or response. Some assessment of the overall performance should be made, however, and writing assignments can be evaluated according to usual class standards.

8. *The teacher should have students memorize if they want to.*

Memorization assignments are desirable when they do not become oppressive or substitute for an understanding of the poem. The teacher should help the youngsters see the advantages of knowing a poem "by heart" and let them follow their own inclinations.

9. *The teacher should help students to develop pride in their work.* During the poetry unit students will accumulate sheets of mimeographed poems, compositions, and other writing efforts. Chances of the papers being scattered on the floor or lost on the playground will be reduced if youngsters are asked to include all poems and assignments in a notebook to be handed in at the end of the unit. The notebook can be evaluated generally and returned to the students so that they may refer to the poems later.

Poems for Grade Seven

By the time children reach the seventh grade, they have been drenched in current popular music rhythms. In this context, sound and beat really get to them. Considering their grounding in this sort of experience, the teacher might well introduce them to poetic sound through popular music. What are their favorites and why? Choices will change from month to month, even week to week. Can they provide recordings for class listening? If the beat were removed, what would remain? Are the words understandable? Do they tell a story? Or do they only reinforce the beat? The analogy between popular songs and poetry will soon be exhausted, and study should be transferred to folk song.

Folk music *is* poetry. Sound, story, picture, and metaphor combine much as they do in the poems students will experience in print, and the individual consciousness expressed in the lyrics is accessible. Included in this sequence are ten songs chosen for their poetic expression and illustration of the folk tradition. "Boll Weevil" typifies several of the ballad characteristics noted by Leach in his *Ballad Book*,[5] and its expression of consciousness parallels that of "John Henry" and contrasts somewhat with "Sixteen Tons." "Tom Dula" leaves so many questions unanswered that the listener is led naturally to the story behind the song, and both this ballad and "Titanic" present models for contemporary ballad writing. The outlaw as hero is celebrated in "Johnie Armstrong" and "Jesse James," and the final selections—"Frankie and Johnny," "Lord Randal," and "Barbara Allen"—are love tragedies.

Throughout the sequence, emphasis should be on the song itself and the listener's response. Students will profit by some background information on the ballad folk, the folk hero, and basic ballad characteristics, but this information should be presented through anecdotes rather than lectures—after the poem has been introduced. For more thorough analysis of folk song, the ballad, and the nature of poetry, the teacher should read some or all of the references listed in the bibliography.

THE BALLAD FOLK

Most of the English ballad texts date from the sixteenth, seventeenth, eighteenth, and even nineteenth centuries, but the oral form emerged earlier—in the Middle Ages. Though many of the English songs reflect the poor man's view of aristocracy, the singers themselves were probably not illiterate. Leach says in his discussion of the ballad folk that "evidence points to the middle class: small farmers, shoemakers, village schoolteachers, nursemaids, tinkers, wives of small tradesmen, innkeepers, drovers."[6]

> Among these too are the itinerant singers of song who go from village to village plying a small trade but concerning themselves largely with singing their stores of songs. Here and there members of the gentry and of the professional and book-educated class became interested in ballads and sang them or wrote them down.[7]

The best ballads, says Leach, are to be found among persons of intelligence and taste. And he offers as a present-day analogy the songs of the Gaelic people of Cape Breton who, though completely literate, live in relative isolation. "They still believe in the fairy folk," says Leach, "and they harbor many more superstitions than do people belonging to the general culture."[8] Out of this way of life, which is analogous to the folk cultures of the past, has come a store of songs, most of them dealing with local events.

In America the folk tradition blends elements from the settlers' original homes with those growing out of life in the new country. Of the ten ballads included here, three of them—"Johnie Armstrong," "Lord Randal," and "Barbara Allen"—are of English origin. But the others are essentially American. Despite certain English borrowings, they developed from situations and events peculiar to this country. For a fascinating discussion of the strands which comprise American folk music, the teacher should read the introduction to Alan Lomax's *The Folk Songs of North America.* "The pedant may search in vain for a 'pure' American folk song," says Lomax.

> "There just ain't no such animal." Our best songs and dances are hybrids of hybrids, mixtures of mixtures, and this may be the source of their great appeal to a cosmopolitan age and the cause of their extremely rapid development.[9]

THE BALLAD ITSELF

A ballad, simply defined, is "a narrative song that fixes on the most dramatic part of its story and impersonally lets the story move of itself, by dialogue and incident, quickly to the end."[10] It is differentiated from other kinds of poetry, not by its origin or the methods by which it was handed down from one generation to another, but by its internal structure and characteristics. Hard and fast categories are misleading, of course, because devices overlap, and there is a tendency for a ballad to change form as it is sung year after year.[11] But it is possible to outline these main characteristics, most of which follow naturally from the ballad's main object of presenting a dramatic story in song.

1. Ballads are more concerned with action than with character, setting, or theme. Action is usually about a single situation, it is plotted rather than episodic (moving rapidly from an unstable situation to a solution), and it is not motivated through character as in most modern stories.

2. The method by which the ballad tells its story is analogous to a film sequence. Narrative is presented "not as a continuous sequence of events but as a series of rapid flashes."[12] This is what Leach calls the "leaping and lingering" technique—in which the ballad leaps over time and space and lingers on the colorful, dramatic scene.[13]

3. Presentation is objective—without moral comment—and on the same level of tension throughout. A consistently casual tone

is used for tragic, brutal, exciting circumstances and the most pedestrian details.

4. As ballads are transmitted from generation to generation, details of the individual man and situation are usually lost, and the appeal moves from the particular to the universal. Anything which might hold up the narrative—including explanation, metaphor, and original phraseology—tends to drop out.

Leach contends that, in a sense, the ballad is the ultimate in dramatic expression. "Here is *a* man becoming man and facing the one moment in life that destroys all or reveals all. What matter the details that bring this moment about? . . . The folk are not concerned with why, for they are not introspective or analytical. Rather they are concerned with the drama of the moment and the character's reaction to it."[14]

TEN REPRESENTATIVE FOLK BALLADS

"THE BALLET OF THE BOLL WEEVIL"

The boll weevil is a tiny cotton borer which destroys the plant by laying its eggs in the young bud. Originally from Mexico, the weevil came into Texas in the 1890's and within a few years had spread across the whole South. The Negro plantation worker saw a parallel between his own life and the plight of the little bug— both were looking for a home. The text which follows is the Mississippi version as anthologized by Hudson[15] and reprinted in *The Viking Book of Folk Ballads.*[16]

1. First time I saw little Weevil he was on the western plain,
   Next time I saw him he was riding a Memphis train.
       He was seeking him a home, a happy home.

2. Next time I saw him he was settin' on a cotton square.
   The next time I saw him he had his family there.
       He was seeking him a home, a happy home.

3. Next time I saw him he was runnin' a spinnin' wheel;
   The next time I saw him he was ridin' in an automobile.
       He was seeking him a home, a happy home.

4. Mr. Merchant said to the farmer, "Well what do you think of that?
   If you'll get rid of little Weevil, I'll give you a Stetson hat."
       He was seeking him a home, a happy home.

5. Mr. Farmer took little Weevil and put him in paris green.
   "Thank you, Mr. Farmer; it's the best I ever seen.
   I'm going to have a home, a happy home."

6. Then he took little Weevil, put him in a block of ice.
   "Thank you, Mr. Farmer; it is so cool and nice.
   I'm going to have a home, a happy home."

7. Mr. Farmer then got angry and sent him up in a balloon.
   "Good-by, Mr. Farmer; I'll see you again next June.
   I'll be seeking me a home, a happy home."

8. Little Weevil took Mr. Farmer, throwed him in the sand,
   Put on Mr. Farmer's overcoat, stood up like a natural man.
   I'm going to have a home, a happy home."

9. Little Weevil said to the sharp-shooter, "Better get up on your feet.
   Look down across the Delta at the cotton we'll have to reap.
   We've got us a home, a happy home."

10. Mr. Merchant said to the farmer, "I can not see your route.
    Got a mortgage on old Beck and Kate; just as well be taking them
        out.
    And bring them home, and bring them home."

11. "Come on, old woman, and we will travel out West.
    The weevils et up everything we've got but your old cotton dress.
    And it's full of holes, it's full of holes."

12. If anybody axes you who wuz it writ dis song,
    Tell 'em it wuz a dark-skinned nigger
    With a pair of blue duckins on
    A-lookin' fur a home,
    Jes' a-lookin' fur a home.[17]

The teacher may introduce "The Ballet of the Boll Weevil" as music by playing the recording by Huddie Ledbetter, Musicraft M-31 (this is recommended by Leach for its authenticity) or one of the other versions: Tony Kraber, Keynote K 104 and Mercury LP, MG 20,008; Bill Bonyun, Folkways FP2; Terry Gilkynson, Decca 5263; Carl Sandburg, Lyrichord LL4. The teacher should provide a mimeographed copy of the ballad for the students to follow as they hear it sung; then, for a more careful study, he should move to the printed version.

Discussion should be guided by carefully selected questions. It should explain unfamiliar language patterns, clarify meaning, and reveal to the students the kind of person living in the poem. What is a weevil? What is unusual about the form of many of the action words in the poem? Why? What is paris green? *Who* is this particular Boll Weevil? How does he show *what* he is? Does he ever lose his good humor? Students should experience the weevil's attempts to "make his mark," to find his home. How do the first three stanzas help us to know Little Weevil? Each of the six views shows him a little higher in worldly status. He is "coming up in the world." How does he react when he is in trouble? Stanzas five, six, and seven show his reactions to the farmer's attempts to get rid of him. Regardless of the problem, Little Weevil never forgets that he is searching for a home. This might be an appropriate time to introduce the word *perseverance*, as a way of describing the weevil.[18]

The "leaping and lingering" technique which Leach finds characteristic of most ballads is found in this folk song. The singer leaps over time and space and concentrates—lingers—on those scenes which present most dramatically the conflicting worlds of the cotton farmer and the weevil. Notice that in stanzas five, six, and seven each stanza represents a single dramatic focus: in each the farmer acts and the weevil reacts. Then between stanzas seven and eight the singer takes the weevil for a giant leap from the balloon in the air to the ground where he throws Mr. Farmer. This leaping characteristic might be pointed out briefly in each ballad selection so that the student may form his own generalization.

Stanzas nine through eleven seem to require clarification. Who is the sharp-shooter? Who are Beck and Kate? What is the meaning of stanza ten? Isn't it rather vague? Does this add to or subtract from our enjoyment of the song? In *The Ballads* Hodgart observes that "however much of the force of ballad imagery comes from our apprehension of its meaning, a great deal nevertheless comes from the very fact that the meaning is not clearly understood at all."[19] In other ballads, too, the children will find vague passages. They should understand that the meaning is unclear to all readers—not just themselves—and that this is characteristic of some portions of many ballads.

Though "Boll Weevil" is complete without the twelfth stanza, these five lines are commonly offered as a conclusion. How do they expand our interpretation of the poem? What clues in the first eleven stanzas would support this way of reading the ballad? With this in mind, what are the new possibilities for interpreting these stanzas? Would the reader have made this comparison without the final lines? Why do students think this ballad has been so popular throughout the years? The teacher should play the recorded selection again so that the students may experience it finally as music and poetry rather than words.

"JOHN HENRY"

Of the American folk heroes, John Henry, the steel-drivin' man, continues to be among the most popular. His story has been sung in many versions, some of which may be familiar to the students. As an introduction to the folk hero, the teacher might want to read to the class Carl Sandburg's "They Have Yarns" or pehaps the chapter on "John Henry and the Machine in West Virginia" in Walter Blair's *Tall Tale America*. The text which follows is from Carl Sandburg's *American Songbag*.

1. John Henry tol' his cap'n
   Dat a man wuz a natural man.
   An' befo' he'd let dat steam drill run him down,
   He'd fall dead wid a hammer in his han',
   He'd fall dead wid a hammer in his han'.

2. Cap'n he sez to John Henry:
   "Gonna bring me a steam drill 'round;
   Take that steel drill out on the job,
   Gonna whop that steel on down,
   Gonna whop that steel on down."

3. John Henry sez to his cap'n:
   "Send me a twelve-poun' hammer aroun',
   A twelve-poun' hammer wid a fo'-foot handle,
   An' I beat yo' steam drill down,
   An' I beat yo' steam drill down."

4. John Henry sez to his shaker:
   "Niggah, why don' yo' sing?
   I'm throwin' twelve poun' from my hips on down,
   Jes' lessen to de col' steel ring,
   Jes' lessen to de col' steel ring!"

5. John Henry went down de railroad
   Wid a twelve-poun' hammer by his side,
   He walked down de track but he didn' come back,
   'Cause he laid down his hammer an' he died,
   'Cause he laid down his hammer an' he died.

6. John Henry hammered in de mountains,
   De mountains wuz so high.
   De las' words I heard de pore boy say:
   "Gimme a cool drink o' watah fo' I die,
   Gimme a cool drink o' watah fo' I die!"

7. John Henry had a little baby,
   Hel' him in de palm of his han'.
   De las' words I heard de pore boy say:
   "Son, yo're gonna be a steel-drivin' man,
   Son, yo're gonna be a steel-drivin' man!"

8. John Henry had a 'ooman,
   De dress she wo' wuz blue.
   De las' words I heard de pore gal say:
   "John Henry, I ben true to yo',
   John Henry, I ben true to yo'."

9. John Henry had a li'l 'ooman,
   De dress she wo' wuz brown.
   De las' words I heard de pore gal say:
   "I'm goin' w'eah mah man went down,
   I'm goin' w'eah mah man went down!"

10. John Henry had anothah 'ooman,
    De dress she wo' wuz red.
    De las' words I heard de pore gal say:
    "I'm goin' w'eah mah man drapt daid!
    I'm goin' w'eah mah man drapt daid!"

11. John Henry had a li'l 'ooman,
    Her name wuz Polly Ann.
    On de day John Henry he drap daid
    Polly Ann hammered steel like a man,
    Polly Ann hammered steel like a man.

12. W'eah did yo' git dat dress!
    W'eah did you git dose shoes so fine?
    Got dat dress f'm off a railroad man,
    An' shoes f'm a driver in a mine,
    An' shoes f'm a driver in a mine.

The teacher should follow the same general method with "John Henry" as was used with "The Ballet of the Boll Weevil." As students follow the words on a mimeographed sheet, he should play a recorded version of the ballad. These recordings are available: Library of Congress, Archive of American Folk Song (AAFS) 15, album 3: Huddie Ledbetter, Asch A-343; Josh White, Decca A-447; Dave Macon, Decca-Brunswick B 1024; Sam Eskin, Folkways 1020; Richard Dyer-Bennett, Asch, 461, Remington 199-34; Bascom Lunsford, *et al.*, Brunswick BL 59001; Legend of John Henry, Folkways LA8; Tom Scott, Signature S-5; Josh White, Decca DL 5082.

In discussing the ballad, the teacher should be sure students understand the dialect word forms. What is meant by the words in stanza one—"John Henry tol' his cap'n/ Dat a man wuz a natural man"? The teacher should help the students to understand that here John Henry is saying that a man counts for something that a machine isn't and that he (John Henry) will die before bowing to any machine. He should remind the students that Boll Weevil, in stanza eight of that ballad, "Put on Mr. Farmer's overcoat, stood up like a natural man." Little Weevil counts for something, too. He is a man. In what sense can we call Little Weevil a man?

The teacher may want to discuss at this point the students' ideas of what makes a man. Is manhood, in this sense, a condition one grows into automatically, or must it be earned? Can a woman be a natural man? How is John Henry similar to Boll Weevil? What was the word we learned earlier to describe Little Weevil? Are there ways in which John Henry is a different sort of person? How might each react in the other's situation? The teacher should lead students to see that these are not characters such as one meets in many stories, because we never know them in detail. The ballad singers have selected events, situations, and details so that we see the character only in his most dramatic moments and then as a sort of generalization. The teacher should point out the "leap" between stanzas six and seven and the way in which the final six stanzas are sort of tacked on after the dramatic climax in stanzas five and six.

The social change which accounted for John Henry's conflict continues today. Some students will have friends and relatives who, like John Henry, have found their own particular skill no match for machines which can work faster and more thoroughly. The teacher may want to go outside the poem into a discussion of change—its effects on persons who are caught up in it and possible ways that one may prepare for the change which he is certain to encounter. Following the discussion, the teacher should play the recorded version again.

"SIXTEEN TONS"*

In the 1940's Merle Travis, son of a Kentucky coal miner, recorded his "Folk Songs of the Hills" album for Capitol records. In addition to the traditional ballads of mining life, the album included two original ballads which, as Lomax says in his anthology,[20] are so clearly in the native ballad tradition that they are now circulating throughout the English-speaking world. One of these is "Sixteen Tons."

1. Now some people say a man's made out of mud,
   But a poor man's made out of muscle and blood,
   Muscle and blood, skin and bones,
   A mind that's weak, and a back that's strong.

   chorus:
   You load sixteen tons and what do you get?
   Another day older and deeper in debt.
   Saint Peter, don't you call me 'cause I can't go,
   I owe my soul to the company store.

2. I was born one mornin' when the sun didn't shine,
   I picked up my shovel and I walked to the mine,
   I loaded sixteen tons of number nine coal
   And the strawboss hollered, "Well, damn my soul!" (chorus)

3. Now when you see me comin', you better step aside,
   Another man didn't and another man died;
   I've got a fist of iron and a fist of steel,
   If the right one don't get you, the left one will. (chorus)

The teacher should introduce the ballad by playing Merle Travis' original version in his "Folk Songs of the Hills" (Capitol album)

---

* Copyright 1947 American Music Inc., Hollywood. Used by permission of American Music Inc. and author. See: *Folk Songs of the Hills*, Capitol 48001. Reprinted by permission of Noma Music, Inc.

or Tennessee Ernie Ford's recording which was popular several years ago. Then he should ask questions like these:

Do you suppose loading sixteen tons of number nine coal is a great feat? How does the person in the poem indicate the physical difficulty of the job? Is coal loaded in this way today? A few points must be clarified. In the last two lines of the chorus—who is St. Peter? Why would he call? Why does the person in the poem ask him not to?

The teacher should help the students to see the progression in the song—the way the person lets us know what he thinks of his world. In the first stanza he tells us what he thinks a man is; in stanza two he talks about himself; and in the final stanza he offers his warning to all the men in the world. Here we see him flexing his muscles. He is letting us know that he has power—that he counts for something. What kind of power is it? Where does it get him? Despite the pride in force and power which the person seems to feel, there is a sense of despair throughout the ballad. Little Weevil always looks to the future—to the home he is seeking. Does the man in this poem work for a future? Why? What is the meaning of the line, "I was born one morning when the sun didn't shine"? Travis conveys in the following words the mixed feelings of those who have derived their meagre lives from the mines.[21]

> I never will forget one time when I was on a little visit down home to Ebenezer, Kentucky. I was a-talkin' to an old man that had known me ever since the day I was born—and an old friend of the family, he says, "Son, you don't know how lucky you are to have a nice job like the one you've got and don't have to dig out a livin' from under these hills and hollers, like me and your pappy used to." When I asked him why he had never left and tried some other kind of work, he said, "Nawsir, you just won't do that. If you ever get this old coal dust in your blood, you're just gonna be a plain old coal miner as long as you live." He went on to say, "It's a habit —sorta like chewin' tobaccer."

The teacher should discuss the condition of despair and its effects on the person who experiences it. How do students account for the humor in the old miner's tobacco analogy? Before playing the ballad again, the teacher should ask students to listen for the regular four beats in each line. Rhythm is more clearly defined in this poem than in the previous two, and students should experience this consciously as a preface to their own ballad writing.

"TOM DULA"*

This is the notice of Tom Dula's death as it appeared in the Statesville, North Carolina, *American* in May, 1868:

> Thomas C. Dula suffered the extreme penalty of the law by hanging, near this place, at 17 minutes past 2 o'clock p.m., on May 1st, having been a second time convicted of the murder of Laura Foster of Wilkes County, more than a year ago. Under the gallows he made a long address to several thousand persons who were present to witness his execution, and avowed preparations to appear in another world. On the night previous to the execution, he made confession of his guilt, which we copy from his own hand.
>
> "I declare that I am the only person that had a hand in the murder of Laura Foster, April 30th, 1868."[22]

The text which follows—Tom's song on the night before the hanging—is from *Folksong: U.S.A.*, copyrighted in 1947 by Frank Warner and John and Alan Lomax. A modified version was popularized several years ago by the Kingston Trio. For other recordings currently available, see *A List of American Folksongs Currently Available on Records*, compiled by The Archive of American Folksong of The Library of Congress.

1. Hand me down my banjo,
   I'll pick hit on my knee,
   This time tomorrow night
   It'll be no use to me.

   chorus:
   Hang down your head, Tom Dooley,
   Hang down your head and cry,
   Hang down your head, Tom Dooley,
   Poor boy, you're bound to die.

2. I met her on the mountain,
   I swore she'd be my wife,

* Words and music collected, adapted, and arranged by Frank Warner, John A. Lomax, and Alan Lomax. Copyright 1947 and 1958 Ludlow Music, Inc., New York, N.Y. Used by permsision.

I met her on the mountain,
And I stabbed her with my knife. (chorus)

3. This time tomorrow,
Reckon where I'll be,
Down in some lonesome valley
A-hangin' on a white-oak tree. (chorus)

4. I had my trial at Wilksboro',
And what d'you reckon they done?
They bound me over to Statesville
And that's where I'll be hung. (chorus)

5. The limb a-bein' oak, boys,
The rope a-bein' strong,
Bow down your head, Tom Dooley,
You know you're gonna be hung. (chorus)

Who is the singer in this ballad? Is the voice of the chorus the same as that of the verses? What is the attitude of the chorus toward Tom? Why does the chorus express sympathy for a self-confessed murderer? One realizes in a first reading that Dula's name is changed by the chorus to Dooley. What circumstances might have accounted for this variation? Students will have little trouble understanding the literal meaning of the ballad, but they will want to know more than they can learn from these five stanzas and the chorus. *Why* did Tom Dooley stab the woman he had sworn to make his wife? In his discussion of the ballad, Lomax says that, despite Dula's confession, members of the community believed that he was protecting a third party—a woman who also had a hand in the slaying. The Lomax account is lively and fun and, though too long to include here, might be read to students as background information.[23]

At this point, as a springboard to the students' own ballad writing and as a valuable exercise in itself, it might be well to explore the similarities between ballads and newspaper stories and the ways the first might be adapted from the second. Both "Tom Dula" and "Titanic," the next ballad the students will hear, were based on actual historical events; and we have seen how social changes, resulting, for example, from the spread of the boll weevil and the invention of the steam drill, have also been used as a basis for song.

From their study of the previous four ballads, students have probably formed several generalizations. They may never have listed the specific characteristics of ballads (such listing is of questionable value), but they know that emphasis is on telling a story dramatically, emphatically, without frills. They have experienced the leaping and lingering technique, the objective presentation, and the spare story line in each ballad they have studied. These are all characteristics of good news stories too. The news story is more particular than the ballad; that is, it deals with a specific rather than a general treatment of persons and events. But comparison of the two ways of handling material should help students to grasp the nature of each form.

Factual accounts of disaster, love conflict, crime—as contained in nearly every issue of most newspapers—are the raw material of folk song. Students have already compared the announcement of Tom Dula's death with the balladists' creation. They should find similar ideas for ballads in current news stories. With the writing project in mind, study of the "Titanic" might center on the way the story of the disaster is told in song. Some students will have had no experience with newspapers in their homes and will need guidance. Aids for developing a unit on newspaper study are available in the sections on newswriting in *Two Units on Journalism for English Classes* and *Teacher's Guide to High School Journalism*.[24] Both publications were prepared for high school teachers, but contain ideas which might be adapted for junior high students.

"TITANIC"

In 1912 the White Star Line *Titanic*, which had been advertised as unsinkable, collided on its maiden voyage with an iceberg and sank with a loss of 1,513 lives. Broadside ballad versions of the disaster appeared in the South immediately. The text which follows was anthologized by White[25] and reprinted in *The Viking Book of Folk Ballads*.[26]

> 1. It was on one Monday morning just about one o'clock
>   When the great *Titanic* began to reel and rock;
>   People began to scream and cry,
>   Saying, "Lord, am I going to die?"

It was sad when that great ship went down,
It was sad when that great ship went down,
Husbands and wives and little children lost their lives,
It was sad when that great ship went down.

2. When that ship left England it was making for the shore,
The rich had declared that they would not ride with the poor,
So they put the poor below
They were the first to go.

3. While they were building they said what they would do,
We will build a ship that water can't go through;
But God with power in hand
Showed the world that it could not stand.

4. Those people on that ship were a long ways from home,
With friends all around they didn't know that the time had come;
Death came riding by.
Sixteen hundred had to die.

5. While Paul was sailing his men around,
God told him that not a man should drown;
If you trust me and obey,
I will save you all today.

6. You know it must have been awful with those people on the sea,
They say that they were singing, "Nearer My God to Thee."
While some were homeward bound,
Sixteen hundred had to drown.

This poem differs from the four previous ones in that it has no central consciousness—no single person living within it. The song is a simple dramatic narrative focused on groups of passengers. We learn nothing of the specific details of the collision or the condition of the vessel itself—only that the poor were the first to go, the passengers sang "Nearer My God to Thee," and sixteen hundred had to drown.

"Titanic" represents one way a news event might be adapted to ballad form. For their first attempt at ballad writing, however, students will need a model with more definite rhythm. The teacher may refer them back to "Sixteen Tons" or acquaint them with the standard four-line stanza of four beats followed by three beats. In this form usually only the second and fourth lines rhyme. Example:

1. Ta tum' ta tum' ta tum' ta tum'
2. Ta tum' ta tum' ta tum'

3. Ta tum' ta tum' ta tum' ta tum'
4. Ta tum' ta tum' ta tum' (rhymes with line 2)

"JESSE JAMES"

Ballad heroes frequently live outside the law. Jesse James, for instance, was a robber and murderer. But his story, as it appeared in the ballad by the anonymous composer known only as Billy Gashade, produced a legend in which the crimes of the hero were absorbed by his courage, daring, and kind treatment of the poor. From movies, television, and popular stories students will be familiar with the legend of Jesse James and his brother Frank. The ballad of Jesse James is available in these recordings: Bill Bonyun, Folkways FP 2; Brownie McNeil, album available from the singer, Trinity University, San Antonio, Texas.

1. It was on a Wednesday night, the moon was shining bright,
   They robbed the Danville train.
   And the people they did say, for many miles away,
   'Twas the outlaws Frank and Jesse James.

2. Jesse had a wife to mourn him all her life,
   The children they are brave.
   'Twas a dirty little coward shot Mister Howard,
   And laid Jesse James in his grave.

3. Jesse was a man was a friend to the poor,
   He never left a friend in pain.
   And with his brother Frank he robbed the Chicago bank
   And then held up the Glendale train.

4. It was Robert Ford, the dirty little coward,
   I wonder how he does feel,
   For he ate of Jesse's bread and he slept in Jesse's bed,
   Then he laid Jesse James in his grave.

5. It was his brother Frank that robbed the Gallatin bank,
   And carried the money from the town.
   It was in this very place that they had a little race,
   For they shot Captain Sheets to the ground.

6. They went to the crossing not very far from there,
   And there they did the same;
   And the agent on his knees he delivered up the keys
   To the outlaws Frank and Jesse James.

7. It was on a Saturday night, Jesse was at home
   Talking to his family brave,
   When the thief and the coward, little Robert Ford,
   Laid Jesse James in his grave.

8. How people held their breath when they heard of Jesse's death,
   And wondered how he ever came to die.
   'Twas one of the gang, dirty Robert Ford,
   That shot Jesse James on the sly.

9. Jesse went to rest with his hand on his breast;
   He died with a smile on his face.
   He was born one day in the county of Clay,
   And came from a solitary race.

After playing the recorded version of the ballad, the teacher should have the students read the ballad in print. Is it possible to piece together the story from these nine stanzas? What questions must be answered if we are to understand the story? Who is Mister Howard? Who is Captain Sheets? Who was Robert Ford? The singer tells us he was "one of the gang." What gang? Why did Robert Ford shoot Jesse James? When we try to answer these questions by tracing pronouns to their noun antecedents, we see that the singer wasn't very exact with pronoun references. He was assuming more specific knowledge of the legend than some contemporary audiences command.

In *The Folk Songs of North America,* Lomax offers this background to the tale of Jesse James, the Missouri outlaw.

> Jesse James led a charmed life, until one day, without reason, he brutally tortured a member of the Ford connection. Robert Ford, one of Jesse's trusted gunmen, swore vengeance. He received a secret promise from the Governor of Missouri that his life would be spared if he assassinated the outlaw. He then paid a friendly visit to James, who was living under the alias of Howard in a little clapboard house in St. Joseph, Missouri.[27]

So Mister Howard is James himself; Ford was a trusted member of the James gang; and the murder was precipitated by Jesse's treatment of one of Ford's relatives or close associates. According to Lomax, Ford shot James in the back of the head when his host's back was turned. Ford was acquitted of the murder, however, collected a $10,000 reward, and left the state. Though Lomax's explanation doesn't account for the reference in the ballad to Captain Sheets, we might conclude that the Captain was the "Ford connection" mentioned by Lomax—the man whose murder began the chain of events.

The person living in this poem—the one through whose eyes we see the tale—is not Jesse James, but the ballad singer himself. Who is the singer? Do we know his name? Do we know what he looks like? Our only knowledge of him as a person is through his interpretation of the story of Jesse James. What qualities does the singer admire in a man? Are there things about his hero that you do not find wholly admirable? Can you imagine a singer with another point of view—a different kind of person telling the story in a different way?

"JOHNIE ARMSTRONG"

In the early sixteenth century the powerful Armstrong clan, led by John Armstrong, brother of the clan chief, raided on both sides of the Scottish border. Though the attacks were primarily against the English, they were embarrassing to King James V of Scotland because he had to admit to the English that the clan was beyond his control. The chronicles tell how King James seized Johnie and his men by promising safe conduct and then had them executed. The English balladist altered the story somewhat. In the following text, which has been adapted from *Wit Restor'd*, 1658, Johnie is an outlaw from Westmorland rather than Gilnockie (his historical home). His forays against the English are ignored. Instead, as the victim of the treacherous Scottish foe, he becomes an English hero.

1. There dwelt a man in fair Westmorland,
   Johnie Armstrong men did him call.
   He had neither lands nor rents coming in,
   Yet he kept eight score men in his hall.

2. He had horses and harness for them all.
   Goodly steeds were all milk-white.
   O the golden bands all about their necks!
   Their weapons, they were all alike.

3. The news was brought unto the king
   That there was such a one as he

That lived like a bold out-law,
    And robbed all the north-countree.

4. The king he writ a letter then,
    A letter which was large and long,
And signed it with his own hand,
    And he promised to do him no wrong.

5. When this letter came to Johnie,
    His heart was as blythe as birds on the tree.
"Never was I sent for before any king,
    My father, my grandfather, nor none but me.

6. And if we go the king before,
    I would we went most orderly;
Let everyman wear his scarlet cloak
    Laced up with silver laces three.

7. Let everyman wear his velvet coat
    Laced with silver lace so white.
O the golden bands all about your necks!
    Black hats, white feathers, all alike."

8. By the morrow morning at ten of the clock,
    Towards Edenburough gone was he,
And with him all his eight score men.
    Good lord, it was a goodly sight to see!

9. When Johnie came before the king,
    He fell down on his knee.
"O pardon my sovereign liege," he said,
    "O pardon my eight score men and me!"

10. "Thou shalt have no pardon, thou traitor strong,
    For thy eight score men nor thee;
For tomorrow morning by ten of the clock
    Both thou and them shall hang on the gallow-tree."

11. But Johnie looked over his left shoulder,
    Good Lord, what a grievous look looked he!
Saying, "Asking grace of a graceless face—
    Why there is none for you nor me."

12. But Johnie had a bright sword by his side,
    And it was made of the mettle so free,
That had not the king stept his foot aside,
    He had smitten his head from his fair bodie.

13. Saying: "Fight on, my merry men all,
    And see that none of you be taine;
For rather than men shall say we were hanged,
    Let them say how we were slain."

14. Then, God wot, fair Edenburough rose,
    And so beset poor Johnie round,
    That four score and ten of his best men
    Lay gasping all upon the ground.

15. Then like a mad man Johnie laid about,
    And like a mad man then fought he,
    Until a false Scot came Johnie behind
    And ran him through the fair bodie.

16. Saying: "Fight on, my merry men all,
    And see that none of you be taine;
    For I will lie down and bleed awhile,
    And then I will rise and fight again."

The teacher may introduce "Johnie Armstrong" as music by playing a recording of the ballad. For a list of available recordings, he may consult *A List of American Folksongs Currently Available on Records* by The Archive of American Folksong of The Library of Congress. The teacher should provide printed copies of the poem for more detailed study. Language in the preceding version should pose few problems as most variant spellings in the original seventeenth-century text have been changed to standard modern forms. Some original spellings have been retained, however—countree, mettle, bodie—so that students may experience the flexibility of English spelling before the eighteenth century. The teacher should be sure students know the meanings of "sovereign liege," "smitten," and "four score and ten."

The story line of "Johnie Armstrong" is simple. Johnie Armstrong is the leader of an outlaw clan. He is summoned by the king with the promise that he will be done no wrong. When Johnie appears with his men, however, the king breaks his promise and orders them hanged. The clan prefers to fight rather than submit to death on the gallows, and in the ensuing battle Johnie is killed. After a class reading of the ballad, the teacher should be sure students have these few points in mind. The teacher might ask a student to summarize briefly the series of events.

What picture do we have of Johnie and his men as they appear before the king? Details are offered throughout the poem—in stanzas one, two, six, seven, eight, and twelve. If the students have not formed in their minds an image of the group, the teacher should reread the ballad to them and ask them to visualize the scene. Why is Johnie so concerned about the appearance of his clan?

What sort of relationship might we expect between an outlaw and a king? As an embodiment of the law, the king would probably oppose a person living outside the law. Historically this has not always been true. Often the king has been unable to control certain of his subjects. But we might expect one who lives by flouting the law to avoid the king. Why, then, does Johnie answer the king's summons? No members of his family have ever been so summoned, Johnie says in stanza five, and he directs his men to wear their finest costumes. What do his words and actions tell us of Johnie's attitude toward the king? Does he trust the king? Does he fear him? Is he in awe? What does he mean when he asks the king's pardon? The teacher should lead the students to see that Johnie's pride seems to overpower his judgment. The teacher should avoid pushing the motivational interpretation too far, however. He should remember that the poem is a ballad, not a dramatic tragedy.

At this point the teacher may want to discuss the concept of honor as it appears in this ballad. Students can easily see that the ballad singer is on Johnie's side, but they will also realize that all evidence is not in Johnie's favor. He is, first of all, an outlaw. He has been stealing and plundering in the north country. Are these socially accepted activities? Today we have laws against stealing and provisions for dealing with robbers. In sixteenth-century England and Scotland thievery wasn't respectable either. How, then, does the singer make us see Johnie as a hero—how does he select for his story those elements which will lead us to accept Johnie as a hero?

The teacher should help students to see that the crux of the matter is the promise of safe conduct which the king makes. To the ballad singer a man's word is his honor, and the king goes back on his word when he tells Johnie that he and his men shall hang. Some readers might quibble that the king only promised "to do him no wrong" and that punishing Johnie for his crimes is just. Such an interpretation is perhaps too literal, however, as

ALLEE CURRICULUM LIBRARY
BUENA VISTA COLLEGE
STORM LAKE, IOWA

the deception has some historical basis and is the situation upon which the ballad turns. So the king becomes a villain, and in the fight which follows, Johnie dies as a hero. If he had been killed by one man his valor might be questioned, but he was downed by a barrage of men. He couldn't possibly escape.

The teacher should point out to students that the form of this ballad approximates the four-line stanza of alternating four- and three-beat lines, which was suggested earlier for their own ballad writing. He should help them to see that the form offers a sort of built-in music which combines with the story to convey the rollicking tale of Johnie's venture and honorable defeat.

"FRANKIE"

False lovers and vengeful women abound in English and American ballad stories. Two sharing this theme—"Frankie" and "Barbara Allen"—are, in Lomax's opinion, America's two most popular ballads. In the earlier versions of "Frankie," several of which circulated in the nineteenth century, the hero's name was "Albert." In the jazz adaptation which became a popular American college song, however, the name was changed to "Johnny." Lomax suggests that "a number of the Frankie-type ballads may have been composed by Negroes and whites in the Mississippi valley, during this period, about a number of similar incidents."[28] The text which follows is the version published in Carl Sandburg's *American Songbag*, 1927.

1. Frankie and Johnny were lovers, O lordy how they could love,
   Swore to be true to each other, true as the stars above;
   He was her man, but he done her wrong.

2. Frankie she was his woman, everybody knows.
   She spent one hundred dollars for a suit of Johnny's clothes.
   He was her man, but he done her wrong.

3. Frankie and Johnny went walking, Johnny in his bran' new suit,
   "O good Lawd," says Frankie, "but don't my Johnny look cute?"
   He was her man, but he done her wrong.

4. Frankie went down to the corner, to buy a glass of beer;
   She says to the fat bartender, "Has my loving man been here?
   He was my man, but he done me wrong."

5. "Ain't going to tell you no story, ain't going to tell you no lie,
   I seen your man 'bout an hour ago with a girl named Alice Bly—
   If he's your man, he's doing you wrong."

6. Frankie went down to the hotel, she rang that hotel bell,
   "Stand back all of you floozies or I'll blow you all to hell,
   I want my man, he's doin' me wrong."

7. Frankie threw back her kimono; took out the old forty-four;
   Roota-toot-toot, three times she shot, right through that hotel door.
   She shot her man, 'cause he done her wrong.

8. Johnny grabbed off his Stetson. "O good Lawd, Frankie, don't
   shoot."
   But Frankie put her finger on the trigger, and the gun went
   roota-toot-toot.
   He was her man, but she shot him down.

9. "Roll me over easy, roll me over slow,
   Roll me over easy, boys, 'cause my wounds are hurting me so,
   I was her man, but I done her wrong."

10. With the first shot Johnny staggered; with the second shot he fell;
    When the third bullet hit him, there was a new man's face in hell.
    He was her man, but he done her wrong.

11. Frankie heard a rumbling away down under the ground.
    Maybe it was Johnny where she had shot him down.
    He was her man, and she done him wrong.

12. "Oh, bring on your rubber-tired hearses, bring on your rubber-tired
    hacks,
    They're takin' my Johnny to the buryin' groun' but they'll never
    bring him back.
    He was my man, but he done me wrong."

13. The judge said to the jury, "It's plain as plain can be.
    This woman shot her man, so it's murder in the second degree.
    He was her man, but he done her wrong."

14. Now it wasn't murder in the second degree, it wasn't murder in
    the third.
    Frankie simply dropped her man, like a hunter drops a bird.
    He was her man, but he done her wrong.

15. "Oh put me in that dungeon. Oh, put me in that cell.
    Put me where the northeast wind blows from the southeast corner
    of hell.
    I shot my man 'cause he done me wrong."

16. Frankie walked up the scaffold, as calm as a girl could be,
    She turned her eyes to heaven and said, "Good Lord, I'm coming
       to thee.
    He was my man, and I done him wrong."

The teacher may introduce the ballad by playing one or more
of the available recordings. An early version of "Frankie and
Albert" has been recorded by Huddie Ledbetter, Musicraft M-31.
This might be compared with a later jazz version of "Frankie
and Johnny." In the preceding printed version there are few unfamiliar language forms; study should center on the story, the
point of view of the ballad singer as he tells the story, and the
values he conveys.

Like most of the ballads in the sequence, this song combines
narrative (stanzas one and two) with specific scenes (stanzas
three and four) and dialogue (stanza five). The teacher should
be sure students recognize the speaker in stanzas five and nine.
He should help them to see that, though the story is told through
several devices, it is directed by a single point of view—that of the
singer. Who is the ballad singer? Is he giving a factual report of
the event or is he inserting some personal opinion? The teacher
should reread stanza fourteen. What is the ballad singer's attitude
toward the murder?

How does Frankie view her crime? Does she consider herself
justified? In stanza sixteen she admits she has done wrong to her
man, but she tells the Lord she is coming to heaven. What does
this indicate of her attitude toward her crime? Does she consider
herself justified? Why? Does the ballad singer agree with Frankie?
Here, as in the outlaw-hero ballads, the criminal is guided by a
code of honor. Johnie Armstrong was wronged when the king
broke his promise; Frankie was wronged when Johnny went out
with Alice Bly. Is the ballad singer suggesting that two wrongs
make a right? Might the story have been told in fewer stanzas?
How would the ballad be changed if all material not necessary
to the story were omitted?

"LORD RANDAL"

Because of the relative difficulty of the final two ballads in this
sequence—"Lord Randal" and "Barbara Allen"—the teacher may

prefer to study them only with average or talented students. Variations of "Lord Randal" are found, as Leach observes, "from Italy to Iceland and from the Slavs to Ireland."[29] The names and other details change, but the basic story remains the same: a young man is poisoned and comes home to die. The text which follows is from Sir Walter Scott's *Minstrelsy of the Scottish Border*, 1802.

1. "O where hae ye been, Lord Randal, my son?
    O where hae ye been, my handsome young man?"
   "I hae been to the wild wood; mother, make my bed soon,
    For I'm weary wi' hunting, and fain wald lie down."

2. "Where gat ye your dinner, Lord Randal, my son?
    Where gat ye your dinner, my handsome young man?"
   "I din'd wi' my true-love; mother, make my bed soon,
    For I'm weary wi' hunting, and fain wald lie down."

3. "What gat ye to your dinner, Lord Randal, my son?
    What gat ye to your dinner, my handsome young man?"
   "I gat eels boil'd in broo; mother, make my bed soon,
    For I'm weary wi' hunting, and fain wald lie down."

4. "What became of your bloodhounds, Lord Randal, my son?
    What became of your bloodhounds, my handsome young man?"
   "O they swell'd and they died; mother, make my bed soon,
    For I'm weary wi' hunting, and fain wald lie down."

5. "O I fear ye are poisoned, Lord Randal, my son!
    O I fear ye are poisoned, my handsome young man!"
   "O yes! I am poison'd; mother, make my bed soon,
    For I'm sick at the heart, and fain wald lie down."

The teacher may introduce "Lord Randal" by playing one of these recordings: Ewan MacColl, H.M.V. B 10259; Burl Ives, Columbia C-186, CL 6058; Jaques Gordon, Decca A-270; Sam Eskin (Croodin Doo) Staff, FM1; Shep Ginades (Welsh), Elektra, 508-B; Richard Dyer-Bennett, Remington, 199-44.

The teacher should begin the study of the printed text by clarifying the language forms which are unfamiliar to the students. "Hae," "wi'," and "wald," for instance, should be explained as dialect forms of have, with, and would. Whereas the ballads that the students have studied before have been combinations of narrative and dialogue or narrative alone, this ballad is developed entirely through dialogue. The teacher should help students to see that the alternating question and answer form is consistent throughout: in the first two lines of each stanza Mother asks a question and in the last two lines Lord Randal replies. What do we know immediately of their social status? His title of Lord indicates that they are members of the aristocracy or upper class. What is the situation? Lord Randal has been hunting with his dogs, he had lunch with his true love, his dogs died, and now he has returned home "sick at heart." How are we to explain the death of his dogs and his own peculiar illness?

What did Lord Randal's love serve him for lunch? Eels boiled in broth, strange as the dish may sound to us, may have been quite a delicacy to Lord Randal. Why did his bloodhounds swell and die? The teacher should remind students of the custom in some areas of feeding animals scraps from the table. Probably the dogs were given leftover eels and broth. At this point, if not before, students will realize that his dogs, too, were poisoned. How does it happen that the dogs have died and Lord Randal lived to reach home? Perhaps the dogs ate more; perhaps the dregs at the bottom of the bowl contained a stronger concentration of poison. Does Lord Randal know when he reaches home that he has been poisoned? Why doesn't he tell his mother immediately? Why does he say he is sick "at the heart" instead of sick at the stomach?

What does this ballad suggest about the world? This is a world in which a young man can be poisoned by his true love—a person whom he loves and trusts. Lord Randal's trust in his love was perhaps similar to a youngster's trust in his mother. When a student goes home to lunch he doesn't expect to have poison in his soup. It has been prepared by a loving mother who would not want to poison him. Such was the confidence Lord Randal had in his true love, and the violation of this trust has made him sick at heart.[30]

"BARBARA ALLEN"

Originally from Scotland, the ballad of "Barbara Allen" has been popular in many parts of the world, particularly in America. Of the many versions, Friedman calls text C from West Virginia the typical American one.[31] The following was adapted from that text.

1. In Scarlet town where I was born,
   There was a fair maid dwellin'
   Made every youth cry, "Well-a-day."
   Her name was Barbara Allen.

2. All in the merry month of May,
   The green buds they were swellin'
   Sweet William on his death bed lay
   For the love of Barbara Allen.

3. He sent his servant to her door,
   To the place where she was dwellin',
   "O Miss, O Miss, O come you quick,
   If your name be Barbara Allen!"

4. O slowly, slowly got she up,
   And slowly she came nigh him;
   She drew the curtain to one side
   And said, "Young man, you're dying."

5. "Yes, I am sick and very sick,
   And grief is in me dwellin',
   No better, no better, I'll never be,
   If I don't get Barbara Allen."

6. "Do you remember the other night
   When you were at the tavern?
   You drank a health to the ladies all,
   But you slighted Barbara Allen."

7. "Yes, I remember the other night
   When I was at the tavern;
   I gave a health to the ladies all,
   And my heart to Barbara Allen."

8. He turned his pale face toward the wall,
   For death was in him dwellin',
   "Goodbye, goodbye, my dear friends all,
   Be kind to Barbara Allen."

9. As she was walking toward her home,
   She heard the death-bell knellin';
   And every stroke it seemed to say,
   "Cold-hearted Barbara Allen!"

10. She looked to the east, she looked to the west;
    She saw the corpse a-coming,
    "O hand me down that corpse of clay
    That I may look upon it.

11. "O mother, mother, make my bed;
    O make it long and narrow;
    Sweet William died for me today,
    I shall die for him tomorrow.

12. "O father, father, dig my grave,
    O dig it long and narrow;
    Sweet William died for love of me,
    And I will die for sorrow."

13. A rose, a rose grew from William's grave,
    From Barbara's grew a briar;
    They grew and they grew to the steeple-top
    Till they could grow no higher.

14. They grew and they grew to the steeple-top
    Till they could grow no higher;
    And there they tied in a true-love knot,
    The rose clung around the briar.

The following recordings are available: L of C, AAFS 66, Album 14; L of C, AAFS 2, Album 1; A. R. Summers, Columbia 408; Richard Dyer-Bennett, Asch 461. After the students have heard the ballad sung, have them hear it read. This poem has fewer dialect forms than "Lord Randal," but some of the expressions will be unfamiliar: "Well-a-day," in line three, for instance. Is this expression common today? What might we say in a similar situation? What do we learn in stanza three of William's social position? As in previous ballads the students have studied, this poem is developed through narrative and dialogue with the characteristic leap between some stanzas.

Is Barbara Allen's reaction to William's illness in stanza four what we might expect? Why does she react in this way? Do you think William's failure to drink to her health is sufficient reason for acting as she does now? What is his defense? Did this misunderstanding have to occur? Might it not have been straightened out so that William could have regained his health and both he and Barbara continued to live? Can men actually die of love? Do you know anyone who has died for love?

In the final two stanzas of the poem we learn that the rose growing from William's grave and the briar growing from Barbara's entwine in a "true-love knot." This is the ballad singer's conventional way of assuring the listener that their love was real and has, in this sense, extended beyond the grave. But it doesn't resolve the central question of the ballad. Why did Barbara act as she did? Does her dying immediately excuse her guilt? Is our reaction to her more favorable then it would be had she lived to love another man?

The ten ballads which have just been considered constitute the sequential poetry program for grade seven. Students should experience many more poems during the year, however, in connection with other literature and language study. Basic elements of sound, story, and point of view have been introduced through the preceding ballads. The second section of the sequence, which is designed for students in grade eight, builds upon this experience.

Poems for Grade Eight

The basic poetry program for grade eight consists of nineteen lyrics arranged for sequential presentation. In "Four Little Foxes," the first in the series, emphasis moves from the elements of story, which are familiar to students from their ballad study, to the way the poet uses words within his poem. "The Eagle" and "A Narrow Fellow in the Grass" provide exercises in visualization as well as some understanding of how a poet creates pictures from words, and "Swift Things Are Beautiful" introduces the effect of quantity or number on movement within the poem. The twelve Japanese haiku, which are presented here in the English translation of Harold G. Henderson, acquaint students with additional poetic structures which they will experience later in more complex forms.

As in the ballad study, selections are arranged according to difficulty. All students should hear and study the first four lyrics and the haiku sequence, but the teacher should decide, on the basis of student interest and response, whether to include the final three selections. "To Earthward" works through a strong central image which must be made accessible to students if they are to grasp what the poem is about. "In Just" provides a sort of exercise in poetic meaning, and "A Hillside Thaw" presents in more complex forms the elements of picture, repetition, and suggestion that students have experienced before.

FOUR LITTLE FOXES*

Lew Sarett

Speak gently, Spring, and make no sudden sound;
For in my windy valley yesterday I found

42

New-born foxes squirming on the ground—
    Speak gently.

Walk softly, March, forbear the bitter blow;
Her feet within a trap, her blood upon the snow,
The four little foxes saw their mother go—
    Walk softly.

Go lightly, Spring, Oh give them no alarm;
When I covered them with boughs to shelter them from harm,
The thin blue foxes suckled at my arm—
    Go lightly.

Step softly, March, with your rampant hurricane;
Nuzzling one another, and whimpering with pain,
The new little foxes are shivering in the rain—
    Step softly.

* From *Covenant with Earth* by Lew Sarett. Edited and copyrighted, 1956, by Alma Johnson Sarett, and published by the University of Florida Press, 1956. Reprinted by permission of Mrs. Sarett.

The teacher should begin by reading the poem to the students. What is happening? What time of year is it? What problem does the poem present? The story is fairly simple, and those few questions should establish the situation. In the first stanza we are introduced to the foxes; in the second we learn how their mother died; in the third the person in the poem tells us what he has done for them; and in the fourth we learn of their present circumstances. Students should note that the story is conveyed in the second and third lines of each stanza, whereas the first and fourth lines are the person's plea to Spring. Each stanza is a snapshot focusing on one aspect of the problem; together they are a series through which the story is told. The teacher should help the students to understand that in this poem the stanza is a word picture, a unit of meaning, rather than an arbitrary division.

What does one feel in reading the poem? What does the person who is telling the story feel? How does he express his feeling? The teacher should help students to see that the narrator assumes a certain position in the poem. He is a sort of guardian to the foxes—offering a plea to circumstances which he cannot control. The question of how feelings are expressed leads to consideration of the way the poet uses words within his poem. Students will understand the meaning of the middle lines in each stanza, but they probably will not grasp the importance to the poem of the first and fourth lines. Here the person interrupts his story to request mild weather so that the foxes might survive. In each stanza the request is varied slightly, but the sentence structure, rhythm, and basic meaning remain the same; and the effect is one of repetition. What does the repetition of words, sounds, and structures within the poem contribute to the reader's experience? What would the poem be without these repeated forms?

Students should be led to understand how the poem is held together by repetitions. Just as one can attach two pieces of material by putting a bit of glue on each and pressing them together, the poet glues his poem together by repeating words, sounds, and structures. Other than the major repetitions in the first and fourth lines, what other forms are repeated? The "s" sounds in the first stanza, the "b" sounds in the second, and the rhymes at the ends of the lines will probably be most apparent to the students. The teacher should avoid an exhaustive search for repeated forms, however. This is only an introduction to the device of repetition. He should conclude the study by rereading the poem aloud.

THE EAGLE

Alfred, Lord Tennyson

He clasps the crag with crooked hands;
Close to the sun in lonely lands,
Ringed with the azure world, he stands.

The wrinkled sea beneath him crawls;
He watches from his mountain walls,
And like a thunderbolt he falls.

As students hear "The Eagle" read, they should try to visualize the scene which the words create. In the first stanza the picture focuses on the eagle as he stands motionless in a context of sun and sky. In the second stanza, the eye of the reader is led to the sea below, back to the bird, and then falls in the last line with the eagle. Students should realize that the poem is organized on the contrasting principles of rest and motion. Whereas the picture in the first stanza is static, both the scene and the eye of the reader are in motion in the second. Tension in each builds toward the final words—"he stands" and "he falls"—which point up the contrast.

How does the poet create his word pictures? Why didn't he write for a first line, "He stood on the cliff"? The teacher should help students understand that the picture is focused by the words which such a matter-of-fact statement excludes—"clasps," "crag," and "crooked hands." As in "Four Little Foxes," the stanzas of this poem are held together and linked by repeated forms. Students will probably note the repetition of "c" sounds in the first stanza and "w" sounds in the second, but the teacher may have to show how the two schemes are linked by "world" in the last line of stanza one and "crawls" in the first line of stanza two. End rhymes also unite the separate stanzas and contrast each with the other.

Because of the detailed picture in this poem, the teacher may want to use "The Eagle" as the basis for an assignment in visualization. Students might be asked to illustrate the first five lines of the poem—the scene before the eagle falls. The teacher should remind them that the words of the poem should offer specific directions for their drawings. After the illustrations are completed, he should help the students to evaluate their powers of visualization by asking these questions of their pictures: Is the eagle watchful? Are his crooked hands visible? Do they clasp a crag? Does he stand as one capable of falling like a thunderbolt? Has the picture a sun? Does the sea crawl beneath the mountain wall on which the eagle stands?

A NARROW FELLOW IN THE GRASS*

Emily Dickinson

A narrow fellow in the grass
Occasionally rides;

* Reprinted by permission of the publishers and the Trustees of Amherst College from Thomas H. Johnson, Editor, *The Poems of Emily Dickinson,* Cambridge, Mass.: The Belknap Press of Harvard University Press, Copyright, 1951, 1955, by The President and Fellows of Harvard College.

You may have met him—did you not?
His notice sudden is.

The grass divides as with a comb,
A spotted shaft is seen;
And then it closes at your feet,
And opens further on.

He likes a boggy acre,
A floor too cool for corn.
Yet when a boy, and barefoot,
I more than once, at morn,

Have passed, I thought, a whip lash
Unbraiding in the sun, —
When, stopping to secure it,
It wrinkled, and was gone.

Several of nature's people
I know, and they know me;
I feel for them a transport
Of cordiality;

But never met this fellow,
Attended or alone,
Without a tighter breathing,
And Zero at the Bone.

After students have heard this poem, the teacher should be sure they recognize the subject. Who is the narrow fellow? Does the poet ever identify him? What clues does she offer? Students should understand that the poem is a sort of riddle which offers several strong picture clues but no positive identification. At what point in the reading did you realize that the poem is about a snake? Here, as in the eagle poem, the writer creates a picture with words. Why does she use the words "narrow fellow" instead of "snake"? What does "rides" in line two suggest of the snake's movement? What does the reference to the whip lash in the fourth stanza add to our picture of the snake? Why does the person in the poem experience "a tighter breathing,/And Zero at the Bone?" What does the word "Zero" mean here? Does it represent zero degrees or naught, nothing? Might it represent both concepts? Is there some evidence that this person is not the poet herself? The teacher should conclude with a final reading of the poem.

SWIFT THINGS ARE BEAUTIFUL[*]

Elizabeth Coatsworth

Swift things are Beautiful:
Swallows and deer,
And lightening that falls
Bright veined and clear,
Rivers and meteors,
Wind in the wheat,
The strong-withered horse,
The runner's sure feet.

And slow things are beautiful:
The closing of day,
The pause of the wave
That curves downward to spray,
The ember that crumbles,
The opening flower,
And the ox that moves on
In the quiet of power.

After students have heard "Swift Things are Beautiful" read aloud, the teacher should lead them to consider what the poet is trying to do in the poem. Each stanza presents a general statement —"Swift things are beautiful," "And slow things are beautiful"— which is expanded by specific examples in the remaining seven lines. Students will probably note that the stanzas are similar in sentence structure, rhyme scheme, and repetition of sounds within the lines. But the differences between the two stanzas will be less apparent. The teacher should read the poem again, emphasizing the swift movement of stanza one and the slower movement of stanza two. How does the poet manage to have her words echo her meaning? How does she make the first stanza swift and the second relatively slow?

How many swift things does she list? How many slow? The teacher should compare the number of sounds (syllables) in the corresponding lines of the two stanzas. He should help the students to see that the poet presents more details more swiftly

[*] Reprinted by permission of The Macmillan Company from *Away Goes Sally* by Elizabeth Coatsworth. Copyright 1934, The Macmillan Company; renewed 1962 by Elizabeth Coatsworth Beston.

(with a fewer number of sounds) in the first stanza. In the second stanza, she slows the movement by presenting fewer details more slowly (with a greater number of sounds). The teacher should reread the poem so that students may experience again the ways that quantity or number can effect movement.

HAIKU IN ENGLISH

The haiku, a brief, seemingly simple poem of oriental origin, offers the beginning student of poetry a sort of microcosm for the study of poetic language. Through the images and rich store of suggested meaning which usually characterize haiku, students can become familiar with some of the basic structures of poetry which they will encounter later in more complex forms. Though the poems are short, the teacher is advised to present no more than four haiku in a single period, and class study and discussion should provide for many readings of each. It is only through repeated readings that these little poems convey their full meaning.

Students will enjoy and respond to haiku without extensive knowledge of their origin or the culture out of which they have come. They should know, however, that—though the poems are now written in many languages—the form is traditionally Japanese. Also, the original Japanese haiku do not have titles, though translators and editors sometimes add titles for English editions. All of the selections in this sequence were written originally in Japanese and are presented here in the English translations of Harold G. Henderson as they appear in his anthology, *An Introduction to Haiku.**

> A whale!
>   Down it goes, and more and more
>   up goes its tail!
>   (Buson, 1715-1783)

What is particularly interesting about the way a whale dives? How does the poet capture this seeming contradiction in his poem? How does he manage to create a "you are there" effect—as

* From *An Introduction to Haiku* by Harold G. Henderson. Copyright 1958 by Harold G. Henderson. Reprinted by permission of Doubleday.

though the reader were on the spot viewing the dive? The teacher
should help the students understand how the poet's use of language contributes to their experience of the dive. In the first line
we sight the whale. In the second line (before the comma) its
body begins the dive, and with the words "more and more," the
tail begins to rise, reaching its highest position in line three. The
poet ends his picture at this dramatic moment—before the whale
disappears beneath the water.

> A giant firefly:
> that way, this way, that way, this—
> and it passes by.
> (Issa, 1762-1826)

Here, again, the poet presents the subject in the first line and
comments on it in the remaining two lines. What impression does
he convey in the second line? How does his use of language help
to create this effect? The teacher should lead students to understand how picture is reinforced by sound in line two and how the
repeated forms contrast with the final statement that the firefly
passes by.

> A trout leaps high—
> below him, in the river bottom,
> clouds flow by.
> (Onitsura, 1660-1738)

Here, as in the whale and firefly poems, the poet offers an objective description. Why does he combine in his picture a trout
leaping out of the water and a reflection of clouds below? Why
not a trout and a bird flying by? What do the trout and the clouds
have in common in this picture? The teacher should help the students to see that each is out of his normal context: usually the fish
is below the surface of the water and the clouds are in the sky.
But in these lines, without distorting what he sees, the poet inverts
their position and presents in an instant of time a picture which
may never recur.

> Leading me along,
> my shadow goes back home
> from looking at the moon.
> (Sodō, 1641-1716)

The person in this poem is walking home after looking at the moon. Why doesn't he say so directly, then, instead of focusing the poetic statement on his shadow? The teacher should help the students to see that the image which the words create—the picture of the person being drawn by his shadow away from the moon—expresses what the poet wants to say about his experience. We are not told that the person responds in a certain way to the moon, that he is hesitant to return to his home, or that he sees in his surroundings a means of expressing his feelings. But all of these meanings and more are suggested by the way the poet makes his statement. Though the Japanese poet did not give his poem a title, Henderson has titled his English translation "Moon Magic." Does his title correspond with your interpretation of the poem? What title would you give if you were translating from the Japanese original?

> Oh, don't mistreat
> the fly! He wrings his hands!
> He wrings his feet!
> (Issa, 1762-1826)

Why is the reader asked not to mistreat the fly in this poem? What sort of fly is he? Is he behaving typically when he wrings his hands? What explanation can you offer for the foot-rubbing motion of flies to which the poet is referring? What parallel is the poet suggesting by describing this motion as hand wringing? How does the poet indicate an even-greater-than-human agitation in the fly?

> These morning airs—
> one can see them stirring
> caterpillar hairs!
> (Buson, 1715-1783)

What is in motion in this poem? Is the poet primarily concerned with caterpillar hairs or with what they indicate? What does he tell us of the morning airs? How forceful are they? How would we experience the airs if we were present with the caterpillar? Would we have to look at the caterpillar to understand the nature of the morning airs? Considering the poet's limitations—the fact that he has only words to work with—how does he help us to experience the morning airs? The teacher should lead the students to understand that the knowledge one gains from the sense of touch cannot be transferred directly into words. The poet must use an indirect, suggestive method, and one such method is to show what effect this "feeling" has upon persons or objects.

Here the airs are strong enough to stir the caterpillar hairs, but not strong enough to move the caterpillar from his position—not strong enough even to disarray his hairs. The reader is able to visualize the caterpillar and to experience through him the nature of the morning airs. The reader should notice, however, that the poet moves away from his picture by using the pronoun "one" instead of "I" in line two, and the word "see" suggests two possible interpretations. Is the person in the poem saying that one can visualize (see in one's mind) such a caterpillar? Might the poet be suggesting both?

> Right at my feet—
>   and when did you get here,
>   snail?
> (Issa, 1762-1826)

The person in this poem notices a snail at his feet and reacts with a typical question—"When did you get here?" In presenting his picture is the poet also suggesting a subtle comparison? Could the snail's arrival be as sudden as the person's recognition? Does a snail arrive anywhere all of a sudden? Some students will be aware from their reading thus far that the writer of haiku often brings together seemingly divergent concepts or ideas. In the poem about the whale we see the tail going up as the fish goes down, in the picture of the trout and clouds the usual positions are reversed, and here a person's quick perception is presented against our previous knowledge of a snail's pace. The experienced reader learns to look for those comparisons and contrasts.

> The falling leaves
>   fall and pile up; the rain
>   beats on the rain.
> (Gyōdai, 1732-1793)

In this picture of falling leaves and falling rain, students should experience a subtle distinction. In what way are the results of the two actions similar? In what way are they different? At this point capable students might be introduced to some of the formal elements of haiku through a comparison of the English translation of this poem with Gyōdai's Japanese original.

Ochiba | ochi
(Falling-leaves | fall)

kasanarite | ame
(piling-up | rain)

ame | wo | utsu
(rain | acc. | beats)

Students should realize that there are no articles or punctuation marks in Japanese, and the usual word order places verbs at the end of the sentence. The language has little accent, syllables are of approximately the same length, and all words end in either "n" or a vowel. In this particular poem, however, there are no words ending in "n." Japanese poetry is unrhymed (repetition of the few word endings would be monotonous), but the verse form— which in haiku is three lines of five, seven, and five syllables respectively—is strictly adherred to. "Wo" in this poem is a structure word indicating that the word before it (ame) is an accusative form. Students should be led to understand that, because of basic differences between languages, translation is more than word substitution, and poetic forms can never be transferred intact from one language to another.

Springtime rain: together
intent upon talking, go
straw-raincoat and umbrella.
(Buson, 1715-1783)

Literally, this poem says that a straw-raincoat and an umbrella are walking and talking in the rain. Is this a usual sort of situation? Are we to assume that this is the poet's meaning? What might we expect to find walking and talking in the rain? Though anyone in our society might wear a raincoat or carry an umbrella, we may suspect that in Japan, at the time Buson was writing, men usually wore raincoats and women usually carried umbrellas. What do the words "together intent upon talking" indicate of the persons involved? If the poet wants to tell that a boy and girl are walking in the rain, why doesn't he say it instead of talking about raincoats and umbrellas?

At this point in their study some students will have realized without having been told that the haiku is a short poem of three lines which suggests a mood or thought through the presentation of a picture. The picture is often sketchy, though, so that the reader must complete it through his own imagination. Those students who compared English translation of the falling leaves poem to the Japanese original realize that, though the differences between the two languages prevent the translation from duplicating the original, the haiku in both languages is short and condensed. The poet must make every word count if he is to present his picture and create his mood in so few words.

With these thoughts in mind, students should return to the raincoat and umbrella poem. What would have happened to the poem if the poet had said in the last line "A boy in a straw-raincoat and a girl carrying an umbrella." Clearly, the line would have been too long for a haiku, and—even if the poet could justify to himself the longer last line—the compressed effect of the poem would have been lost. A poet writes within a certain frame to gain a certain effect, and if he varies the form, he can expect a corresponding change in his poetic effect. Why didn't the poet omit the reference to the straw-raincoat and umbrella, then, and mention only the boy and girl? Such a last line would be brief, but not really condensed, because it would lack the information that the boy was wearing a straw-raincoat and the girl was carrying an umbrella. The picture would lose its focus and much of its force. It is at this point—when the poet is unable to make so few words mean all that he has to say—that he represents one object by another. He expands the meaning of certain words by having them represent, or stand for, themselves and also something else. He offers clues for interpretation and counts on the reader's experience, knowledge, and ability to help him understand the meaning.

> Old, and crippled by years
> do I seem?—Even mosquitoes
> buzz close to my ears!
> (Issa, 1762-1826)

What do we know of the person in this poem? We know that he is old, and we may suspect that a mosquito is buzzing close to his ear. About the latter we can't be sure, though—perhaps this general statement was prompted by no particular mosquito. More important to the person than the fact of the mosquito is what it suggests of his own condition, and most important to the reader is what the poem suggests of the person and of old age in general. At this point students should be able to differentiate between the explicit statement of a poem and its implications—between what it says and what it suggests. The person in this poem says that he seems old; even mosquitos buzz close to his ears. This is the poem's explicit statement and any "meaning" beyond this is implied or suggested.

It is frequently in the area of suggested meaning, however, that poems are most forceful. What does this poem suggest of this particular old person? Do mosquitos buzz close to the ears of old persons only? Would a young person attribute such close buzzing to his old age? Can you recall instances in which your elderly relatives or friends have viewed common everyday situations in terms of their age? Students should realize that, though practiced readers of poetry will differ in their interpretations of poetic suggestion, one should not assume that all readings have equal merit. A fair reading requires experience, knowledge, imagination, and discipline from the reader.

> Just three days old,
> the moon, and it's all warped and bent!
> How keen the cold!
> (Issa, 1762-1826)

What situation has prompted the writing of this poem? What time of year is it? It is winter, and the moon—which is three days old—is beginning to lose its full shape. The poet says it is all warped and bent. What does the poet suggest has caused the moon to warp? Do you share his opinion, or do you have another explanation? Does the poet intend us to accept his explanation as fact? If he does not expect us to believe that the cold has caused the moon to warp, why does he say it? The teacher should help students understand that the poet is using the cause and effect relationship to tell us something of both the cold and the moon. How cold is a cold which can warp the moon? What things can be bent and warped by cold? If cold alone can damage only those things which embody life, what is the poet suggesting of the moon?

> They were called "Sir"
>   when they were being raised—
>   these silkworms were.
>   (Issa, 1762-1826)

What is the poet saying in this poem? Why were the silkworms called "Sir"? Is there anything in the poem to indicate the reason for their being addressed in this way? A Japanese person living during the time of Issa would have no trouble understanding this little poem, but a contemporary American reader requires some background information. As Henderson explains in his *Introduction to Haiku*, "Silkworms were of vital economic importance to many Japanese households and, in recognition of the fact, were often given the title *sama*, a term of respect which can have more affectionate connotations than 'sir'" (p. 136). The English word "sir" is the translator's approximation of the Japanese "sama." Are the silkworms in this poem still being raised? Are they still being called "sir"? Students should recognize the implications of the past tense of the verb. What future can the silkworms expect? What comparison is the poet suggesting by his simple statement that the worms "were called 'Sir'"?

At this point the teacher may want to encourage students to write some haiku of their own.[32] From their study of the preceeding poems, students should realize that haiku usually suggest a mood or thought through the presentation of a picture. They should also know that, though the original Japanese poems have seventeen syllables arranged in three lines of five, seven, and five syllables each, American writers often vary this form slightly because of the differences inherent in the two languages. To reinforce what the students have already experienced in their study, the teacher may want to offer these specific writing suggestions:

1. Limit the subject. It is impossible to treat a complex situation in so few syllables. Focus instead on a simple picture, mood, or thought.

2. Use pictures which either exist or could exist. Have a clear image of the picture—either before you or in your mind—before you write.

3. Use only those words which are essential. Unnecessary words will fog the picture and reduce the poetic impact.

4. Consider the haiku form a model rather than a set of rigid requirements. Use rhyme, if you like, and feel free to vary the number of syllables in the lines.

Shiki, the nineteenth-century Japanese poet, advised the beginning writer of haiku to be natural and direct. Write to please yourself, he said, as only in this way can you hope to please others (Henderson, p. 161).

TO EARTHWARD*

Robert Frost

When stiff and sore and scarred
I take away my hand
From leaning on it hard
In grass and sand,

The hurt is not enough:
I long for weight and strength
To feel the earth as rough
To all my length.

The preceding lines comprise only the last two stanzas of Frost's eight-stanza poem. Because the strong central image in these final lines is more accessible to eighth-grade students than the total poem or similar images in other poems, one is probably

* From *Complete Poems of Robert Frost*. Copyright 1923, 1930, 1939 by Holt, Rinehart and Winston, Inc. Copyright 1951, 1958 by Robert Frost. Reprinted by permission of Holt, Rinehart and Winston.

justified in presenting a shortened version. After the students have heard the stanzas and read them slowly to themselves, the teacher should ask them to think back to a time when they have leaned on a hand in the grass or sand for several minutes. How did the hand look after it was taken away? How did it feel? Students will probably recall that their arm as well as hands were stiff and sore. Was the feeling altogether unpleasant? Why does the person in this poem say that the hurt is not enough? In the final three lines of the poem the person tells us that he longs for the strength to press his whole body to the earth till it is stiff and sore and scarred as his hand was. For their own experience, many students will recognize this longing to press themselves against the earth—to feel an external pain strong enough to balance the unrest inside.

How does the poet manage to convey his meaning? The first stanza is one long phrase building to the statement that "The hurt is not enough"; the remaining lines expand this idea. Students should note that the entire eight-line poem is a single sentence. How is the poem held together? Students will probably note the repeated "s" sounds in the first stanza and the rhymed lines, but they may not grasp the cohesive force of the single image or movement within the poem. The teacher should help them to understand that the momentum building toward and leading from the first line of the second stanza works with the central image toward unity.

IN JUST*

e. e. cummings

in Just-
spring   when the world is mud-
luscious the little
lame balloonman

whistles   far   and wee

and eddieandbill come
running from marbles and

---

* From *Poems 1923-1954* by e. e. cummings. Copyright, 1923, 1951, by e. e. cummings. Reprinted by permission of Harcourt, Brace & World, Inc.

piracies and it's
spring

when the world is puddle-wonderful

the queer
old balloonman whistles
far   and   wee
and bettyandisbel come dancing

from hop-scotch and jump-rope and

it's
spring
and
        the

              goat-footed

balloonMan   whistles
far
and
wee

Who is the person living in this poem—the one through whose
eyes we see the world of eddieandbill, bettyandisbel, and the
queer old balloonman? What do we know of the person? Can we
describe the way he looks? The way he feels? The teacher should
help the students to understand that though we know nothing of
his physical appearance, his age, or his life outside the poem, we
understand and experience with him his reaction to a certain sort
of day in spring. What is the source of his joy and energy? Have
you reacted similarly to a day in spring? How does one express in
words such an unnameable experience? How does the poet manage?

With this last question in mind, the teacher should direct the
students to the poem as it appears in print on the page. How does
the arrangement of words differ from that of other poems in the
sequence—"The Little Foxes," for instance, or "To Earthward"?
Some words which usually occur singly are combined in this poem
(eddieandbill, bettyandisbel) or hyphenated (mud-luscious,
puddle-wonderful), while others which usually occur consecu-
tively are widly spaced (whistles   far   and wee). There are no
punctuation marks, only two capital letters, and the arrangement

of lines is highly irregular. Is the poet merely playing games, or are there reasons for his unorthodox forms?

Students should note the details of the person's world—the little lame balloonman (queer, goat-footed, whistling), the puddles (wonderful, mud-luscious), and the running, dancing children. Students should understand some of the ways point of view, details, and language work together in this poem. The tumbling effect of "eddieandbill" and "bettyandisbel," for instance, reflects both the actions of running and dancing and the person's sense of freedom and joy. What is the effect of the hyphenated forms? Of the peculiar spacing? How do these devices influence movement within the poem?

Why is the balloonman described as "goat-footed"? If students are unfamiliar with Pan, the Greek god of forests, pastures, flocks, and shepherds, the teacher should refer them to a dictionary or encyclopedia. Do other details in the poem indicate a connection between the balloonman and the god Pan? Why is the allusion particularly appropriate to the time of year?

A HILLSIDE THAW*

Robert Frost

> To think to know the country and not know
> The hillside on the day the sun lets go
> Ten million silver lizards out of snow!
> As often as I've seen it done before
> I can't pretend to tell the way it's done.
> It looks as if some magic of the sun
> Lifted the rug that bred them on the floor
> And the light breaking on them made them run.
> But if I thought to stop the wet stampede,
> And caught one silver lizard by the tail,
> And put my foot on one without avail,
> And threw myself wet-elbowed and wet-kneed
> In front of twenty others' wriggling speed,—
> In the confusion of them all aglitter,
> And birds that joined in the excited fun
> By doubling and redoubling song and twitter,
> I have no doubt I'd end by holding none.

* From *Complete Poems of Robert Frost*. Copyright 1923, 1930, 1939 by Holt, Rinehart and Winston; copyright 1951, 1958 by Robert Frost. Reprinted by permission of Holt, Rinehart and Winston.

It takes the moon for this. The sun's a wizard
By all I tell; but so's the moon a witch.
From the high west she makes a gentle cast
And suddenly, without a jerk or twitch,
She has her spell on every single lizard.
I fancied when I looked at six o'clock
The swarm still ran and scuttled just as fast.
The moon was waiting for her chill effect.
I looked at nine; the swarm was turned to rock
In every lifelike posture of the swarm,
Transfixed on mountain slopes almost erect.
Across each other and side by side they lay.
The spell that so could hold them as they were
Was wrought through trees without a breath of storm
To make a leaf, if there had been one, stir.
It was the moon's: she held them until day,
One lizard at the end of every ray.
The thought of my attempting such a stay!

The teacher should introduce "A Hillside Thaw" by reading it aloud to the students. He should direct their attention during a second reading with these questions: What is happening in the poem? What are the silver lizards? According to the person in the poem, why have they appeared? Do you agree with his explanation? At what point did you realize that the lizards are not real? What is the central contrast of the poem? How is it handled? Students will probably realize that to answer these questions satisfactorily, they must focus more closely on individual lines and phrases. Emphasis here should be on fairly detailed explication, but—insofar as possible—interpretation should be elicited *from* students rather than offered *to* them.

The first five lines present the puzzle of ten million silver lizards out of snow and also the person's confession that he "can't pretend to tell the way it's done." In the next three lines he offers a comparison ("It looks as if . . ."), which he qualifies in the nine-line sentence which follows. What do we experience in this first stanza? What do we see? What do we feel? What word pictures does the poet paint? Why can't the person expect to halt the lizards? What is the antecedent of "this" in the first line of stanza two? What powers does the person attribute to the sun? To the moon? Why does he call the sun a wizard and the moon a witch? What is the antecedent of "It" in line 16 of stanza two? What do lines 13-15 tell us of the moon? At this point students may want to reconsider or expand their answers to the earlier questions.

Depending on student interest and response, the teacher may want to pursue in this poem other elements of poetry that students have experienced previously in more simple lyrics. How does the picture in stanza one differ from the one in stanza two? In what other poems have students experienced the motion-rest contrast? How does movement in lines 9-17 differ from that in the lines before and after? How does the poet manage this effect? Why? What suggested meanings are conveyed by the words wizard and witch in reference to the sun and moon? Are these suggestions made explicit anywhere in the poem? How is the poem unified: what forces hold it together? The teacher should help students to understand how picture, movement, repetition, and suggestion work together in this poem.

This concludes the sequential poetry program for students in grade eight. Lyrics were selected and presented to reinforce past experiences—with sound, beat, story, and point of view—and to introduce elements of picture, word choice, and suggestion. The selections and questions for grade nine will build on all of these experiences.

Poems for Grade Nine

The third section of the basic poetry program contains ten lyrics recommended for students in grade nine. Emphasis in these poems moves to include metaphor, symbol, and tone as well as the elements considered in grades seven and eight. As in previous study, students are led to an awareness of the consciousness within the poem and the importance of this "person" to the formation of the work. In "Prayers of Steel," "The Heart," and "A Poison Tree" poetic suggestion becomes symbol, functioning in each case as an expression of personal identity. The lines from Solomon and "Spring" evidence two minds at work on similar material for dissimilar purposes with resulting differences in tone. And "fate is unfair" presents, through a particularly engaging persona, yet another sort of tone. In "Mending Wall" the poet works through cliché in the definition of a certain kind of mentality and in the last poems in the section, "Auto Wreck," "Ozymandias," and "God's Grandeur," students experience in more complex forms elements of poetry which they have experienced in other poems in the sequence.

PRAYERS OF STEEL*

Carl Sandburg

Lay me on an anvil, O God.
Beat me and hammer me into a crowbar.
Let me pry loose old walls.
Let me lift and loosen old foundations.

---

* From *Cornhuskers* by Carl Sandburg. Copyright 1918 by Holt, Rinehart and Winston. Copyright 1946 by Carl Sandburg. Reprinted by permission of Holt, Rinehart and Winston.

Lay me on an anvil, O God.
Beat me and hammer me into a steel spike.
Drive me into the girders that hold a skyscraper together.
Take red-hot rivets and fasten me into the central girders.
Let me be the great nail holding a skyscraper through blue
nights into white stars.

Discussion of this poem should direct students first toward a literal reading. What do we know of the speaker or person through whom we experience the prayers? What is he saying? What is an anvil, a girder, a rivet? When students recognize the logical impossibilities of a literal reading—that a person cannot become a crowbar or a steel spike, for instance—they should be directed toward the poem's suggested, symbolic meaning.

What kind of person lives in this poem? To what extent does his prayer reveal his own nature? How does he view himself in relation to the God to whom he prays? What meanings are conveyed by the word "old" in stanza one? By the "steel spike" and "great nail" in stanza two? What force is to loosen old foundations and build new structures? How would the person participate in this leveling and building process? Is his role entirely passive? How does the prayer change from the first stanza to the second? In the first stanza the person asks to be used in disruptive revolutionary action; in the second he asks to participate in rebuilding. Does the person's concept of himself change? Does his relationship to his God change? What are the "prayers of steel"? In the most literal sense each line of the poem is the person's prayer. What further meaning does the poet suggest by his reference to their being made of steel? Students should understand that the skyscrapers themselves are embodiments of prayer. They represent or symbolize the creative process in which the person asks to participate.

How does the poet convey his meaning? The lines, each a sort of sentence prayer, are cumulative, expressing the processes of destruction (stanza one) and creation (stanza two). Students should recognize the similarities in both sentence structure and word choice between the two stanzas and also the way the poet builds toward the final line, the person's final plea, by increasing progressively the length of the lines. Each line begins with an imperative action word followed immediately, except in line eight, by the personal pronoun "me." Thus, the relationship between the person and his God, one in which God acts upon the person at the person's own request, is reinforced in each line of the poem.

Students should notice the poet's use of color in the final two lines—"red-hot rivets," "blue nights," and "white stars." What further meanings are suggested by these particular colors? Do other details in the poem suggest an American setting? Ninth grade students may lack comparative knowledge of cultures, but they should realize that the wrecking and building process, which is present to some degree in all societies, is particularly characteristic of life in the United States. The teacher should not overemphasize the patriotic implications of the poem, however. Though the implications are there, the persons in the poem might have the same conception of himself and his God in another national setting. Emphasis should be on understanding the position of the person within his world—his affirmation of a process in which he is an instrument of a greater moving force.

THE HEART*

Stephen Crane

In the desert
I saw a creature, naked, bestial,
Who, squatting upon the ground,
Held his heart in his hands,
And ate of it.
I said, "Is it good, friend?"
"It is bitter—bitter," he answered;
"But I like it
Because it is bitter,
And because it is my heart."

There are two persons present in this poem—the one through whom we experience the incident ("I") and the naked, bestial creature to whom he speaks. Where does their conversation take

* Reprinted by permission of Alfred A. Knopf, from *Collected Poems* of Stephen Crane.

place? What is the creature doing when the first person sees him? What might be our question if we came upon a creature squatting upon the ground, holding his heart in his hands, and eating of it? What is the first person's question? Students will realize from the nature of his question that the first person accepts the creature's behavior without questioning the credibility of one who would hold his heart in his hands and eat of it. This nonliteral response to the situation suggests to the reader that a metaphorical reading of the poem may be required. The person is not censuring or challenging with his question, but attempting to get at the nature of the creature's experience.

What is this experience? Is it good? No, it is bitter. Why, if the experience of eating his heart is bitter, does the creasure persist? He likes it *because* it is bitter and because it is *his own*. At this point students must move from a literal to symbolic reading of the poem—from attention to what the words denote to what they suggest and represent. In addition to the clues to interpretation provided by the poet, they will have to draw upon their knowledge of their own behavior and what they have been able to learn of others. For what reasons might one enjoy an action which is painful to him? Do you know persons who enjoy torturing themselves? Have you experienced this sort of joy yourself? Why is the creature eating his heart? Why not his liver or some other portion of his body? Students should be able to identify the symbolic meanings which attach to the word heart and realize how the poet makes these meanings work in his poem.

The dominant image of a creature eating his heart, projected against a desert setting, is the poem's unifying force. By what internal device does the poet mold this picture and single verbal exchange into a whole? Students will recognize the repetition of "h" sounds in the fourth and final lines and "b" sounds in the last four lines. These repeated forms hold the lines together as does the direct progression of the three sentences from setting to question to answer. And the spare language of the poem, the sense of all unnecessary words having been cut away, reflects the stark nature of the creature's experience.

A POISON TREE

William Blake

I was angry with my friend:
I told my wrath, my wrath did end.
I was angry with my foe:
I told it not, my wrath did grow.

And I water'd it in fears,
Night and morning with my tears:
And I sunnèd it with smiles,
And with soft deceitful wiles.

And it grew both day and night,
Till it bore an apple bright;
And my foe beheld it shine,
And he knew that it was mine.

And into my garden stole
When the night had veil'd the pole:
In the morning glad I see
My foe outstretch'd beneath the tree.

What is the meaning of the phrase "I told my wrath" in line two?
Students should realize that meaning here is analogous to that
in the expression "I told the truth." That is, the speaker tells someone *about* his wrath. Whereas he vents the wrath which he feels
toward his friend, however, he keeps to himself the wrath which
he feels for his foe. In this last case he is, as we might say, nursing
a grudge. What is the meaning of the word "wrath"? Why do you
think the poet chose this word instead of anger? Do you think that
anger is a kind of wrath, or is wrath a kind of anger? What sort of
anger is wrath? The teacher is reminded that in medieval schemes
wrath is one of the seven deadly sins: Anger in itself is neither
good nor bad, but wrath is sinful.

What sort of behavior is represented in the second stanza? How
might a person cause his wrath to increase? Why are the images
of cultivation and growth particularly expressive of the person's
behavior? What do lines three and four of stanza three further
suggest of the relationship between the person and his foe? Why
did the foe steal into the garden? What has happened to him
there? How does the person in the poem react? Students may de-

tect in the "apple bright" and the garden allusions to the garden of Eden. Pursuit of the parallel is not very meaningful in this context, however, without reference to the mythological frame within which Blake worked.

In what ways is the person in this poem similar to the creature of the previous one? Are their experiences comparable? How are they dissimilar? Students should recognize in each consciousness a bitter sort of self-indulgence—turned in upon itself in the first poem and directed toward another in the second. By what devices has the poet unified this last poem? Is there an image here comparable to that of the creature eating his heart? How do the central images of the two poems differ? Whereas the first is fairly static, the second develops in the course of the poem: Beginning as wrath, the anger is watered and sunned into a poison tree. The person's burgeoning wrath, as symbolized by the growth of the lethal tree, is the central unifying force of the poem.

How might we describe the language used by the person in this poem? Are sentence structure, vocabulary, diction, and stanza form obstacles to understanding? Is the consciousness within the poem of comparable simplicity? Why, then, do you think the poet has chosen such simple poetic forms? The teacher should help the students recognize the sort of tension between the terrible experience within the poem and the almost childlike simplicity of the language which conveys it.

POEM OF SPRING FROM SONG OF SOLOMON (2:10-13)

> Rise up, my love, my fair one,
> and come away.
> For, lo, the winter is past,
> the rain is over and gone;
> The flowers appear on the earth;
> the time of the singing of birds is come,
> and the voice of the turtle is heard in our land:
> The fig tree putteth forth her green figs,
> and the vines with the tender grape give a good smell.
> Arise, my love, my fair one,
> and come away.

Who is the speaker of these lines and to whom does he speak? What time of year is it? From what specific details do you conclude that it is spring? What is the meaning of "lo" in the second sentence? Students should know that this word is used, much as "listen" in present usage, to call attention. What is the "voice of the turtle"? This reference is to the sound of the turtledove—a small dove distinguished by its affection for its mate—whose presence is considered a harbinger of spring. What is the person's message to his love? Because it is spring, he says, you should come with me.

Elements of the poem are ordered to reflect the relationship between the season and the mood of the speaker. Line one is the person's plea, lines two and three develop his argument, and line four repeats his original plea. Is the person's argument logical? Might a decision to come away follow logically from his catalog of the characteristics of spring? Is his argument persuasive? Why? How do images of sight, sound, touch, and smell contribute to the mood of the poem? How is the poem held together? The basic unit is the poetic line, and essential forms of one line parallel corresponding forms in that and other lines. The second and third lines, for instance, are composed of seven descriptive statements, parallel in structure and linked only by commas or the word "and." The final line restates the first with a single variant: "Rise up" in line one becomes "Arise" in line four, thus enclosing and unifying the person's plea. Students should be led to understand the way these repeated forms work with the series of images to produce the person's persuasive appeal to his love.

SPRING*

Edna St. Vincent Millay

To what purpose, April, do you return again?
Beauty is not enough.
You can no longer quiet me with the redness
Of little leaves opening stickily.
I know what I know.
The sun is hot on my neck as I observe
The spikes of the crocus.
The smell of the earth is good.

* From *Collected Poems*, Harper & Row. Copyright 1921, 1948 by Edna St. Vincent Millay. Reprinted by permission of Norma Millay Ellis.

It is apparent that there is no death.
But what does that signify?
Not only under ground are the brains of men
Eaten by maggots.
Life in itself
Is nothing,
An empty cup, a flight of uncarpeted stairs.
It is not enough that yearly, down this hill,
April
Comes like an idiot, babbling and strewing flowers.

Here, as in the preceding poem, the speaker is addressing a specific person. To whom does he speak? How does the person addressed in this poem differ from the fair one in the preceding poem? Here the poet speaks to April as though the month were a person capable of understanding and responding to his words. What tone is established in the first line? What are the immediate indications that the poet is questioning fundamental assumptions—that this will not be another joyous celebration of the return of spring? What do the words "no longer" in line three indicate of the person's past attitude toward spring?

What characteristics of April are given in the first nine lines of the poem? What sort of appeal does each of these make to the reader? Students will identify images of sight, sound, smell, and touch similar to those in the poem from Solomon. Are the images used for the same purposes in both poems? What is the meaning of the word "apparent" in line nine? What sort of images does the poet present in the remainder of the poem? Students should realize that "apparent," used here in the basic sense of "according to appearances or seeming," is a pivot word in the poem, separating appearances from the poet's apprehension of reality. The final images of the poem—offered as real indices of life—are, ironically, images of death and emptiness.

The central irony in this poem turns on associations already present in the minds of both poet and reader. Spring is generally considered a time of growth and resurgence—both literally and metaphorically, of joy and faith in the forces of life. And the manifestations of spring commonly function in art and in popular consciousness as symbols of perpetual (in the sense of recurring) life.

In this poem, however, the entire symbolic apparatus is rejected, and the images of spring point instead to the gap between what seems to be and what is. What is the general tone of the poem? How might we account for the force with which the person presents his argument? The teacher should lead the students to understand the significance of the person's past associations ("no longer" reference in line three) to his present intensity.

FATE IS UNFAIR[*]

Don Marquis

in many places here and
there
i think that fate
is quite unfair
yon centipede upon
the floor
can boast of
tootsies by the score
consider my
distressing fix
my feet are limited
to six
did i a hundred
feet possess
would all that glorious
footfullness
enable me
to stagger less
when I am
overcome by heat
or if i had
a hundred feet
would i
careening oer the floor
stagger
proportionately more
well i suppose
the mind serene
will not tell

[*] From *the lives and times of archy and mehitabel* by Don Marquis. Copyright 1918 by Sun Printing and Publishing. Reprinted by permission ot Doubleday & Co., Inc.

destiny its mean
the truly
philosophic mind
will use
such feet as it can find
and follow calmly
fast or slow
the feet it has
where eer they go

archy

The person in this poem has signed his name at the end. What do we know of Archy other than his name? His feet are limited to six, though "yon centipede" has "tootsies by the score." Why is Archy's distressing fix humorous? Are you distressed that your feet are limited to two? What is a centipede? After students have identified these few details from the poem, they should be told that the lines are from a longer poem by Don Marquis, and Archy is a cockroach. He types his poem without capital letters, because he can't hold down the shift key while hopping from one letter key to another.

What sort of person is Archy? Does he question his position in the world? What does his phraseology ("yon centipede," "tootsies by the score") indicate of his attitude toward his subject? What is the tone of his complaint? Students should realize from his lilting lines and happy phraseology that Archy maintains a sort of good-humored detachment from these matters of fate. This attitude and his acknowledgment in line twelve of his own six feet suggest to the reader that perhaps Archy's words should not be taken literally.

The teacher should lead students to understand the development of Archy's argument from his statement that fate is quite unfair, to the evidence he offers in support of his statement, to his supposition about the serene and philosophic mind. What meanings do we usually attach to "serene" and "philosophic?" Are we to accept his final supposition at face value? Is he resigned to his limited feet? What does the phrase "such feet as it can find" indicate of his attitude? Does this represent a change in tone from the beginning? How are we to interpret the word "feet"?

Why are the lines arranged as they are? Where does the first sentence end? How do you know? What sort of signals substitute for punctuation marks? Students should understand how the stress patterns within the lines indicate the way the words are to be read. These function for the capital letters and punctuation marks which the "philosophic" cockroach omits.

MENDING WALL*

Robert Frost

Something there is that doesn't love a wall,
That sends the frozen-ground-swell under it,
And spills the upper boulders in the sun;
And makes gaps even two can pass abreast.
The work of hunters is another thing:
I have come after them and made repair
Where they have left not one stone on a stone,
But they would have the rabbit out of hiding,
To please the yelping dogs. The gaps I mean,
No one has seen them made or heard them made,
But at spring mending time we find them there.
I let my neighbor know beyond the hill;
And on a day we meet to walk the line
And set the wall between us once again.
We keep the wall between us as we go.
To each the boulders that have fallen to each.
And some are loaves and some so nearly balls
We have to use a spell to make them balance:
"Stay where you are until our backs are turned!"
We wear our fingers rough with handling them.
Oh, just another kind of outdoor game,
One on a side. It comes to little more:
There where it is we do not need the wall:
He is all pine and I am apple orchard.
My apple trees will never get across
And eat the cones under his pines, I tell him.
He only says, "Good fences make good neighbors."
Spring is the mischief in me, and I wonder
If I could put a notion in his head:
"*Why* do they make good neighbors? Isn't it

* From *Complete Poems of Robert Frost*. Copyright 1923, 1930, 1939 by Holt, Rinehart and Winston, Inc. Copyright 1951, © 1958 by Robert Frost. Reprinted by permission of Holt, Rinehart and Winston, Inc.

Where there are cows? But here there are no cows.
Before I built a wall I'd ask to know
What I was walling in or walling out,
And to whom I was like to give offense.
Something there is that doesn't love a wall,
That wants it down." I could say "Elves" to him,
But it's not elves exactly, and I'd rather
He said it for himself. I see him there
Bringing a stone grasped firmly by the top
 In each hand, like an old-stone savage armed.
He moves in darkness as it seems to me,
Not of woods only and the shade of trees.
He will not go behind his father's saying,
And he likes having thought of it so well
He says again, "Good fences make good neighbors."

Like Stephen Crane's "The Heart," which students read previously, this poem presents two persons—the one through whom we experience the situation and the neighbor with whom he speaks. In the beginning line the person states generally that "Something there is that doesn't love a wall." How has he reached this conclusion? What specific evidence does he offer to support his claim? What do we know of the neighbor? Do we learn of him through his own words and actions or from those of the first person? Why does the neighbor say that "Good fences make good neighbors"? Does he offer any evidence to support his statement? How does he reply to the person's question—"Why do they make good neighbors"? Why does the speaker want to let his neighbor "say it for himself"? Why not tell him outright? The person says his neighbor "will not go behind his father's saying." What does he mean? How does the image of "an old-stone savage armed" contribute to our knowledge of the poem? What sort of darkness does the neighbor move in?

Do good fences make good neighbors? Can you imagine situations which might have led the neighbor, his father, or grandfather to have reached such a conclusion? Is the generalization useful to the neighbor in this situation? Does it offer him intelligent direction? Is it a precise description of reality? What is the general tone of the poem? Is it serious? In what ways is it humorous? Is the tension between the person and his neighbor sustained throughout? The teacher should lead students to understand how their relationship is formed and limited by the kind of person each man is.

AUTO WRECK*

Karl Shapiro

Its quick soft silver bell beating, beating,
And down the dark one ruby flare
Pulsing out red light like an artery,
The ambulance at top speed floating down
Past beacons and illuminated clocks
Wings in a heavy curve, dips down,
And brakes speed, entering the crowd.
The doors leap open, emptying light;
Stretchers are laid out, the mangled lifted
And stowed into the little hospital.
Then the bell, breaking the hush, tolls once,
And the ambulance with its terrible cargo
Rocking, slightly rocking moves away,
As the doors, an afterthought, are closed.

We are deranged, walking among the cops
Who sweep glass and are large and composed.
One is still making notes under the light.
One with a bucket douches ponds of blood
Into the street and gutter.
One hangs lanterns on the wrecks that cling,
Empty husks of locusts, to iron poles.

Our throats were tight as tourniquets,
Our feet were bound with splints, but now,
Like convalescents intimate and gauche,
We speak through sickly smiles and warn
With the stubborn saw of common sense,
The grim joke and the banal resolution.
The traffic moves around with care,
But we remain, touching a wound
That opens to our richest horror.

Already old, the question Who shall die?
Becomes unspoken Who is innocent?
For death in war is done by hands;

* Copyright 1941 by Karl Shapiro. Reprinted from *Poems 1940-1953*, by Karl Shapiro, by permission of Random House, Inc.

Suicide has cause and still birth, logic;
And cancer, simple as a flower, blooms.
But this invites the occult mind,
Cancels our physics with a sneer,
And spatters all we know of denouement
Across the expedient and wicked stones.

This poem begins immediately after an auto accident. Discounting the title, at what point does the reader realize the reason for the silver bell, the ruby flare, and the pulsing light? What purposes do the first fourteen lines of the poem serve? How does the poet suggest issues of life and death without using either of the words? What images of life and death appear in the opening stanzas? How does each contribute to the poet's picture? The teacher should lead students to understand how images of organic life ("beating, beating"; "Pulsing . . . like an artery") work with those of injury and death ("mangled," "little hospital," "bell . . . tolls once") to expand the reader's experience of the accident.

The person in the poem doesn't appear until the second stanza, when we learn that he and others are present at the scene—walking, deranged, among the cops. Was the person involved in the wreck? How do you know? What are the meanings of "gauche," "banal"? What is the "stubborn saw of common sense"? Students should realize that the word "saw" as used here means a "saying." How does the expression "empty husks of locusts" expand our understanding of the accident? How do the persons present react? Why has the poet chosen to compare their throats with tourniquets? Why does he speak as though their feet were bound with splints? Students should understand the poet's use of figurative language in the third stanza—his description of emotional reactions in terms of convalescence. How does this particular imagery contribute to the impact of the poem? What is the "wound" which the persons touch in the eighth line of stanza three?

The last stanza, which comments on the wreck, is the most difficult section of the poem. Here the poet moves from descriptions of the scene and the reactions of those involved to abstract questions of "who?" and "why?" What the the meanings of "occult," "denouement," "expedient"? How are we to interpret line seven—"Cancels our physics with a sneer"? What is the tone of this final stanza? What conclusions has the poet drawn?

OZYMANDIAS

Percy Bysshe Shelley

I met a traveler from an antique land
Who said: Two vast and trunkless legs of stone
Stand in the desert. Near them, on the sand,
Half sunk, a shattered visage lies, whose frown,
And wrinkled lip, and sneer of cold command,
Tell that its sculptor well those passions read
Which yet survive, stamped on these lifeless things,
The hand that mocked them and the heart that fed;
And on the pedestal these words appear:
"My name is Ozymandias, king of kings:
Look on my works, ye Mighty, and despair!"
Nothing beside remains. Round the decay
Of that colossal wreck, boundless and bare
The lone and level sands stretch far away.

In this poem students meet in more complex forms elements which they have experienced before. As meaning may not be immediately accessible, careful, directed reading is essential. Who is speaking in the poem? Students should distinguish between the person who introduces the traveler in the first sentence and the traveler himself, whose narration comprises the rest of the poem. What is the meaning of "antique" in the first line? What is a "visage"? A "pedestal"? The sentence beginning in line three and ending with line eight presents a syntactical problem which students must resolve before proceeding in their interpretation. How do the final phrases (line eight) work in the sentence? Whose is the hand that mocked them? Whose heart fed?

Students have learned in writing assignments that a modifying phrase surrounded by commas can be lifted from the sentence (with commas) without destroying the basic meaning of the sentence. How would this sentence read if, "stamped on these lifeless things," were removed? Without the modifying phrase it becomes clear that the final phrases are objects of the word "survive"—that the passions survive (in the sense of outlast) the hand and the heart. The hand that mocked these passions belonged to the artist who portrayed Ozymandias as a sneering commander. The heart that fed the passions was that of the king himself. What did Ozymandias accomplish? What did the artist accomplish? What was neither able to control? What remains, after the years, of the statue, the man after whom it was modeled, and the artist? Is the work itself permanent? Is there evidence that it, too, will pass away?

A poet chooses a pattern which will help him to express his meaning. How do pattern and idea work together in this poem? Is progression within the poem consistent, or do the lines fall into logical divisions? Students should recognize the break between lines eight and nine: the first eight lines tell what the traveler said and the last six lines repeat the words on the pedestal. Does the tone change from the first part to the second? What relationship do the parts bear to each other? Is our understanding of the inscription (lines 9-14) increased by our knowledge of the setting (lines 1-8)? What aspects of meaning are revealed only when setting and inscription are considered together? Students should realize that the poem's central irony—its contrast of the power which was with that which has endured—hinges on the juxtaposition of the two sections.

At this point in their study of "Ozymandias"—after discovering the octet-sestet pattern and how it works in this particular poem— students might be told that "Ozymandias" (wih its fourteen lines breaking between eight and nine) is a kind of sonnet. The specific kind of sonnet or the ways this poem differs from traditional models need not be explained. Only after students have read and studied many sonnets will such distinctions be meaningful.

GOD'S GRANDEUR

Gerard Manley Hopkins

The world is charged with the grandeur of God.
   It will flame out, like shining from shook foil;
   It gathers to a greatness, like the ooze of oil
Crushed. Why do men then now not reck his rod?
Generations have trod, have trod, have trod;
   And all is seared with trade; bleared, smeared with toil;
   And wears man's smudge and shares man's smell: the soil
Is bare now, nor can foot feel, being shod.

And for all this, nature is never spent;
　　There lives the dearest freshness deep down things;
And though the last lights off the black West went
　　Oh, morning, at the brown brink eastward, springs—
Because the Holy Ghost over the bent
　　World broods with warm breast and with ah! bright wings.

This poem is considerably more difficult than others in the sequence, and therefore is recommended only for capable ninth-grade students. The teacher should begin by reading the poem aloud to the students and allowing them time to reread it silently. Then he should move to close line by line examination. What is the meaning of "charged" as it is used in line one? To what is the grandeur of God compared in lines two and three? Each line begins with a descriptive metaphor ("It will flame out," "It gathers to a greatness,"), which is then expanded by a direct comparison ("like shining from shook foil," "like the ooze of oil"). Because words are tightly compressed, the images are not easily visualized. What shines from foil when it is moved from side to side? Under what circumstances does oil gather to a greatness? Why has the poet chosen these particular images? What do they suggest of the grandeur of God?

What is the meaning of "reck" as used in line four? What is the essence of this question? How does it grow out of the preceding three lines? What is the central image of the sentence beginning with line five? Are the lines to be interpreted literally? How do you know? What has been the result of man's foot upon the world? What is the effect of his actions on man himself ("nor can foot feel, being shod")? Students should understand the poet's implication that in searing, smearing, and smudging the natural world, man has lost his sensitivity—his ability to feel.

In what sense do the final six lines represent a redirection of the poem? What are the positives to be weighed against the negatives of the preceding lines? How are we to read the concluding metaphor? What forces are represented by "the last lights off the black West"? What does morning symbolize? To what is the Holy Ghost compared in the last two lines? How is the tension between man's bent for destruction and nature's persistent freshness accounted for by the final image? By what means is the natural balance maintained? Though knowledge of the circumstances under which the poem was written are not essential to critical understanding, students might benefit from knowing that Hopkins was a Jesuit priest writing within the frame of traditional Christian thought.

To help students understand the pattern of "God's Grandeur," the teacher might ask of this poem questions similar to those asked finally of "Ozymandias." How do pattern and idea work together? Are there logical divisons within the poem? Here the break in thought is underlined by the stanzaic break. Does the tone change from the first part to the second? What relationship do the parts bear to each other? How would the poem differ if it were to end with line eight? What other poem within your experience follows a design similar to this? Comparison of this poem with "Ozymandias" should help students grasp the basic potentialities of the form and some variations possible with it. At least students can experience in these two poems a relationship between external pattern and the development of idea.

The preceding program was designed as an introduction to the study of poems for students in grades seven, eight, and nine. Selections were made on the basis of poetic merit and accessibility to students of this age. They were arranged sequentially—from the simple and concrete to the more complex—so that the study of each poem would build on past knowledge and lead to more complete understanding. Questions following each poem were formulated to lead students toward critical generalizations and toward an understanding of the position of the poet in relation to his material.

To the extent that learning at all levels must build on past knowledge, the study of poems in the upper grades will be sequential, too. But emphasis may now move away from an ordered presentation of poetic structures toward a more thorough critical study of individual poems. With their experiences of the basic program as a foundation, students in grades ten, eleven, and twelve should be able to approach fairly difficult poems with confidence and some degree of sophistication.

NOTES

1. For an enlightening discussion of the nature of poetry, read Josephine Miles' "Reading Poems" in *What to Say about a Poem . . . and other essays.*

2. In his Inaugural Lecture before the University of Oxford on June 11, 1956, W. H. Auden listed among the questions which interest him most when reading a poem: "What kind of a guy inhabits this poem? What is his notion of the good life or the good place? His notion of the Evil One? What does he conceal from the reader? What does he conceal from himself?"

3. Mary Elizabeth Fowler suggests that, for junior high school students, enjoyment of many poems is preferable to close technical study. *Teaching Language, Composition, and Literature* (New York, 1965), p. 270. And David Holbrook, in his discussion of the nonacademic student, suggests that "bulk is the essential in all imaginative work in English, so we must read to our pupils a large number of poems." *English for Maturity* (Cambridge, 1961), p. 79. Neither Fowler nor Holbrook would suggest presenting a large number of poems in a small period of time, however. (See suggestion on p. 3 for pacing the assignments.)

4. The reference here is to John Ciardi's critical anthology, *How Does a Poem Mean?* (Boston, 1959).

5. MacEdward Leach, ed., *The Ballad Book* (New York, 1955), p. 4.

6. Leach, p. 9.

7. Ibid.

8. Ibid.

9. Alan Lomax, *The Folk Songs of North America* (New York, 1960), p. xvi.

10. Leach, p. 10. This section is written for the teacher—to help him lead students toward some basic generalizations. In no case should definitions precede study of individual ballads.

11. Leach, p. 5.

12. Hodgart, p. 28.

13. Leach, p. 4.

14. Ibid.

15. A. P. Hudson, *Folksongs of Mississippi and Their Backgrounds.* (Chapel Hill, N. C., 1936), p. 199.

16. Albert B. Friedman, ed. (New York, 1956), pp. 320-21.

17. Though not a part of the original Mississippi text, this final stanza is a common conclusion.

18. Even slow students are stimulated by new difficult-sounding words provided they are presented individually and in a context which they can understand.

19. Hodgart, p. 37.

20. Lomax, p. 282.

21. As printed by Lomax, p. 282.

22. Reprinted by Lomax, p. 262

23. Lomax, pp. 262-63.

24. These were published in 1964 and 1965, respectively, by the Indiana State Department of Public Instruction in cooperation with The Newspaper Fund of *The Wall Street Journal*. The first publication was distributed to all high school teachers of English in Indiana and the second was made available to all high school journalism teachers in the state.

25. N. I. White, *American Negro Folk Songs* (Cambridge, 1928), p. 347.

26. Pp. 323-24. Editor Friedman says the text "probably goes back to . . . a tinted broadsheet, vended regularly in Negro districts before World War I for five cents."

27. Lomax, p. 346.

28. Ibid., p. 558.

29. Leach, p. 81.

30. Prof. William H. Wiatt of Indiana University suggested this approach to "Lord Randal" in his TV presentation of the poem to a class of secondary students.

31. Friedman, p. 88.

32. *American Haiku* (P.O. Box 73, Platteville, Wisconsin) is a "little magazine" devoted entirely to the publication of haiku in English.

BIBLIOGRAPHY

Brooks, Cleanth and Robert Penn Warren. *Understanding Poetry*. 3rd ed. New York: Henry Holt, 1960. In this anthology, which assumes that "if poetry is worth teaching at all it is worth teaching as poetry," the authors discuss many poems in specific analytical terms. Though designed for college students, this is an invaluable source for the professional teacher of English whose commitment is to poetry as poetry.

Ciardi, John. *How Does a Poem Mean*. Boston: Houghton Mifflin, 1959. This critical anthology, which considers the nature of poetry by reference to many specific poems, is a stimulating introduction for the teacher-student of poetry.

Fowler, Mary Elizabeth. *Teaching Language, Composition, and Literature*. New York: McGraw-Hill, 1965. As the title indicates, this is a comprehensive discussion of recent trends and developments in the school English program. Mrs. Fowler's comments on the teaching of poetry are particularly valuable.

Friedman, Albert B., ed. *The Viking Book of Folk Ballads of the English-Speaking World*. New York: Viking, 1956. In the introduction to this collection Friedman discusses ballad form and origin.

Henderson, Harold G. *An Introduction to Haiku*. New York: Doubleday, 1958. This "anthology of poems and poets from Basho to Shiki" contains Henderson's English translations of more than 375 haiku along with his commentary on the poems and the original Japanese texts. An invaluable guide to the teacher or student of haiku and poetry in general, the book is available as a Doubleday Anchor Original paperback.

———. *Haiku in English*. Japan Society, New York, 1965. This little paperback discusses the writing of haiku in English and summarizes the current American interest in the form. A section on "Writing and Teaching Haiku" is particularly valuable to the teacher.

Hodgart, M. J. C. *The Ballads*. London: Hutchinson's University Library, 1950. 2nd ed., 1962. This is a brief readable discussion of ballad form, history, and scholarship with specific reference to some ballad texts.

Holbrook, David. *English for Maturity*. Cambridge: Cambridge University Press, 1961. Holbrook's blending of theory and practical advice is directed toward teachers of English in England's secondary modern schools (as contrasted to the more academically oriented grammar schools). The poetry teaching suggestions in chapters five and six, however, should be valuable to all teachers of English. He considers poetry the heart of any English program.

Leach, MacEdward. *The Ballad Book*. New York: Harper, 1955. Here in one volume is a comprehensive collection of ballads from England, Scotland, and America. The selected list of available ballad recordings, which appears in an appendix, is particularly valuable to the teacher.

Lomax, Alan. *The Folk Songs of North America*. New York: Doubleday, 1960. This comprehensive history of folk songs in America contains words, music, and background of more than 300 songs. Lomax, a recognized authority, has also written *Mister Jelly Roll, Folk Song: U. S. A.,* and *Harriett and her Harmonium*.

Perrine, Laurence. *Sound and Sense*. 2nd ed. New York: Harcourt, Brace & World, 1963. This was written for college students as an introduction to the serious study of poetry. It is an appropriate first book for the English teacher whose background in poetry is insufficient.

Wimsatt, W. K., Jr. *What to Say about a Poem . . . and other essays.* Champaign, Illinois, 1963. In addition to Wimsatt's title essay, this paperback publication of the National Council of Teachers of English includes "Reading Poems" by Josephine Miles and "The Importance of Tone in the Interpretation of Literature" by Laurence Perrine.

Part II
DRAMA*

░░░

Like the basic poetry sequence, the drama program for grades
seven through nine builds on the students' previous experience
with the elements of story. "Action and Narration," the first unit
in the series, is designed to help students grasp the essential differences between narrative and dramatic form. The play version of
Stephen Vincent Benét's "The Devil and Daniel Webster" must by
its very nature differ from the author's earlier narrative version of
the same story, and the changes that Benét makes in adapting
his material from one form to another reflect the peculiar requirements of each.

In her critical explication, Professor Mary Alice Burgan out-
lines for the teacher a method of comparative study. She considers
the formative influence of narrative voice in de Maupassant's "The
Necklace" and Poe's "The Tell-Tale Heart," as well as Benét's
short story. By contrast, she examines the ways Benét's dramatic
version works to compensate for the lack of a narrative point of
view. Finally, in the writing assignments which conclude the unit,

---

* It has not been the purpose of this program to offer detailed day-by-day
lesson plans for the teacher. Rather, writers of the program have attempted
to present a critical and pedagogical basis for the development of units of instruction. The role of the teacher in forming the materials for his own class
is crucial. The aims of sound courses of study can be realized only by
qualified teachers in their classes.

she engages students in some of the crucial creative tasks that writers of short stories and plays must face.

Built on "Action and Narration" and recommended for students in grade eight are two plays about Abraham Lincoln—*Abe Lincoln in Illinois* by Robert E. Sherwood and *The Last Days of Lincoln* by Mark Van Doren. Students experience in these plays the ways history can be fashioned into dramatic form. Though Sherwood and Van Doren have selected different incidents from the life of Lincoln, the themes of the plays, insofar as they relate to the central character, are similar. By comparing the ways two playwrights have interpreted for the stage the massive issues of slavery, secession, civil war, and reconstruction, students should become more aware of both the limitations and the potentialities of dramatic literature.

In grade nine students read two Shakespearean history plays, *Richard III* and *Henry V*. Action in both of these is dominated and unified by the central character, so that the plays are less diffuse and consequently more accessible to young readers than many of Shakespeare's history plays. As with the Lincoln plays, emphasis is on careful reading of the texts. In the Shakespeare unit, however, students are led from the specific plays toward basic critical generalizations about history plays. Concern here, as in all sections of the junior high school literature program, is with workable distinctions rather than with *a priori* definitions.

The writers of these materials have attempted to provide teachers with a critical and pedagogical basis for their class instruction. The critical essays in the three units are written for the teacher to serve as focal points for the development of units of instruction. The study questions which follow each essay are formulated, for the most part, to lead students toward the critical generalizations expressed in the essay. Both essays and questions are designed to respect the integrity of individual works and at the same time to acquaint students with basic structures underlying all dramatic literature.

Class activities should lead students toward an understanding of how the elements of drama—plot, character, action, setting, theme, and language—work together in individual plays. For example, the writing assignment in "Action and Narration" which pertains most specifically to drama requires students to visualize an opening scene for a play version of "The Necklace." Only by assuming the position of a playwright and solving some of his initial problems of setting, character, and action can students adapt the story from narrative to dramatic form. Further writing assignments requiring creative or critical participation may be formulated from individual study questions of the other units. As in the other sequences of this course of study, the teacher should use the ideas which seem to him valuable and supplement them with the methods which have been successful for him in the past.

Action and Narration:
An Approach to the Drama
and the Short Story

MARY ALICE BURGAN

Assistant Professor of English
Indiana University

The discussion of the short story and the one-act play in this unit attempts to suggest ways of building an awareness of the possibilities of fiction upon the student's natural interest in such elements of storytelling as suspense, vividness of action, spectacular effects, and the excitement of plot. If the student can learn to analyze the manner in which a particular story takes its hold on him, he is well on his way to a discovery of the satisfaction in those elements of literature which make for another, deeper kind of entertainment—a kind which outlasts the pounding of the pulses, or the pleasure of solving a puzzle, or the tickle of excitement that modifies the terror of a good "thriller."

To take advantage of the beginning student's spontaneous encounters with these highly dramatic elements of literature, the unit begins with a comparison between the short story and drama: the story and the one-act play versions of Stephen Vincent Benét's "The Devil and Daniel Webster" have been chosen because the story has been widely anthologized and the play is readily available in paperback (*24 Favorite One-Act Plays*, ed. Bennett Cerf and Van H. Cartmell, Dolphin Books: Doubleday, Garden City,

N. Y., 1963). The comparison of these works is intended only to provide a model, however, for comparisons of any more current fiction and drama which the teacher may wish to substitute. Frequently television will offer a dramatization of a famous short story; in the past it has presented Bret Harte's "The Outcasts of Poker Flat," and one major network has announced future plans for a dramatization of Katherine Ann Porter's "Noon Wine." Another possibility for comparison lies in collections of short stories drawn from televison series; there are two such collections from "The Twilight Zone." Movies can provide other occasions for the comparison of a dramatic with a narrative version of a story; *To Kill a Mockingbird* is only one example of such a possibility. In short, the teacher who wishes to make use of the suggestions offered in the initial discussion here may want to keep watch over the local television and motion picture offerings for worthwhile dramatizations which will have the appeal of currency with his students.

The additional stories treated in this unit have been chosen for their special kind of dramatic appeal, even though the drama in them is not the drama of the stage. Guy de Maupassant's "The Necklace" and Edgar Allan Poe's "The Tell-Tale Heart" have been chosen because their appeal lies in a characteristic emphasis upon a dramatically simple situation, a working out of that situation largely in terms of swift and vivid action, and a basic dependence upon the creation of relatively "theatrical" effects like surprise and terror in the reader. These are stories the beginning student may enjoy with many of the same responses that are elicited by the movie or the television screen, and an analysis of those responses can lead to a fuller understanding of the stories themselves as well as of the nature of narrative art in general.

One major difference between the narrative and dramatic versions of a story will usually lie in the fact that the narrative account must have a constant voice—the voice of the narrator. That voice may be neutral, it may be characterized by a special idiom or a particular bias, indeed it may turn out to be the voice of a major character in the story; but because it is a sequential mode—unlike drama, which is also spatial and pictorial—there is a constant presence in narrative of some kind of voice which places action, setting, character, and scene in a continuum; and in most stories that voice cannot help but influence meaning. It will interpret, if only through selection and rejection of detail, the special emphases to be noted. In the play, unless the dramatist uses a chorus or a chorus figure, as does Thornton Wilder with the Stage Manager in *Our Town*, there is no such constant interpreter present; the force of the story must come through scenes which are significant enough in themselves to force the playgoer to assume the role of interpreter. This is not to imply that action is negligible in the narrative mode; modern story-writers, less and less content that any single narrator could have the wisdom to interpret definitively the whole of a tale for the reader, have attempted to make their narratives as "scenic" as possible. Nevertheless, they cannot avoid the narrative voice as fundamental for their particular mode, and the reader's attention to the characteristics of that voice will often provide a valuable key to the interpretation of a story. The formative function of the narrative voice in establishing the context, intensity, focus, and sequence of action in a short story may finally lead the reader to his best understanding of theme; moreover, the operation of the narrative voice, as it variously occurs in "The Devil and Daniel Webster," "The Necklace," and "The Tell-Tale Heart," illustrates a tremendous variety—a short story can be a dramatic essay on American history, an almost scientific notation of the ascendency of fate, or a case study of a demented mind.

If we survey the differences between the story and play versions of "The Devil and Daniel Webster," we can see how the voice of the narrator may be established and adjusted to the action of the story in order to provide context and focus. The voice that speaks in Stephen Vincent Benét's short story is the voice of a native New Hampshireman who is passing on to the reader a "tall tale" which has been current for a long time in his particular section of the country. In his first sentences the writer enables him to introduce himself and place his tale geographically, while giving the impression of an informal, rambling chat with the reader.

It's a story they all tell in the border country, where Massachusetts joins Vermont and New Hampshire.

> Yes, Dan'l Webster's dead—or, at least, they buried him. But
> every time there's a thunderstorm around Marshfield, they say
> you can hear his rolling voice in the hollows of the sky.

Aside from setting the background of the story in time and space,
these first lines begin to give the narrator character, even though
he plays no part in the plot itself. But the role he does play is
important: he provides the context, emotional and historical as
well as geographical, of the tale he is telling. He sounds the note
of native pride and patriotism which will become a motivating
force in the later action of the story when Jabez Stone is acquitted
by a jury of native American villains after Daniel Webster has
stirred their pride and patriotism deeply. Moreover, this particular
narrator serves in the initial characterization of the central actor
in the story, for his emphasis on the legendary quality of Daniel
Webster and his continual allusions to Webster's struggles to save
the union from dissolution in the troubles which preceded the
Civil War focus the reader's attention immediately on the emotional and historical aura of the man he is talking about. The first
anecdote he recounts about his hero gathers all these qualities
together and thereby prepares for their illustration in the action
which follows:

> And they say that if you go to his grave and speak loud and
> clear, "Dan'l Webster—Dan'l Webster!" the ground'll begin to
> shiver and the trees begin to shake. And after a while you'll hear
> a deep voice saying, "Neighbor, how stands the Union?" Then you
> better answer: the Union stands as she stood, rock-bottomed and
> copper-sheathed, one and indivisible, or he's liable to rear right out
> of the ground. At least, that's what I was told when I was a
> youngster.

The creation of a narrative voice which can combine the idiom
of a particular locale with a sense of the whole history of the
nation helps to show that Webster was not only a man of great
political power who had one major concern—the preservation of
the integrity of his country—but also that he was human enough
to inspire the affectionate and gossipy reminiscences of his neighbors. In the light of this interest in Daniel Webster's character
and vocation, the story of Jabez Stone, the poor farmer who sells

his soul to the devil in a moment of discouragement, will provide only a secondary interest: the climactic action of "The Devil and Daniel Webster" will be the great trial scene in which Webster is the central mover of events. The emphasis there is on the patriotism and natural love of freedom which his eloquence can re-evoke even for the members of the ghostly and biased jury which the devil has provided to try Stone's case. As far as plot is concerned, Stone's situation seems most important for its agency in providing a dramatic illustration of the power of Daniel Webster: his own feelings about his plight, the feelings of his wife, the emotion of his situation—all take second place to the portrait of the great New England lawyer given by the admiring, historically conscious New Hampshire narrator.

The centrality of Daniel Webster in the narrative version of Benét's fiction is further emphasized by the action which follows the trial and concludes the story. The devil offers to tell Daniel Webster's fortune for him. Webster agrees, and in the passage that follows, the devil foresees all the troubles Webster will have in the future—the defeat of his ambition to be President, the death of his two sons in the Civil War, and his loss of popularity among his own constituents because of his advocacy of moderation over the abolition dispute. At the end of this prophecy, however, Webster asks the devil if the Union will survive. When the devil answers yes, Webster roars with laughter, and says, "For, by the thirteen original colonies I'd go to the Pit itself to save the Union!" This episode is absent from the play, and its absence is one mark of a shift in interest which the dramatic form seems to have required in adapting the story for the stage. The theme in the story version, with its emphasis on the character and mission of one man, seems to be the preservation of the Union in a time of great troubles through the devotion of a simple man to the ideals of American freedom. When we turn to the play, however, we find that it virtually deletes this interpretation of the life of Daniel Webster, shifting its interest to Jabez Stone's plight as a man and creating roles for Stone's wife and neighbors, as well as for Daniel Webster, in freeing him from his bargain with the devil.

The play begins with the wedding of Jabez and Mary Stone, and the opening scene which conveys this fact to the audience also shows what substitutes the absence of a narrative voice might require in setting up a play. The historical importance and significance of Daniel Webster will have to be made clear through action or not at all; there is no one available in the play to give his whole biography through anecdote and summary. The play must set up some background, however, in its opening scene. The scene opens on the day of Jabez Stone's wedding; it is the main room of the Stone farmhouse, and the room is filled with typical New England characters milling around, dancing to the tune of the fiddler, and talking about the typical New England dishes that are to be served for the wedding supper. "Oysters for supper! . . . And layer cake—layer cake—" Clearly the playwright has decided to make use of a kind of chorus of townspeople to do the job which his narrator had performed in the story, and in the midst of the chorus dialogue which follows, a note of mystery is struck; one old man says, "Wonder where he got it all—Stones was always poor." And a neighbor replies, "Ain't poor now—makes you wonder just a mite." The gossip continues until it has risen to a high pitch, becoming a kind of chant which is to be delivered in time with the dance music. The audience overhears from the crowd of wedding guests what it needs to know in order for the action of the play to progress, and in the process the chanting suspicions of the chorus figures point to Jabez Stone's past and its possible secret depths.

The chorus not only sets the background, then; it also heightens the personal dimensions of the story of this man who has sold his soul to the devil. Frequently the chorus speaks in what is almost free verse, and achieves an emotional intensity almost entirely absent from the fictional version of the tale. For example, when the devil arrives at the wedding celebration, he indicates his unusual origins by playing a strangely exciting tune on the fiddle; the townspeople slowly begin to recognize who he is; and in a rising chorus they accuse Jabez of having committed a terrible sin. "Jabez Stone—Jabez Stone," they cry, "answer us—answer us." At last they leave in panic, having seen the truth of the situation, and do not return until the end of the play, when they young man imperiled by a wrong choice and redeemed by the loyalty of his wife. That is not, to be sure, all there is to the play; but the lovers' ordeal secures an effect which comes easily to playwrights, and it appears in this case to have filled in for an effect which is very hard to transpose from the printed page to the theater. With a few expert narrative strokes, the short-story writer can evoke the interest of Webster's character and some sense of its peculiar relation to the New England mind. Lacking comparable means, the playwright works toward a different end, evoking the pathos of Jabez Stone's situation, and a sense of his commonplace—though touching—relation to his wife. In other words, the vivid familiar sentiments of melodrama replace the subtler, more abstract concerns of fiction when Benét puts his characters on stage—thus he loses much of his freedom to interpret them for us.

Explicit commentary is perhaps the most obvious expression of the narrator's license to control his reader's response, but the sophisticated modern writer tends to make rather sparing use of this privilege. He would rather suggest than declare, and his resources of suggestion are flexible almost beyond comparison with those of a playwright, whose chorus can only intrude at some cost to the progress of the action, and whose occasional flashbacks —as in Arthur Miller's *Death of a Salesman*—are at best a somewhat clumsy approximation of that easy entry into the character's mind which the writer of fiction takes for granted. As Daniel Webster searches for the right note to strike in his final appeal before the jury, an offstage voice points up the meaning of the crisis for the theater audience. The reading audience, on the other hand, discovers what it feels like to plead this case before this jury:

> For it was him they'd come for, not only Jabez Stone. He read it in the glitter of their eyes and in the way the stranger hid his mouth with one hand. And if he fought them with their own weapons, he'd fall into their power: he knew that, although he couldn't have told you how. It was his own anger and horror that burned in their eyes; and he'd have to wipe that out or the case was lost. He stood there for a moment, his black eyes burning like anthracite. And then he began to speak.

drive the devil off with muskets, flails, and b
surge of the townspeople onto the stage is nee
spectacular resolution for the whole drama.

To a limited extent, then, the chorus may assum
a narrator—commenting on the action, helping to
appropriate mood, and indeed surpassing the narra
immediacy and emotional force. If we now examine t
characters as they appear before us on the stage, we v
notice a corresponding gain in their capacity to rivet ou
to the events they enact. But we will also find those
have lost so much of their original quality that they now
almost a different story. Jabez Stone's opening lines, whicl
that Daniel Webster is coming to the wedding, are quickl
What follows is a dialogue between Jabez and Mary, now
together on stage, in which the sympathies of the audienc
emphatically directed to the love between these two young
ple. Mary is plainly proud of her man; and her man, althot
he seems uneasy about something, lets it be known that no mat
what may chance to happen, "It was all for you."

This romantic interest, which Benét neglects to develop in hi
short story, turns out to be central to the stage version of "The
Devil and Daniel Webster." When Mary learns that her bride-
groom has sold his soul, she assures him of her unselfish devotion.
"Do you think it's the place makes the difference to a woman?
I'd—I'd have kept your house. I'd have stroked the cat and fed
the chickens and seen you wiped your shoes on the mat. I wouldn't
have asked for more. Oh, Jabez—why didn't you tell me?" Again,
when Webster asks her to make the sacrifice of withdrawing when
the devil arrives, she bravely complies. Nor does her absence
deprive her of all part in the action of the trial. At a crucial moment, just before Webster's final appeal to the jury, her voice is
heard off stage saying, "for love is strong as death," an utterance
which seems to inspire the orator to his highest flight.

Mary, in short, supplies the play with a motivating force which
would positively interfere with the main undertaking of the short
story. A piece of fiction which is very nearly an essay, a nostalgic
excursion into American folklore, has become a melodrama about

The writer here has no need to invent an action capable of reveal-ing the significance of this tense moment. He can present a totally inward state of mind without the slightest halt in the rush of his story toward its climax.

By pointing out the changes entailed in dramatizing "The Devil and Daniel Webster," even though Benét himself carried out the necessary revisions, we can show our students that to strip a short story of everything but its action is in fact to make it into a new story, which no longer means quite what it meant before because there are certain kinds of meaning that it can no longer express. Yet we cannot rest comfortably in this demonstration. Having made clear that action is only one factor among various others, how shall we describe its cooperation with the rest? A close look at two short works famous for their action, Guy de Maupassant's "The Necklace" and Edgar Allan Poe's "The Tell-Tale Heart," may help to clarify that question. In both cases, the nature of the narrative voice is ultimately the surest clue to the meaning of what happens.

If such a statement seems easy enough to apply to one of Poe's tales, it is harder and perhaps more instructive to test it on one of de Maupassant's. When we recall "The Necklace," we are apt to visualize a sequence of dramatic scenes, tersely rendered in flawless, transparent prose. Indeed, the transparency is so fine that we seem at first to be dealing with a narrator whose great virtue consists in his refusal to assert himself at all. "What hap-pens" is simply that a clerk's wife borrows a diamond necklace to wear to a party, loses it on the way home, replaces it with a costly duplicate—keeping both the accident and the substitute a secret from the rich friend who lent her the necklace—and endures a lifetime of desperate poverty as she and her husband struggle to pay the vast sum which the duplicate cost them. The story ends with the miserable couple discovering that the lost "dia-monds" were really paste imitations, worth a tiny fraction of the debt contracted to replace them. The reader is stunned by this abrupt ending; he has been engaged by the pathos of Madame Loisel's shift in fortune, and suddenly, if there is any more to

be said about Madame Loisel's life, he must make it up for himself: the story does not ask him—hardly even permits him—to go
that far. The fact that her life has been ruined has been deeply
confirmed by the concluding revelation that it has been ruined
in vain, and the suddenness of the revelation is designed to prevent the reader from questioning it; indeed in one of its most
characteristic effects, de Maupassant's surprise ending seems designed to halt all questions about the role of fate in the lives
of the unlucky.

On the first reading a beginning student will probably miss
the relation between the problem of fate and the surprise ending
of "The Necklace," but de Maupassant's skill will have assured
his participation in the shock of the sudden reversal. Taking this
participation for granted, then, we might begin to direct his
attention backward in class discussion. We might investigate the
way the story's episodes lead to the final action. De Maupassant
takes great pains to show Madame Loisel hesitating before she
chooses the necklace, and finally making a perfect selection after
giving up the search. Then in his depiction of the great party he
gives a glittering emphasis on her triumph, evoking the mystifica-
tion her beauty inspires and accenting it by showing her dull
husband half asleep at the end of the ball. An analysis of these
details may lead the student to see de Maupassant's art in ar-
ranging the situation so as to heighten the contrasts in Madame
Loisel's strange story and to show, in doing so, a whole world
dominated by surprising contrasts because it is ruled by fate.

The surprises of fate are seen throughout to be malevolent or
unlucky. Madame Loisel, we are told in the first lines of the
story, "was one of those pretty and charming girls born, *as though
fate had blundered over her, into a family of artisans*" (italics
added). Beauty and charm are gifts of fortune, mocked by the
absence of other gifts which fortune withholds. But positive acts
of choice seem to fare no better. For example, the young couple
have earnestly sought the honor which leads to their undoing.
Monsieur Loisel bears their invitation home in triumph: "I had
tremendous trouble to get it. Everyone wants one; it's very select,

and very few go to the clerks. You'll see all the really big people there."

The two other objects of eager pursuit in the story are the necklace itself and the glorious dress which Madame Loisel buys for the occasion at the expense of the little money her husband has saved for a hunting trip. The finery has taken all her calculation; her reward is to attend the party in a sort of masquerade. A middle-class housewife has become a Cinderella: "She was the prettiest woman present, elegant, graceful, smiling, and quite above herself with happiness. All the men stared at her, inquiring her name, and asked to be introduced to her. All the undersecretaries of state were eager to waltz with her. The Minister noticed her." Such ironies hint that fate is always ready to put people in their places, but especially those persons who feel that their place is not a rightful one and therefore go about trying to change it. It may be, indeed, that fate is not blind but attends only to what is required to preserve the status quo. All will go well with a man who accepts his appointed state in life, but he is asking for trouble if he pretends to be something higher. In "A Piece of String," to cite another example of de Maupassant's theme, the peasant who picks up a piece of string and then tries to hide his miserliness in doing so is accused of having stolen a wallet in the act and must spend the rest of his life trying to get people to realize the truth of his miserliness.

In "The Necklace," which is essentially a dramatic story, the surprises have been so well built up in their dramatic economy and concreteness that the main thing we remember about Madame Loisel is simply what *happens* to her—in short, the action. We have already begun to see that this action is linked with the thematic import of the story; nevertheless, there is a voice which "tells" this story, and when we stop to listen to it closely, we can analyze its peculiar bearing on the way the action has been presented and the assumptions which the story as a whole makes about the inevitable role of surprises in human life.

The narrative voice is strangely unnoticeable in this story, which seems at first to depend so heavily on inspiring our pity.

The voice has no pity of its own; it is there simply to tell about Madame Loisel as clearly as possible, not to draw attention to itself. It is the voice of the impersonal narrator—one who will delineate the motivations of his characters but one who will not comment on them, one who will never say, for example, whether they are good or bad. Despite the care in setting up Madame Loisel's situation so that it will illustrate all that it can offer of irony and bad luck, the main function of the narrator is to prepare for the surprise; he never stops to weep for the poor heroine or to ask the reader to weep for her. In short, the narrator seems intent upon refusing to register any emotion, and this characteristic is best illustrated by his failure to make any comment at all on the surprise that ends the story. In a world ruled by fate, it is useless to comment. Indeed, the narrator of "The Necklace" seems to have set himself up as a kind of scientific observer; he seeks to provide a well-documented case study rather than to highlight the tragedy in a study of human aspiration come to grief.

There is an aspect to "The Necklace" other than action and narration, of course; there is the aspect of characterization. But although de Maupassant fleshes out his characters with details which help the reader to see them as individuals rather than as types, we have begun to see that this story is based on idea more than on character. It would, for example, be somewhat distorting to try to show the action of this story deriving from character—to show that Madame Loisel *deserved* the fate that came to her because she was a very vain and materialistic woman; the emphasis does not lie upon her so much as upon what happened to her. The surprise ending focuses that emphasis sharply and definitively.

In the third story we have to look at here, Edgar Allan Poe's "The Tell-Tale Heart," there is a surprise ending, but from the first line of the story, that ending is modified; the emphasis of the story on character is set by the fact that the main protagonist is speaking. The story is a mystery story, to be sure, but it retains one mystery long after the reader has found the answer to the most obvious secret at the end. The second mystery is the mystery of the character of the narrator: "True! — nervous — very, very, dreadfully nervous I had been and am; but why *will* you say that

I am mad?" Both mysteries begin with this opening statement, and they go on building to a climax that explodes with the very last line of the story, revealing both that the murder has been discovered, and that in its discovery lies the truth and mystery of the narrator's madness. " 'Villains!' I shrieked, 'dissemble no more! I admit the deed! — tear up the planks! — here, here!—it is the beating of his hideous heart!' "

Then there are two major sources of interest for the reader in "The Tell-Tale Heart" which coincide at the very end of the story. In the matter of action alone there is the suspense of committing a crime and then getting away with it. The reader is drawn into the narrator's fascination with this problem because he sees all the action through the narrator's coolly calculating eyes. Because he has been there, the narrator can tell with all its vividness what happened—the stops and starts in the night, the breathless waiting at the door, the endless listening to the old man's heart, and then the sudden surge of fury in which the deed is done. The act of murder is described almost photographically, taken down first hand from the senses of its main mover, and this intimacy involves the reader in a strange kind of sympathy with the narrator. When the police arrive, the reader himself is ready to hope that they will be deceived; one source of shock at the end is the narrator's giving his whole secret away, suddenly disbelieving his own plan of action.

The reader's shock at the twist of plot at the ending of "The Tell-Tale Heart" initiates a second discovery, one that bears upon the deeper, more lasting mystery of the story. For he rediscovers at the end of the tale that the real issue of the story is not simply physical suspense but the truth of the fact that the nervousness which the narrator has remarked in himself in the opening lines is indeed madness. Of course, the reader has sensed some suspension of normality throughout the story, but it is part of Poe's art that the narrator's grasp on normality has almost left him by the end. The art of the story lies in the vividness with which the action has been described and in the suspense which waits for the last realization that such vividness could come only from a demented mind. When we return to the beginning, then, our task will be to look at the startling action not for itself but for the clues it is able to give about the nature of the narrator and the meaning of his murder of the old man.

Students, especially those who have enjoyed the shock and horror of "The Tell-Tale Heart" fully on a first reading, may find it difficult to understand why they have to go back to the beginning again. But here is where their analysis of their own reactions to the surprise ending might help them to see that there is more to a story than plot alone. A good storyteller like de Maupassant or Poe will always help us to drive home that fact, because no first reading can ever catch all the significance that is there. On a rereading of Poe's story, for example, it becomes evident that the narrator has given some clues as to where he is now in time and space, and those clues tell the reader that he has already been found out, that he has not deluded the police. The time of the telling is well after the deed he recounts; there is also a listener who seems to have been arguing with the narrator for some time, so that the story is framed as an answer to some accusation. Moreover, the accusation has to do with a disease against which the narrator is trying to defend himself; he says that it had "sharpened my senses—not destroyed—not dulled them." In recalling the deed, the narrator acts as a lawyer, building up his case with logic and irrefutable evidence. His urgency in insisting upon detailed, patient analysis of his motives and those of the old man man forms a dramatic interest not only in the murder itself but also in the presentation of his case. The listener's involvement is a product of the drama of the defense as well as the horror of the murder narrative. Looking at the defense, we see that its emotion indeed parallels the emotion which accompanied the deed itself, in its progress to the last climax. The narrator, we realize, is telling about *and* reenacting the crime; his final shriek of terror belongs not only to the scene with the policemen on the morning after the murder; it also belongs to the scene with the listener on this day of the telling of the story.

The listener, then, is unraveling not only the mystery of the act but that of the man who perpetrated the act. And so the surprise of the final terror entails his realization that the act has been found out, and also that one so calm as this narrator should have lost his control. It is in this kind of surprise that Poe's art as a portrayer of demented consciousness lies—the surprise, which he can finally create in his reader, that illustrates how easy it is to become involved in the kind of madness of the narrator if only that madness is given voice. The logic and vividness which Poe gives the voice of the madman can make that voice seem very sane until the surprise ending in which a horrible crime reveals without doubt that the narrator's vividness and reason are really the most threatening forms of distortion and irrationality. "The Black Cat" and "The Cask of Amontillado" provide other superb examples of this kind of effect.

What we can begin to show a class through approaching the tale a second time, looking at the relation of the narrator to the action, is the source of the horror they experience in reading Poe. But perhaps we can go even farther by asking what the horror in this story signifies. From the point of view of action alone, horror seems to rise from the fact that events have turned bad when a successful issue to them was in reach. But that is hardly all, and looking at the story from the point of view of the narrator, we recognize that the horror lies in the cool "reasonableness" of his insanity. Finally, however, we might ask about the meaning of the narrator's motivation. What is there about the old man which has caused the narrator to commit the crime and then to confess to it?

One striking fact about the ending is that it is caused by the dead man. Surely the beating of his heart beneath the floorboards is a figment of the narrator's imagination, but that figment itself is a reality which ruins all his plans. And somehow through *his* belief in the tell-tale heart, the listener believes in it too. Then what compelled the narrator to still that heart in the first place? He says at the beginning that it was nothing: "I loved the old man. He had never wronged me." The only "wrong" to be avenged is the torment of the old man's eye. Nevertheless, as the story progresses, we can begin to pick up other aspects of the narrator's motive. "Never before that night had I *felt* the extent of my own powers—of my sagacity. I could scarcely contain my feelings of triumph." He seems to have been moved by an urge to assert his power over another; there is sheer pleasure in feeling that he is in control, especially in control of another's fears. So when the old man groans, he says, "Many a night, just at midnight, when all the world slept, it has welled up from my own bosom, deepening, with its dreadful echo, the terrors that distracted me. I say I knew it well, I knew what the old man felt, and pitied him, although I chuckled at heart."

The narrator's drive for power over life and death, power to inspire fear in another, ultimately expresses his own fear, his own sense that there are forces over him which he cannot control. In his madness he has located those forces in the old man's blind eye, but the ending reveals that he has not triumphed over them. He must renounce his triumph through confession, and in doing so he unwittingly affirms the limitations of any man's drive to dominate his fears through trying to destroy their source. His confession asserts with all vehemence that what the old man has signified still exists.

The madman is one who has let his own terrors goad him into becoming an instrument of terror for the unoffending beings who surround him. What Poe manages so powerfully to suggest in having him tell his own story is that his madness is similar to sanity. His perversity is understandable—disturbingly so for the reader—and his ruin is shockingly inevitable. He has defied the laws which rule all men, and he has done this with the full and self-destructive belief in their pursuit of him. It is the self-destructiveness of his act which plunges the reader into a most horrifying encounter with the mysteries of human action and conscience in this story.

It is difficult to forecast how far a given group of students may penetrate into the depths of Poe's story, but it does seem feasible to take most classes *beyond* the surprise-ending horror—a task which means taking them *into* the surprise ending with great care. In a good story this analysis will show a great deal about the purely dramatic skill of the writer. His mastery in presenting vivid episodes, building up suspense, and preparing for a final revelation which makes his point with dramatic impact must match that of the playwright. But a study of the setting up of action in a short story will reveal also how much the short-story writer is aided by the narrative voice—his unique resource for focusing the reader's attention on the theme of his story.

The play version of "The Devil and Daniel Webster" illustrates some of the substitutes a playwright may have to use for the narrative voice; other more experimental modern plays have explored less conventional methods for extending the possibilities of the drama to control the spectator's involvement and focus. It should be noted here, however, that the drama's most experimental device for helping to approximate the intimacy of the story is the flexibility of the film. It is in alluding to this form of drama frequently that the teacher can make some of his best points about the nature of both the short story and the play. The modern film dramatist can use the camera eye to focus his action. The movies provide a much more intimate working out of theme in relation to action and character than does the stage. There is, for example, a fine animated cartoon version of "The Tell-Tale Heart" which uses the narrator's voice, throwing abstract, violent images on the screen to evoke the action. Through this medium an attempt is made to visualize the mind of the mad narrator, and with the use of effective sound effects the result is almost overpowering. Moreover, any film director who takes great care with the effects of his camera can help to show a student one of the most crucial lessons he can learn in his first analyses of fiction, or of any art—that the interest of what he reads lies not only in the excitement of the raw emotions it can arouse in him but also in the meaning it can attach to those emotions through forming and directing them toward an exploration of the deeper issues of his life.

STUDY QUESTIONS

1. At one point in the story version of "The Devil and Daniel Webster," the devil refutes a legal maneuver by proving that he is as true an American as anyone else. Reread that passage and then explain how Webster uses it to call for a jury trial of his client. What bearing does the Constitution have on the proceedings?

2. In the middle of the trial Daniel Webster gets angry and

decides to try to trick the jury. Why does he decide not to? What does he decide to do? Can you show how his final decision about the kind of speech he does make is related to his decision earlier to go by the Constitution?

3. Compare the last paragraph of Daniel Webster's speech to the jury with his reaction to the devil's prophecy that his life will be a failure in the future. How do the two passages fit together?

4. The story version of "The Devil and Daniel Webster" does not give us much of a picture of Jabez Stone's wife. Look at the opening speeches in the play version and tell what she is like. To guide your discussion here, it might be well to think of her as a complex character, that is, one who can possess two qualities which might seem to contradict each other. What would you call two of these qualities in Mary Stone? Find one speech in which they are best illustrated.

5. Just as Mary Stone has changed in the play version of Benét's story, so has Jabez. Do you find him more admirable in the play? Why?

6. Early in "The Necklace" de Maupassant has Monsieur Loisel come into the house and exclaim about the stew his wife has planned for supper. Why does he add this small detail? Can you find other details like this in the author's depiction of Monsieur Loisel?

8. At the end of the great ball Madame Loisel has a chance to wait while her husband calls a cab for them. Why does she refuse to do so? What is the effect of her refusal?

9. From the last picture we see of Madame Loisel, would you say that she had learned the lesson of the story? Pick out the details of her description which illustrate your answer.

10. It is often difficult to talk about the language in which a work is written, but you can tell a great deal by the length and kinds of sentences which a passage of prose uses. What happens to the sentences in the last two paragraphs of "The Tell-Tale Heart"? How does the change that takes place in them bear on what is happening in the story?

11. Why is the narrator of the Poe story so anxious to have the police sit in the very room in which the old man is buried? Can

you connect this audacity with his motive for the murder and the telling of the story itself?

SUGGESTED WRITING ASSIGNMENTS

1. Pretend that you are beginning to write a horror story in the style of Edgar Allan Poe; you are at the paragraph in which you want to set your scene so that the reader will really get a physical sense of it. It is dark, so you cannot use visual details; you must write your paragraph using *only* details of hearing and of touch.

2. You have been contracted by a television studio to write a version of "The Necklace" for the stage. Write a description of what the stage set will look like, and then give a paragraph in which you tell who will make the first speech, where your version will begin in the story, what other scenes you plan to use, and any other major changes you think will be necessary.

3. Rewrite the first paragraph of "The Tell-Tale Heart" using a narrator other than the madman to tell the story.

Two History Plays

Abe Lincoln in Illinois
by Robert E. Sherwood

The Last Days of Lincoln
by Mark Van Doren

ROY L. FELSHER

Formerly Assistant Director
of the Indiana University
English Curriculum Study Center

Nations are fascinated by their own heroes and heroines. The few verifiable facts about these persons are supplemented by a core of legends—often of folk origin—which may then be expanded in song, poetry, or drama. Playwrights frequently work with legendary figures. From England and France, for example, have come Anouilh's *The Lark,* Bolt's *A Man for All Seasons,* Eliot's *Murder in the Cathedral,* and Shakespeare's plays of the English kings. Among the American contributions to this genre are plays about Lincoln, Roosevelt, and Daniel Webster. The Lincoln plays now under consideration—*Abe Lincoln in Illinois* and *The Last Days of Lincoln*—are both based on fact. But the interpretation of fact, including much of its human significance, originates in legend.

To be capable of such treatment, a legend must contain elements of vital concern to a modern reader—elements which clarify modern problems or sustain modern beliefs. In other words, the legend must be alive. The legend of Johnny Appleseed has not inspired a history play. There was a real Johnny Appleseed, and a legend grew up about him expressing the frontiersman's relation to the wilderness. But the wilderness has now disappeared, and the men who cleared, farmed, and cultivated it have been replaced by machines. Few persons today identify with the figure of Johnny Appleseed; for the writer of history plays, his legend is dead. By contrast, the legend of Abraham Lincoln is very much alive, not because the historical records are more plentiful (in fact, abundant records can inhibit the growth of legend), but because Lincoln has come to symbolize much that is still meaningful American experience.

In both of these plays about Lincoln, the playwright consciously and deliberately builds upon the Lincoln legend. Though there is no conclusive evidence that Lincoln was attracted to Ann Rutledge, that he proposed to her, or that she accepted his proposal, Sherwood devotes considerable attention to their romance. Within a historical vacuum, the playwright has built a captivating episode which conveys much of his interpretation of Lincoln's character. The result may not be good history, but it is wonderfully effective theater.

An appealing characteristic of the popular image of Lincoln is his sense of humor—which was generous, pungent, always self-effacing. There are many historical examples of Lincoln's humor, of course, but there are also stories in the Lincoln vein which, though not his, might have been. For instance, there is Van Doren's version of an incident aboard the Union vessel *Malvern* during a Presidential visit: The admiral had not realized that Lincoln was so tall, and his stateroom was too short. So, one day when Lincoln had gone ashore, the admiral had his crew lengthen both bed and cabin by a foot. The admiral anticipated some recognition for his maneuver, but hardly the one he received. "Admiral, I think I've shrunk a foot!" was Lincoln's observation the next morning. Did Lincoln actually say this? Perhaps not—but the comment fits the popular conception of what Lincoln might have said on such an occasion.

The major themes in both Lincoln plays are slavery, secession, civil war, and reconstruction. These are standard historical conflicts but rarely are such large issues effectively dramatized. It would be inconvenient to set two great armies maneuvering on the stage or to present a full-scale debate in the halls of Congress. But once the playwright is committed to these momentous issues, he must find ways to present them on the stage. Sherwood and Van Doren solve the problem in a similar fashion—by reflecting the national struggle in the personal struggle of the central character.

Sherwood's method can be illustrated by Lincoln's speech in Act II, scene iv.

> ". . . you talk about civil war—there seems to be one going on inside me all the time. Both sides are right and both are wrong and equal in strength. I'd like to be able to rise superior to the struggle—but—it says in the Bible that a house divided against itself cannot stand, so I reckon there's not much hope. One of these days, I'll just split asunder, and part company with myself—and it'll be good riddance from both points of view."

Here the Civil War is dramatized as an internal conflict within Lincoln himself. The echoes of his famous "house divided" speech suggest that this private experience be understood in larger, more public terms. Throughout the play Lincoln's public problems are reflected in his private life. His love for Ann Rutledge suggests his political idealism, and his reluctance to marry Mary Todd corresponds to his reluctance to enter politics. Sherwood constantly emphasizes the parallels between Lincoln's "private" and "public" selves; and even when the experience seems most private—as in the "house divided" speech—there are important public implications.

Though he shares Sherwood's general method, Van Doren presents specific issues differently. In scene iii Lincoln is visiting Grant's headquarters to discuss the terms of surrender. We have already learned that the Senate is clamoring for vengeance and wants Union troops to occupy the entire South. Lincoln, who prefers a more moderate course, is talking to Admiral Porter about some abandoned kittens that he found near the army camp:

LINCOLN: Admiral, I believe they *are* Confederates. Does this
          mean I should hang them? . . .
PORTER: It could, but I suspect you never will.
LINCOLN: Why not? Their claws are sharp.
PORTER: They could be clipped, and then no one need worry—
          Not now, at least. Of course they would grow again.
LINCOLN: So I should hang them? You say I never will. There
          might be others, though, waiting to do it while my
          back was turned—or thinking how to shame me for not
          doing it myself. I wonder how much chance these kit-
          tens have.

The kittens have come to symbolize the defeated Confederate
army, and Lincoln's thoughts about the kittens reveal the conflict
in his own mind about what to do with the South. Neither the
"house divided" monologue nor the kitten scene has any basis
in historical fact. Both incidents suggest overwhelming public
conflict, however—in a way that is dramatically effective.

QUESTIONS ON *ABE LINCOLN IN ILLINOIS*

ACT ONE (SCENES I-III)

1. Does the grammar lesson strike you as an effective way to
begin the play? How do the grammatical "moods" assist the ex-
position? Which of Lincoln's own "moods" are revealed in this
opening scene?

2. What is the significance of the name of Lincoln's teacher,
Mentor Graham?

3. Ben Mattling is described as a veteran of the Revolutionary
War. In view of the date (mid-nineteenth century) and the place
(Illinois), is it likely that Lincoln would encounter such a veteran?
As Ben Mattling is not an actual historical figure, why do you think
Sherwood wanted him in this scene? How does his presence affect
the historical authority of the play?

4. In scene ii the characters appear to be divided into two camps
—one led by Jack Armstrong and the other by Ninian Edwards.
How does the playwright dramatize the antagonism between these

men? Is their argument prompted by a private or political disagreement? With which group are you most sympathetic? What can you infer about Abe Lincoln from the fact that he is respected by both groups? Do Jack Armstrong and Ninian Edwards admire him for the same reasons? Which do you think has a truer appreciation of Abe's character?

5. Scholars disagree about the importance of Ann Rutledge in Lincoln's life. No one knows for sure whether Abe proposed to Ann Rutledge and, if so, whether he was accepted. Why do you think Sherwood included this episode? Was he merely providing the kind of "romantic interest" to which the audience had become accustomed in other plays? Or does the episode illuminate an aspect of Lincoln's character which might not otherwise be apparent?

6. In scene iii Bowling Green is reading *The Pickwick Papers* by Charles Dickens. After reading one passage aloud, Nancy Green says, "He sounds precisely like *you,* Bowling." This scene is supposed to take place in 1835, and Dickens' novel was not published until 1836. Do you think this is carelessness on Sherwood's part, or did he alter the chronology for a purpose?

7. Ann Rutledge appears on stage for only a few moments, yet she is supposed to have influenced Lincoln decisively. Although Ann says little, a great deal is said about her by the other characters. Compare the views of Bowling Green, Nancy Green, and Lincoln himself. Who do you think comes closest to the truth? Do we know enough about Ann Rutledge to judge the accuracy of these opinions? Is it possible that the playwright intended an element of mystery in his characterization of Ann? If so, why?

ACT TWO (SCENES IV-VIII)

1. Stage directions guide the director and actors in staging a play. Usually these directions pertain to specific details, but sometimes they offer guides to interpretation as well. At the beginning of Act II, the directions offer this description of Lincoln: "He is only thirty-one years old, but his youth was buried with Ann Rutledge." What might the actor who is playing Lincoln learn

from this remark? How could it contribute to a director's interpretation of the play?

2. In a conversation with Billy Herndon, Lincoln indicates that he does not favor the abolitionist crusade against slavery; in conversation with Mr. Green, he admits that he doesn't want to seek high office; and later he tells Josh Speed that he wouldn't want to bear any responsibility for starting a civil war. Do these positions conflict with the popular image of Lincoln? Why do you think they have been recorded here? Do Lincoln's thoughts on these subjects undergo any important change in the course of the play?

3. What first attracts Lincoln to Mary Todd? Why do you think he is reluctant to marry her? Is there an intentional parallel between Lincoln's reluctance to marry and his reluctance to enter politics? What accounts for his hesitation in each case?

4. Mary Todd Lincoln is seldom treated sympathetically by historians. She is remembered as a hot-tempered shrew who destroyed Lincoln's domestic happiness with her constant bickering. Is she treated sympathetically in this play? Does the play suggest that, in some way, Mary was necessary to Lincoln's greatness? What did Mary supply which seemed to be lacking in Lincoln's character?

5. Sherwood's play focuses on both the private and public lives of Lincoln. We see him as suitor, husband, father, and friend, as well as congressman, senatorial candidate, and future President. Does his private or public life receive most emphasis in the play? Was the playwright successful in merging these two aspects of his hero?

6. Consider this passage from Act II, scene iv: "You talk about civil war—there seems to be one going on inside me all the time. Both sides are right and both are wrong and equal in strength. I'd like to be able to rise superior to the struggle—but—it says in the Bible that a house divided against itself cannot stand, so I reckon there's not much hope." Lincoln is obviously speaking of his "private" life; but the passage also has implications for his development as a "public" figure. What famous utterance of Lincoln's later life is echoed in this passage? Can you find other

instances where the same technique is used to bind together Lincoln's "private" and "public" selves?

ACT THREE (SCENES IX-XII)

1. The public debate between Lincoln and Douglas did take place, of course, and much of the material in this scene is from the record of those debates. Which of the debaters is most logical? Which is most persuasive? Must a successful political speech be persuasive as well as logical?

2. Mr. Crimmin describes Lincoln as "one of the smoothest, slickest politicians that ever hoodwinked a yokel mob." He goes on to describe Lincoln's favorite strategy. "Ask him about the labor problem, and he replies, 'I believe in democracy.' Ask him views on religion, and he says, 'Love thy neighbor as thyself.' Now—you know you couldn't argue with that. . . . I tell you, gentlemen, he's a vote-getter if I ever saw one." Is this an accurate description of the conversation that Mr. Crimmin has just over-heard? Is his observation about Lincoln's manner of dealing with questions wholly true, or partly true, or wholly false? Explain your answer.

3. As the final returns come in, Josh Speed makes the startling declaration that Lincoln does not want to win the election. What circumstances surrounding the election might cause Lincoln to react in this manner? What elements in Lincoln's character might foster such an attitude? When has he reacted this way in a similar situation?

QUESTIONS ON *THE LAST DAYS OF LINCOLN*

SCENES I-III

1. Abraham Lincoln—the central character in this play—does not appear in the first scene. However, each of the characters on stage says something about him. Why do you think the playwright introduces Lincoln in this way?

2. Though there is no evidence at this point concerning the attempted assassination, each observer has his own theory. Some are sure it was the result of a conspiracy; others are just as certain it was an isolated act of madness. Are both theories believable

under the circumstances? What important information is revealed to the audience as these theories are discussed?

3. The play opens with the oppressive atmosphere that surrounds a dying man. But scene ii introduces some light comedy, as the two secretaries joke—"not to his face"—about ways of addressing the President. Is the comedy out of place here? Or is the playwright justified in shattering the gloominess of the opening scene?

4. In scene ii the President is referred to by various names: Tycoon, Despot, Dictator, Butcher, Mr. Presidency, Mr. President, Lincoln and—the final word of the scene—Abe. Why are all of these names used? What different attitude does each convey? Might we say that the names suggest the various attitudes in the nation?

5. What particular purpose do the kittens serve in scene iii? Why doesn't Lincoln openly discuss terms of surrender?

6. To whom does Admiral Porter refer when he says "they" want vengeance? Is he speaking for other military men, or is this merely a way of expressing his own opinions without standing responsible for them?

SCENES IV-VI

1. In scene iv the name-calling begins again. Lincoln is surrounded by the voices of praise and blame: "Savior," "Father Abraham," "Nero," "emperor," "hypocrite." Is there any truth in these charges? Isn't the Lincoln legend, in large part, the story of a savior? Isn't Lincoln's conduct before Stanton and the senators almost dictatorial?

2. Robert, the Negro butler, fails to recognize Lincoln because the President does not correspond to the image he has formed from the stories he has heard. In what other ways does the action of the play undercut the charges and countercharges that are flung at Lincoln?

3. Literary allusions appear several times in the play. Announcing the visit of three senators, Lincoln says, "I must ask you to leave me alone with Shadrach, Meshach, and Abednego." Lincoln addresses Stanton as "Mars" and is himself called "Uriah" (a

reference to Uriah Heep in *David Copperfield*). Must one know the Bible, mythology, and Dickens to enjoy the play? How does knowledge of these allusions contribute to one's understanding?

4. Which of Lincoln's qualities is most evident when he confronts the patriots of the North? What aspect of his character is most apparent when he talks with the partisans of the South? Why do you think the playwright places Lincoln in these contrasting situations?

5. Important characters are introduced late in the play. Stanton and Senator Chandler, for example, do not appear until scene v. Why do you think they were not introduced earlier?

6. All the characters comment on the sources of Lincoln's great strength. Do you believe that one of these speaks with particular authority or comes closest to the truth? Does any one speaker seem to express the attitude of the playwright?

7. *The Last Days of Lincoln* begins and ends with the assassination; scenes ii through v are one long flashback. Why do you think the writer chose this plan for his play? Does the final scene advance the action beyond the point reached in scene one? Would the play be as effective if it were presented chronologically, without the first scene?

PAPERBACK TEXTS

Sherwood, Robert E., *Abe Lincoln in Illinois*. Scribner Library.
Van Doren, Mark, *The Last Days of Lincoln*. Hill and Wang, Inc. Washington Square Press, (contained in *Three Distinctive Plays About Abraham Lincoln*).*

* This volume contains, in addition to the Van Doren play, *Prologue to Glory* by E. P. Conkle and *Abraham Lincoln* by John Drinkwater. *Prologue to Glory* is concerned entirely with the brief period that Lincoln spent in New Salem, Illinois. Stress is on the rural background from which Lincoln emerged and upon the first indication of those qualities which distinguished him in later life. *Abraham Lincoln* is a more ambitious work which attempts to dramatize the period when Lincoln was at the height of his powers—from the time he agreed to become a candidate for the office of President to the day he was shot in Ford's theater. Should the recommended works not be available, either of these plays might be substituted.

Two Shakespearean History Plays

Richard III
Henry V

ROY L. FELSHER

The first section of this unit examines the history play as a dramatic form; the next two sections provide brief commentaries on *Richard III* and *Henry V*. These are followed by study questions which amplify many points raised in the commentaries. The unit concludes with a bibliography for teachers.

THE HISTORY PLAY

The term "history play" is sometimes used to refer to any dramatic work which is set in the past, but such reference is not entirely accurate. One could assemble a group of Shakespeare's plays—all of them set in the past—which included comedies and tragedies as well as genuine histories. Little would be gained and many valuable distinctions would be lost if we permitted the time factor to become the sole criterion for distinguishing history plays. There is a better and more precise way to use the term.

It will be easiest to introduce the term "history play" by analogy. Students can appreciate the difference between a private relationship involving, say, an individual and his family and a public relationship such as that between the President and Congress.

These categories are not entirely independent of each other, but it is easy enough to distinguish between a world of private experience and a world of public affairs. The same distinction can be used in other ways. Most drama is "private" in the sense that it is chiefly concerned with the personal affairs of daily life—affairs which directly concern only a small group of persons. But there is a significant number of plays that are concerned with "public" men and "public" issues and that turn upon events which have significance for an entire people or nation. These are the true history plays.

Originally, the distinction between ordinary drama and the history play was derived, by analogy, from two branches of philosophy: *politics*, which is the study of values and morality in public life, and *ethics*, which examines values and morality in private life. The history play will stress politics more than ethics, and concentrate upon action that has public rather than private consequences. Of course, this is primarily a matter of emphasis. Shakespeare's *Richard III* is about an English king and is usually recognized as a history play, but *King Lear*, which is about another English king, is not. *Lear* is a tragedy. The distinction may seem capricious until we remember that one play emphasizes politics and the other ethics—one stresses public events and the other private acts. In other words, to speak of a play as a "history play" says more than that it is simply set in the past. It indicates, in general terms at least, how the matter of the play is developed.

The two Shakespearean plays which are recommended for grade nine are both "history plays" in this sense. *Richard III* is a study of unprincipled ambition, and in the central character we have Shakespeare's portrait of an almost totally corrupt and evil king. By contrast, *Henry V* is a study of responsible leadership, the king-as-hero, and it may represent Shakespeare's conception of an ideal ruler. In both plays the action is brisk. There is a wealth of historical detail, an abundance of pageantry and spectacle, an immense variety of characters and incidents. Yet these are not difficult plays to read, because in each case the larger-than-life figure of the king dominates the action and provides focus amid the changing pattern of events. Although the king occupies this center of interest at all times, it would be misleading to suggest that the emphasis in these plays is biographical. The main thrust of the action is not inward, to an examination of psychological subtleties, but outward, to the dangerous political arena and the great affairs of state. In the history play emphasis is on public events and their public consequences.

The remarks which follow direct attention to some of the important themes in *Richard III* and *Henry V*. These remarks are necessarily brief. For more detailed critical discussions of these plays, the teacher is directed to the bibliography at the end of the unit. As was indicated in "Two History Plays for Students in Grade Eight," students can read and appreciate a history play without much knowledge of the history of the period.

NEMESIS IN *RICHARD III*

Richard III has often been called a "one-man show." Richard himself dominates the stage, and it is his wit, energy, and humor which give the play its tremendous theatrical vitality. In recent stage productions it has been customary to eliminate some of the minor characters to give the role of Richard even greater prominence; and in critical discussions, too, the character of Richard has been emphasized, analyzed, even psychoanalyzed, to an unusual degree. All this is understandable, but it is not quite fair to Shakespeare's play. Most dramatic works are more important than their parts, and it is a mistake to treat a character—even so formidable a character as Richard—as though he were somehow liberated from his dramatic context.

Richard III is a history play, and it is primarily concerned with public acts and with the great political forces that are released by a struggle for the crown. The immense destructive energy of Richard has meaning only within this context. While there is no single voice in the play quite so impressive as Richard's, there is still much to be said about the force, or combination of forces, which eventually topples him. An effective classroom presentation will surely consider the force of Richard's character, but it should also consider this greater force which accounts in the end for his ruin.

THE CHARACTER OF RICHARD

One can trace Richard's development easily, for it has the parabolic sweep of an exhilarating rise to power followed by an almost immediate decline. In the first scene Richard announces that he wants to be king, and he applies himself to the task with cunning, gaiety, and total self-assurance. His brother Clarence stands between him and the throne, so Clarence must be eliminated. His enemies at the court are divided, so he exploits their differences to dispatch them one by one. In all, Richard is responsible for the murder of nine persons in this play—not to mention the casualties of a civil war—and, judged by this simple quantitative measurement, he is probably the most colossal villain in all of Shakespeare's plays. Yet, despite his unabashed wickedness, Richard is a strangely attractive figure. At the conclusion of the play, and in retrospect, we will judge him harshly. But in the actual performance, we suspend judgment and allow ourselves to be carried along by the main force of the drama—even though this force is the diabolical will of Richard himself.

To what extent do we identify with the villain in this play? The matter may provoke some controversy in a ninth grade class. Asked simply whether Richard is a good man or not, a good king or not, a student will have little difficulty arriving at a judgment. But if we go beyond this level of easy generalization and examine specific dramatic situations, the student's response is likely to be more complex. Consider some typical situations— Richard's encounter with Anne (I, ii), with Hastings (III, iv), with the Mayor of London (III, vi), with Elizabeth (IV, iv). In each of these encounters Richard behaves characteristically. He delights in intrigue; he deceives his enemies; he takes a positive pleasure in making them suffer. If we have any sympathy with Richard at such moments, it probably has less to do with our evaluation of his behavior than with what might be called the psychology of the audience.

Richard is so completely without conscience that we may admit
to a subversive pleasure in seeing the ordinary rules of society
so outrageously flouted. There is an anarchic streak in all of us
which is indulged better in the theater than in actual life. Perhaps
we also feel that in each of these confrontations the persons whom
Richard deceives are not really worthy of our admiration. It seems,
in fact, that most of the other characters in the play are rather
stupid. Not, of course, in the schoolroom sense, but in all those
areas of sophistication that enable one to penetrate beyond social
disguises to a true estimate of character. Richard is a master of
social disguise, and adopts an appropriate pose before each of his
enemies. Anne sees only "Richard, the adoring lover"; Hastings
sees "Richard, the loyal comrade"; the Mayor is fooled by "Richard, the god-fearing monarch"; and Elizabeth succumbs to "Richard, the father of kings."

Of course, *we* know that Richard is not to be trusted, but all of
the other characters are taken in. There are moments when Richard's hypocrisy is so gross, his contempt for the judgment of others
so evident, that we cannot help being amused at his success. What
must the audience think as Richard declares in fulsome tones:

My tongue could never learn sweet smoothing words (I, ii, 169).
Cannot a plain man live and think no harm (I, iii, 51)?
I am too childish-foolish for this world (I, iii, 142).
I do not know that Englishman alive with whom my soul is any
   jot at odds . . . (II, i, 69-70).

Here the dramatic irony is so broad that we can almost see
Richard winking at the audience. At such moments we must
enter into collusion with the villain, for the alternative would be
to identify with those who are so easily deceived. There is an
adage to the effect that all men would rather be thought knaves
than fools, and perhaps it is also true that, forced to identify with
a fool or a knave, we choose the knave every time.

These easy victories attest to the fact that Richard is a very
theatrical villain. Could anyone really believe him "a plain man
. . . too childish-foolish for this world"? Probably not; but it makes
for excellent theater. It is this same theatricality, however, which

denies Richard the status of a tragic hero. His brilliant rise to power is due, in part, to a lack of worthy opposition; and when Richmond finally appears—rather late, in Act V—Richard is no match for him. No one could deny Richard's shrewd intelligence or his tremendous energy, but this is one instance in which we do not feel that "character is fate." Richard's character is such that only an unusual set of circumstances made his rise possible; and when these circumstances change, his downfall is inevitable. If *Richard III* were a tragedy, this would be harsh criticism; but as it is a history play, the reverse is true. The history play demonstrates that there can be drama in the force of events.

THE FORCE OF NEMESIS

In Greek myth the goddess Nemesis dispensed the just retribution of the gods. It was she who saw to the destruction of proud and evil men who overstepped the proper bounds of human conduct. Of course in the Elizabethan age men did not worship the pagan goddess, but the ideas that she stood for were very much alive for Shakespeare and his contemporaries. Elizabethan historians like More, Hall, and Holinshed (from whom Shakespeare learned the story of Richard) believed that the Christian God took an active role in the historical process, and that evil conduct, especially when it involved royalty, would provoke divine punishment. There is a very useful study of these beliefs in Tillyard's book (listed in the bibliography); but here we may cite as evidence a single passage from Holinshed. It describes the murder of Prince Edward, an event which is mentioned in *Richard III* and which is to have important consequences in that play. Holinshed writes:

At which words king Edward said nothing, but with his hand thrust him from him, or (as some saie) stroke him with his gentlet; whom incontinentlie George, duke of Clarence, Richard duke of Glocester, Thomas Greie marquesse Dorset, and William lord Hastings, that stood by, suddenlie murthered; for the which cruell act, the more part of the dooers in their latter daies dranke of the like cup, by the righteous justice and due punishment of God.

In a sense, this is what *Richard III* is about. God is active within history, and a crime against the royal family is sure to call forth divine retribution. Each of the historical figures mentioned by Holinshed reappears as a character in Shakespeare's play—Edward, Clarence, Richard, Grey, Hastings—and each is subdued by the "righteous justice and due punishment of God."

This notion of history-as-retribution will help to explain certain matters of treatment and emphasis in Shakespeare's play. The central story is of Richard, but attention is also given to the corrupt and servile courtiers who, like Richard, forget principle in their quest for power. All of them will be swept away in the course of the action, and this multiplication of ruin broadens and deepens the implications of Richard's own downfall. There is the sense that all England is being purified. It is to be expected that ninth grade students will be a little vague about the historical record, and perhaps a bit confused by the large roster of kings and courtiers who make a brief appearance on the stage; but this is not really essential information.

The main thrust of historical events can be examined in a few pivotal figures. Queen Margaret, for example, is a spokesman for the play's underlying theory of history. In the great scene where she hurls curses at the assembled courtiers (I, iii), Margaret provides the fullest possible statement of this tit-for-tat crime and punishment scheme. Each of the courtiers has been guilty of past misdeeds, here neatly itemized, and each is assured of future punishment. Of course, at this point no one is unduly alarmed at Margaret's prophecy; but as the play progresses it is clear to everyone that these predictions are being fulfilled. Margaret is a voice out of the past, a victim of just such wickedness as is being enacted before us, and her presence at the court testifies to the power of the past over the present. The other characters may pretend to ignore her, but she cannot be ignored.

Dreams in this play show ways that the past may rise up and point an accusing finger at the present. There are three such dreams, or nightmares, brought on by stricken conscience. Clarence dreams of his death (I, ii), Stanley dreams of Richard's actual intentions (III, ii), and, at the climactic moment in the play, Richard dreams of his own destruction (V, iii). Long before Freud had charted the unconscious, Shakespeare realized that dreams can present highly charged images that have been suppressed by the conscious mind. Shakespeare's three dreamers would like to dismiss this communication as idle fancy or the "mockery of unquiet slumbers," but in each case the terror felt in the dream state is too real to be denied. The dreams couple feelings of guilt for some past crime with a sudden presentiment of death; just as the action of the play insists that crime will inevitably bring forth retribution.

In Richard's dream at Bosworth Field we have the fullest statement of these themes. The dream is a highly stylized, almost ritual performance, where each of Richard's victims steps forward to bless the fortunes of Richmond's army and proclaim the certain death of Richard. It concludes with Buckingham's assertion,

> God and good angels fight on Richmond's side;
> And Richard falls in height of all his pride.

The dream restates the connection between guilt and death, crime and retribution, and it suggests that powerful and even supernatural forces are gathering to insure Richard's doom.

Finally, there is the appearance of Richmond. An Elizabethan audience would know that Richmond founded the Tudor dynasty, that he was the grandfather of Queen Elizabeth I, and that his reign ended the civil strife so evident in this play. Moreover, Richmond is doing God's will when he advances to meet Richard. In his prayer before the battle he acknowledges that he is serving a higher power.

> O Thou, whose captain I account myself,
> Look on my forces with a gracious eye;
> Put in their hands thy bruising irons of wrath,
> That they may crush down with a heavy fall
> The usurping helmets of our adversaries.
> Make us thy ministers of chastisement,
> That we may praise thee in the victory (V, iii, 107-13).

Out of context this may appear rather self-righteous, but within the context of Shakespeare's play, Richmond fulfills precisely that office which he claims—he is God's champion. The force that finally topples Richard is nothing less than the just retribution of God. It seemed weak perhaps in the fitful curses of Margaret; it gathered strength and supernatural sanction in the three prophetic dreams; it swells to a magnificent triumph in the person of Richmond. The final defeat of Richard's army cannot be attributed to any weakness in the commander, for Richard fights magnificently to the last. But the force which opposes him is invincible.

If we choose to approach *Richard III* as a character study, we need not look beyond its one dominant figure; but if we want to approach the play on its own terms, as a history play, we must consider this working out of God's will in English history.

PATRIOTISM IN *HENRY V*

Henry V is frequently described as an epic drama about England's greatest king. It is a patriotic offering which celebrates "warlike Harry" and his famous victories in France. It has always been a popular play, and never more so than at moments of national peril, like the last war, when Englishmen responded enthusiastically to Shakespeare's portrayal of an indomitable English hero. In recent years, however, the patriotic fervor of *Henry V* has begun to seem one of its least attractive qualities. It has been charged that patriotism always implies a measure of bias, of self-congratulation that is incompatible with the best drama.

One thinks of typical war movies where the enemy never gets a fair hearing, where the cast is always divided between "us" and "them," and where "we" are always brave, noble, self-sacrificing and handsome; while "they" are selfish, unscrupulous, brutal, and ugly to boot. It must be confessed that there is an element of such bias in Shakespeare's play. English soldiers are noble and upstanding men, and Henry himself is "the mirror of all Christian kings," while the French are merely degenerate courtiers, and their king, as compared to Henry, is a milksop. Is it true, then, that Shakespeare has cheapened his play by a direct appeal to patriotic sentiment and produced little more than a piece of nationalistic propaganda?

HISTORICAL RECORD AND CRITICISM

We should say, first, that there is considerable justification for the patriotism of *Henry V* in historic fact. Henry was one of the great English monarchs, and he did conquer a large part of France. There was also a major battle at Agincourt, where the English won an important victory over the French. All this is a matter of record and a source of justifiable pride for Englishmen. Yet it remains for us to decide whether in this case pride has not given way to presumption, and a proper celebration of English heroism been turned into a one-sided account of men and affairs. These are proper matters for literary discussion since they do not involve a study of historical materials, but rather a judgment about what Shakespeare did with these materials.

In the first scenes we are presented with the official reason for the war—or perhaps we should say the reasons, since there is more than one explanation offered. The first, and simplest, states the matter in terms of power politics: England is strong, France is weak; therefore, England should invade France. This position is stated by Westmoreland:

> Never King of England
> Had nobles richer and more loyal subjects,
> Whose hearts have left their bodies here in England
> And lie pavilion'd in the fields of France (I, ii, 126-29).

The English nobles thirst for new conquests and all favor an aggressive war. The Church, however, has a more subtle policy. In scene 1, the Archbishop of Canterbury explains that he is prepared to offer Henry a large sum of money for the French war if, in return, the king will reconsider a bill which authorizes the confiscation of Church property. Henry reconsiders and accepts the bribe. Then, in a long pedantic speech, which may appear irrelevant in view of the transaction we have just witnessed, the Archbishop assures Henry that the war is justified and that he has a legitimate claim to the French throne. This is the "official" reason for the war. Finally, a French ambassador arrives with an insulting gift from the Dauphin.

Up to this point Henry has listened patiently to the arguments of Church and State, but has not committed himself. The gift of tennis balls, however, shatters his composure, and, in an explosive outburst prompted by this personal affront, he makes his formal declaration of war. It may be possible, at this point, for class discussion to isolate the true cause of the war. Can we say that Henry is justified for invading France because he is the legitimate heir to the French throne? Or is this merely a pretext devised by the Archbishop to save Church property? Can we say that Henry is a statesman who wisely defers to the political pressures within his kingdom? Or is he merely a man of weak character who plunges into war because he is offended by the Dauphin's gift? These questions must certainly be faced before we can evaluate the quality of patriotism in Shakespeare's play. Our view of heroic exploits on the battlefield may depend finally upon whether we decide that the war was undertaken for just or dishonorable reasons.

Shakespeare's portrayal of the English soldier provides further evidence that a critical intelligence is at work on these historical materials. There is, to be sure, considerable attention to the heroic virtues. The English are magnanimous in victory, resolute in adversity, and veritable supermen on the battlefield. One obvious indulgence of patriotic sentiment is the casualty list produced after the battle of Agincourt (IV, viii), which lists ten thousand Frenchmen slain and only twenty-nine English. But, setting this aside, it is difficult to believe that Shakespeare intended a one-sided view of the English forces. Even before the army embarks for France there is evidence that not all Englishmen aspire to heroic conduct. At court there is the conspiracy of Cambridge, Scroop, and Grey, who attempt to murder the king for French gold (II, ii). In addition there is corruption at the level of the common soldier. The subplot which traces the fortunes of Nym, Bardolph, and Pistol through the war gives special prominence to a mean and disreputable element in Henry's army. Pistol does not disguise his motives for following the king:

> Let us to France; like horse-leeches, my boys,
> To suck, to suck, the very blood to suck (II, iv, 57-58)!

Pistol and his friends find the war a splendid opportunity for acquiring booty. These characters are frequently cited as an example of "comic relief," but the comedy they provide is of the dry, sardonic sort. Pistol's call to arms is funny, in part, because it serves to deflate the more extravagant rhetoric of the court, bringing us back to the mean realities of warfare. While other characters speak nobly of the heroic code, we learn that Bardolph has been caught stealing from a church (III, vi) and observe Pistol making his craven demands for ransom (IV, iv). In this ironic underplot Shakespeare gives us the seamier side of patriotism.

HENRY IN ACTION

There is even an element of criticism directed against the king. Most of the time we see him through the eyes of the Chorus or his devoted circle of courtiers, and they are lavish in their praise. But we also see him in action. There is a significant contrast between the claim that Henry is "the mirror of all Christian kings" and our own view of Henry before the town of Harfleur (III, iii), where he threatens the inhabitants with death and destruction, with babies tossed upon English spears and women ravished by lusting soldiers. And it is this same Christian king who can declare of his newly won prisoners.

> we'll cut the throats of those we have,
> And not a man of them that we shall take
> Shall taste our mercy . . . (IV, vii, 66-69).

There is a streak of bloodthirstiness in Henry that does much to offset the constant praise that is showered upon him. Of course, it may be argued that this is a war, and that in wartime there is a necessary and inevitable slackening of moral standards. This is precisely Henry's argument. We meet it in his famous rallying cry before the gates of Harfleur: "Once more into the breach, dear friends, once more. . . ." But even famous speeches need to be carefully examined.

> In peace there's nothing so becomes a man
> As modest stillness and humility:
> But when the blast of war blows in our ears,

> Then imitate the action of the tiger;
> Stiffen the sinews, summon up the blood,
> Disguise fair nature with hard-favor'd rage;
> Then lend the eye a terrible aspect;
> Let it pry through the portage of the head
> Like the brass cannon; let the brow o'erwhelm it . . .
> Now set the teeth and stretch the nostril wide,
> Hold hard the breath, and bend up every spirit
> To his full height! On, on, you noblest English . . . (III, i, 3-17).

It is wonderful rhetoric; but before we allow ourselves to be carried away, we might want to examine what Henry is saying. Is it really true that men should follow one scale of values in peace and an entirely different scale of values in war—that all soldiers must exclude "fair nature" and imitate the action of a beast? If this is so, then Henry can remain a model of heroic conduct. Shakespeare does not overtly criticize his royal hero; but the materials for such criticism exist if we choose to use them.

THE CRUCIAL SCENE

The crucial scene of the play, certainly, is the dialogue between Henry and Williams (IV, i). Henry wanders in disguise through the army and soon gets into an argument with one of his common soldiers. This argument raises once more the question of the justice of the war. Williams points out how heavy must be the responsibility of the king when innocent men are sent off to fight and perhaps die in the king's wars.

> WILL. But if the cause be not good, the king himself has a heavy reckoning to make, when all those legs and arms and heads, chopped off in battle, shall join together at the latter day and cry "We died at such a place"; some swearing, some crying for a surgeon, some upon their wives left poor behind them, some upon their children rawly left. I am afeared there are few die well that die in a battle; for how can they charitably dispose of any thing, when blood is their argument? Now, if these men do not die well, it will be a black matter for the king that led them to it; whom to disobey were against all proportion of subjection.

Perhaps this is an unanswerable argument. It has probably occurred to all fighting men, whatever the nation they fight for, whatever the cause they serve. For in most cases the common soldier cannot be expected to know all the reasons for a war; he leaves that to his government.

We have already seen that Henry, as king, had left the justice of his cause to the Archbishop of Canterbury (I, ii). If we take this back a step farther and reexamine the Archbishop's motive for wanting the war to proceed, we are up against a disturbing possibility. It is at least possible that Henry is deceived and that he has no legal claim to the French throne. If this be so, then far from being a patriotic extravaganza, this play may be Shakespeare's ironic portrait of a misguided king who commits his subjects to an unjust and aggressive war.

It is not necessary, however, to take such a thoroughly ironic view of the play. As a patriotic work it is successful by the test that counts: the audience will be gratified by Henry's stirring speeches and by a smashing English victory. If there is much here to suggest that Shakespeare stops short of unqualified approval of his characters and the cause they serve, there is also much to suggest his warmhearted admiration for the courage and resourcefulness of the English nation. The Nym-Pistol-Bardolph subplot may suggest that patriotism is the last refuge of scoundrels, but there is also the Fluellen-Jamy-MacMorris subplot to show that men from all parts of the kingdom can forget their petty differences in a common effort for the king. Perhaps there is a double standard of judgment implicit in this play.

One can judge the action by a patriotic standard, which is ultimately a standard of success and in which case all the victorious English must be judged favorably. Or, one can insist upon more durable human values, like justice and charity, in which case even the most successful characters are not above criticism. Shakespeare accommodates both standards in his play. He clearly indicates the faults of his characters and yet he loves them. A critical appraisal of this play ought to distinguish between approval of these characters because of such faults, and approval despite such faults. The former is the way of a narrow-minded patriotism; the latter is the deeper and more humane patriotism which emerges from Shakespeare's play.

QUESTIONS ON *RICHARD III*

Act I

SCENE I

1. How do Richard's opening lines launch the drama? What do they tell us about past events and events to come?

2. What do Richard's words when he is alone on the stage tell us of his character (1-41)? Does he regard himself as a peaceful man or a warrior, a cautious man or a gambler, a hero or a villain? Cite specific passages.

3. Can you accept Richard's estimation of his own character at face value? Or do you require further evidence? Does the action of this scene tend to confirm or deny Richard's self-portrait?

4. How does Richard manage to get Clarence imprisoned?

SCENE II

1. Why does Lady Anne despise Richard? And why does she finally submit to him?

2. Comment upon Richard's statement to Anne:

> I never sued to friend nor enemy,
> My tongue could never learn sweet smoothing words.

Does Anne believe this? Does the audience believe it? Where have we already seen Richard's accomplished use of "sweet smoothing words"?

3. The battle of wits between Richard and Anne is conducted in a traditional and highly stylized verse form. It is a sort of verbal fencing match, or line-for-line repartee, in which the characters retort sharply to each other while attempting frequent reversals of meaning. For example:

> ANNE. I would I knew thy heart.
> RICH. 'Tis figur'd in my tongue.
> ANNE. I fear me both are false.
> RICH. Then never man was true.

Are these quick retorts appropriate to the dramatic situation? How does Richard get the better of Anne in this exchange? Note that

Shakespeare uses this writing technique again in the interview between Richard and Elizabeth (IV, iv, 34ff).

1. How would you describe the atmosphere at court? Are the nobles united behind the king, or are they divided by factions and petty intrigues? Does Richard seek to promote unity or to find new occasions for discord?

2. Queen Margaret is a pivotal figure because she confronts each character with his past crimes. What is the significance of the past in this play? Can it be safely forgotten, or do past events continue to have repercussions in the present? How does Margaret serve to keep us aware of the past?

3. In this scene Margaret hurls curses at the assembled courtiers, predicting the fate of each. What end does she predict for Richard? Is he at all disturbed by the prophecy?

1. Why is Clarence frightened by his dream? Is the dream merely an idle fancy, or does it develop from actual circumstances of Clarence's life? Is it in any way prophetic?

2. Why do the two murderers deplore conscience? In what sense does conscience "make a man a coward"? Which of the murderers do you think is more cowardly?

3. What appeal does Clarence make to the murderers? Is it successful?

Act II
SCENE I

1. How does King Edward propose to unite his divided kingdom? What promises does he exact from the courtiers?

2. How does Richard manage to rekindle the old feuds at court?

1. Whom does Buckingham side with in the feud?

SCENE III

1. Do the citizens of London contribute substantially to the plot? Why are they introduced at this point?

2. Are there significant distinctions recorded in the characterization of First, Second, and Third Citizen? Do they, perhaps, represent different currents of opinion among the populace?

3. Is Shakespeare's interest in history limited to the affairs of aristocrats, or does it extend to the whole of England? Explain your answer.

Act III

SCENE I

1. Who is the legitimate heir to the throne after the death of King Edward? Is the young prince at all suspicious of Richard? How does he show this mistrust?

2. What does Richard promise Buckingham as a reward for his services?

SCENE II

1. What was Lord Stanley's dream?

2. Hastings dismisses the dream as a "mockery of unquiet slumbers." What does he mean? Is his opinion confirmed by events?

3. Compare Stanley's dream with the earlier dream of Clarence (I, iv). How is their content similar? In what sense are these dreams prophetic?

4. Comment upon Shakespeare's use of the dream as a structural device. Does it heighten anticipation? Does it foreshadow future events? If you were to encounter further dreams in this play, would you be inclined to dismiss them as idle fancies, or would you examine them carefully for a clue to future events?

SCENE III

1. What fate had Margaret predicted for Rivers, Grey, and Vaughan? Is the prediction fulfilled?

SCENE IV

1. What fate had Margaret predicted for Hastings? Is this fulfilled?

2. Do Rivers, Grey, Vaughan, and Hastings suffer innocently, or is this punishment for their past crimes?

3. Is this relationship between crime and punishment merely accidental? Can it be explained entirely in terms of human motivation and conduct? Or is there the suggestion of a supernatural force directing this retribution?

SCENE V

1. How does Richard attempt to justify the murder of Hastings? Does he convince the Lord Mayor of London? Does he convince the audience?

SCENE VI

1. This scene consists of fourteen lines spoken by a Scrivener. What is a Scrivener? If you were directing a production of the play, do you think that this brief scene could be eliminated, or do you think it is a necessary part of the action? Explain your answer.

2. What "palpable device" does the Scrivener condemn?

SCENE VII

1. Why must Richard have popular support in order to advance his claim to the throne? How does he attempt to get this support?

Act IV
SCENE I

1. How do the women react to the news that Richard has been crowned king? Do they have any power to prevent this?

2. Who is Richmond? Why does Elizabeth advise Dorset to leave the court and join Richmond's forces?

SCENE II

1. Richard acknowledges (3-7) that no man has served him better than Buckingham, but in this scene Buckingham deserts

Richard and flees the court. Why? How is this a fulfillment of Margaret's prophecy?

2. Comment on Richard's line: "I am not in the giving vein to-day." In this context does the statement suggest an element of strength or weakness in Richard's character?

3. Who is Tyrrel? What crime does he commit for Richard?

SCENE III

1. Contrast the murder of the young princes with the murders of Hastings (III, iv) and Clarence (I, iv). All of these murders are ordered by a king. Is the king's command a sufficient justification for murder, or is there a power still higher than the king's which must be obeyed? What is the testimony of the murderers in each case?

SCENE IV

1. How do the women react to the news that the princes have been murdered? Note that Margaret takes joy in the partial fulfillment of her prophecy: Rivers, Grey, Vaughan, Hastings, and the young princes all meet the fate she had predicted for them. What further events has Margaret predicted?

2. Richard's interview with Elizabeth is written in the same verse form as one of Richard's earlier conversations with Anne. Why is the form appropriate to this dramatic situation? What argument enables Richard to triumph in this battle of wits?

3. What indications are there that Richard is beginning to lose control of himself and his kingdom? What dramatic purpose is served by the conflicting reports of the messengers? Is the confusion on the stage intended to mirror the confusion in the kingdom?

Act V
SCENE I

1. What had been Margaret's prophecy for Buckingham? Is it fulfilled? Does Buckingham proclaim against his fate, or does he accept it as a just retribution for his sins?

2. Compare the state of England under King Edward and King

Richard. What evidence is there that the nation as a whole has suffered as a result of Richard's policies?

SCENE III

1. This scene introduces a deliberate and formal contrast between Richard and Richmond. How does the stage setting facilitate this contrast? What parallel events take place in each camp? What are the qualities of each leader?

2. Richmond describes himself as God's "captain," and he calls his soldiers God's "ministers of chastisement." How does this serve to confirm a popular Elizabethan view of God's involvement in history?

3. Describe the dream-figures that appear to Richard and Richmond on the eve of the battle. What effect do they have on each man? How does this dream resemble other dreams which have appeared earlier in the play? Be specific.

4. Which of the following views do you take and why? This dream sequence is (a) poor theater, because it is too stylized and not at all realistic; it is impossible for two persons to have exactly the same dream, (b) good theater, because the deliberate stylizing adds an element of unreality that is quite appropriate for a dream. Moreover, this element of unreality suggests that powerful and even supernatural forces are gathering to insure Richard's downfall.

5. Contrast the orations of the commanders to their soldiers. To what attitudes and emotions does each appeal? What arguments does each advance to support his cause?

SCENE IV

1. "A horse, a horse, my kingdom for a horse." Is this a cry of despair or defiance? Explain.

SCENE V

1. Comment upon Richard's victory speech (16 ff). Does Richard seek personal vengeance, or does he subordinate self-interest

to the interest of the kingdom? Could Richard have made this speech had he been the victor?

2. Who is the hero of this play? Is it Richard? Or Richmond? Or England itself?

QUESTIONS ON *HENRY V*

Act I

PROLOGUE

1. What is the function of the chorus? What expectations does it arouse in the audience? How does it set the scene?

SCENE I

1. What impending bill is under discussion? Why do the Bishop and the Archbishop oppose this bill?

2. What do we learn about King Henry before he appears on the stage? What information are we given about his youth, his character, his most recent behavior?

SCENE II

1. What is the reason for the long discussion of the "Salic Law"? On the basis of the evidence presented here, does Henry have a legitimate claim to the French throne? Or is he determined to invade France in any case and is merely searching for a pretext?

2. What is the Dauphin's gift? How does Henry respond to the insult?

3. Which of the following interpretations seems to you most valid? Support your answer with illustrations from the text.

Henry a) has a just cause for invading France, since he is the legitimate heir to the French throne,

b) has no just cause to invade France, but he does have the shrewdness to seek a pretext for invasion from the bishops,

c) is no statesman, but declares war simply because he is offended by the Dauphin's gift,

d) yields to the pressures of a militant nobility, and therefore is a man of weak character.

Act II

PROLOGUE

1. What is the popular response to Henry's declaration? Does the speaker seem at all concerned about the justice of the war? Is his the voice of reason or the voice of patriotic fervor?

2. What plot have the French devised in order to forestall the war?

SCENE I

1. Describe Nym, Bardolph, and Pistol. Why do you think these characters speak prose, whereas the courtiers of Act I spoke verse?

2. Why does Shakespeare dramatize these unimportant incidents in the lives of rather unimportant men? Do they make any substantial contribution to history? How would you justify their inclusion in a history play?

SCENE II

1. Is there any failure of nobility and honor among the English lords? How do you account for the conspiracy of Cambridge, Scroop, and Grey? Who paid them? To do what? Are they successful?

2. What king-like qualities does Henry exhibit when he unmasks the conspiracy?

SCENE III

1. Does the nobility of the court have any parallel among the citizens? Do the mean motives of the conspirators have any parallel among the citizens? Give examples.

2. Near the end of the scene Pistol declares:

> Let us to France; like horse-leeches, my boys,
> To suck, to suck, the very blood to suck!

Do other characters, from the court or the town, share these motives? Do they depart for France in search of honor or booty? Do they care whether the war is just?

SCENE IV

1. In what respects does the French court differ from the English court? Does King Charles have the authority among Frenchmen that King Henry has among the English? Support your answer with specific evidence from the play.

Act III

PROLOGUE

1. How far does the Chorus advance the action? Why is Henry at Harfleur? What offer has he refused? How would the effect be changed if these incidents were dramatized rather than simply recorded by the Chorus?

SCENE I

1. Henry's oration to his soldiers has long been one of the most admired scenes in the play; but some readers object to his praise of war and cruelty on moral grounds. Do you think that Shakespeare intended an implied criticism of Henry, or is the content of the speech justified by the dramatic situation? Why?

SCENE II

1. Gower, Fluellen, Jamy, and MacMorris represent respectively the English, Welsh, Scots, and Irish soldiers in Henry's army. What aspect of speech or behavior identifies each soldier with his homeland?

2. Is there any evidence of traditional rivalries among these men? Give examples. Does the war serve to emphasize their differences or to bring them together for a common purpose?

SCENE III

1. Describe the speech that Henry makes before the gates at Harfleur. What fate does he promise the citizens of that town if they fail to surrender? Does the speech suggest that war is an altogether noble and rewarding pursuit, or does it present the more sordid side of warfare? Which view do you think gets the more emphatic statement in this play?

SCENE IV

1. Why does the French princess attempt to learn English? Do you think she would bother if she were sure the French would win the war?

SCENE V

1. What is the mood of the French court? Why has the French king failed to engage Henry in a battle?

SCENE VI

1. Why is Bardolph to be hanged?

2. What is Pistol's argument in his friend's behalf? What is Fluellen's reply? Is it more important to exercise discipline or charity in a time of war? Why?

SCENE VII

1. The Dauphin says that his horse is like *Pegasus*, that its hoofs are as musical as the pipes of *Hermes*, and that it is a beast fit for *Perseus*. Can you explain these mythical allusions? In what way does the explanation add to your appreciation of this passage?

2. What evidence is there that the French are overconfident on the night before the battle?

ACT IV

PROLOGUE

1. How does the Chorus attempt to create a mood of suspense? Is this genuine, or is it rather the mock-suspense of one who anticipates a favorable conclusion? Remember that everyone in Shakespeare's audience already knew the outcome of this famous battle.

SCENE I

1. Henry discusses the impending battle with the nobility and with the common soldiers; which group is more eager for the battle and more steadfast in its loyalty to the king?

2. Why does Henry assume a disguise as he walks about the camp?

3. What qualities does Henry exhibit by his willingness to enter into debate with a common soldier? Who do you think wins the debate?

4. Williams is clearly not eager for the battle, nor is he entirely loyal to the king. Why doesn't Henry rebuke him?

5. What do you think of Williams' statement that the king has "a heavy reckoning to make" if "the cause be not good"? On the basis of the evidence presented in Act I, *is* the cause good? Why?

6. Describe Henry's soliloquy on ceremony. In what respects is the king like other men? In what respects is he different? Does Henry relish the difference? He speaks of the peasant, who

> from rise to set
> Sweats in the eye of *Pheobus;* and all night
> Sleeps in *Elysium;* next day after dawn,
> Doth rise and help *Hyperion* to his horse,
> And follows so the ever-running year . . . (289-93).

What is his attitude toward the peasant? How do the mythical allusions aid the expression of this attitude?

SCENE III

1. Rhetoric has been defined as "the art of influencing the thought and conduct of one's hearers." Examine Henry's speech (18-67) as an example of rhetoric. What is Westmoreland's original position? How does Henry's speech influence Westmoreland's thought and conduct? Is the speech directed primarily to the hearer's intellect or to his emotions? What elements in the speech have the greatest rhetorical force? Give examples.

2. Why does Henry tell the French herald that he will never buy his freedom with ransom? What effect does this have on the English soldiers?

SCENE VII-VIII

1. What is Henry's reaction to the news that defenseless English boys have been slaughtered? Is he right to order that the French

prisoners be killed, or has he lost his customary cool judgment in the heat of battle?

2. Why does Henry avoid a direct confrontation with Williams? Does Williams conduct himself honorably in the argument with Fluellen?

3. At the conclusion of the battle Henry claims that "God fought for us" and orders a *Te Deum* sung on the battlefield. Is this merely an official gesture, or does it confirm a deeply held Elizabethan belief about the action of God in history?

Act V

1. Some critics have complained that the ceremonious conclusion of Act V, and especially Henry's wooing of Katherine, is anticlimactic after the great battle scenes and is a poor conclusion for the play. Do you agree? Or would you argue that after Henry has proven his mettle as a warrior and displayed the virtues of war, he is now given an opportunity to demonstrate the virtues of peace and thus prove himself an ideal king?

BIBLIOGRAPHY

A. GENERAL SCHOLARSHIP

Tillyard, E.M.W. *Shakespeare's History Plays.* New York: Macmillan, 1944. Also available in Collier Paperback, 1962. A standard reference work; good introduction to Elizabethan ideas about history; discussion of individual plays.

Waith, Eugene M. (ed.), *Shakespeare: The Histories.* Englewood Cliffs, N. J.: A Spectrum Paperback, 1965. Essays on the history play as a dramatic form, together with critical studies of each play.

B. *Richard III*

Goddard, Harold C. *The Meaning of Shakespeare.* Chicago: Phoenix Paperbacks, 2 vols., 1960. Examines the play as a character study with tragic dimensions.

Rossiter, A.P. "Angel With Horns: The Unity of *Richard III*" in *Shakespeare: The Histories* (ed.) Waith. Examines the theme of divine retribution.

Van Doren, Mark. *Shakespeare.* New York: Henry Holt, 1939. Also available as an Anchor paperback, 1953. Attention to verse and prose styles found in the play.

Goddard, op. cit. Views the play as an ironic and highly critical study of the king.

c. *Henry V*

Van Doren, op. cit. Condemns the play for its "direct and puerile appeal to the patriotism of the audience."

Walter, J.H. "Introduction to *Henry V*" in *Shakespeare: The Histories* (ed.) Waith. Defends the play as a successful portrait of the ideal king.

Part III
NOVEL SEQUENCE*

The novels recommended for study in grades seven through nine are presented here as a sequence. Selections are arranged, in general, according to difficulty so that succeeding works build upon those which have gone before. For example, in ... *and now Miguel,* the first in the nine-novel sequence, students experience a simply told yet highly perceptive story with a minimum of characters. *The Witch of Blackbird Pond,* the second in the series, adds subplot, a larger cast of characters, and a number of interrelated themes. Whereas in the first novel events are seen through the eyes of the central character, the narrator in the second is a third person living outside the story, yet reflecting sometimes the attitudes of the central character. Experience of the second selection builds upon that of the first and leads naturally to the third, *The Light in the Forest,* which offers more subtle implications and a changing point of view. The sequence proceeds in this incremental way through *Shane, The Red Pony, Tom Sawyer, The Pearl, Great Expectations,* and *To Kill a Mockingbird.* Each novel is read for

---

* It has not been the purpose of this program to offer detailed day-by-day lesson plans for the teacher. Rather, writers of the program have attempted to present a critical and pedagogical basis for the development of units of instruction. The role of the teacher in forming the materials for his own class is crucial. The aims of sound courses of study can be realized only by qualified teachers in their classes.

its own particular value, but against the background of the preceding novels.

Within this frame the teacher is free to adapt the program for his own class. For instance, an average group might read the first two novels in grade seven and begin novel study in grade eight with *The Light in the Forest*. An academically talented group might complete the first three novels in grade seven and be ready in grade eight for *Shane*. Slower students might progress only to *The Red Pony* or *Tom Sawyer* by the end of grade nine. A flexible program of this sort requires coordination between levels and classes, of course, and will probably be most successful with classes which are fairly homogeneous. But adaptation is a task for individual departments. The purpose here has been to outline a basic sequence—a kind of system for studying the novel.

Like the basic poetry sequence and the drama program, the novel sequence for grades seven through nine assumes only that students have experienced the elements of story. Whereas the poetry program seeks to develop in students an awareness of the influence of person or voice in poetry, the novel sequence directs students toward the functions in that genre of narrative point of view. Character, incident, plot, setting, theme, language—elements common to poems and plays as well as fiction—are examined here for the particular ways they can work together in a novel. Progression in this program, as in the poetry and drama programs, is generally from the simple to the complex, from the concrete to the abstract.

The materials which follow are offered as tools for the teacher. The essays are directed toward the teacher rather than the student and should serve as focal points for the development of units of instruction. The questions are designed for the students to lead them toward the critical generalizations expressed in the essay. Within the discipline of the overall sequence, writers of individual units were free to develop their own explications. Each of the units, it should be emphasized, represents only one of many possible approaches to the teaching of that particular novel.

On the basis of the critical essays and questions, then, the teacher should formulate daily assignments and activities to lead students toward greater understanding of the concepts involved. Writing assignments patterned after those suggested in "Action and Narration," for instance, might help students to grasp the basic requirements of longer fiction. Further writing assignments based on individual discussion questions might help them to interpret the subtleties of character or theme, or to detect individual strands of plot and examine how they combine in the novel in question. Vocabulary study is essential during the junior high school years, and passages from literature provide working models of the ways context can determine and modify meaning.

For other novels which pilot-school teachers have recommended for junior high school students, see the list at the end of the sequence.

Teaching . . . *and now Miguel*

VIRGINIA OLSEN BUSH

Formerly Research Associate
in the Indiana University
English Curriculum Study Center

. . . and now Miguel, by Joseph Krumgold, is a very simply told story about a boy's first entrance into the adult world. Miguel, as both narrator and central character, dominates the book. Through the language and the narrative style we are led into Miguel's own world, viewing his story wholly from his own point of view so that we come to have a complete and noncritical sympathy with him. Through him we experience his longings, his confusion, and his final joy, which together form the meaning of this novel.

"I am Miguel." Significantly, these are the first words the narrator speaks to us, for he conceives of his problem as that of trying to resolve the difficulty of "being Miguel"; and our problem, as readers, is to understand what being Miguel means. To him, the problem of being Miguel is the set of desires and capabilities which forms and sets limits to his personality and its patterns of behavior.

Miguel is twelve years old and a member of the Chavez family. He longs to be accepted as a man and to be allowed to work as a "pas*tor*" alongside the rest of the men of his family. This longing achieves symbolic representation in his mind in his wish to go to the Sangre de Cristo Mountains. As he himself realizes at the end of Chapter 6, it is no good for him to go there by himself; the meaning comes from joining the others as they take the flock to summer pasture in the mountains. Miguel finds, however, that longing often comes into conflict with the demands of reality: before he can go to the Sangre de Cristo the others must know that he is ready, that he knows enough to be of help with the sheep, and then he must wait until it is time. This conflict arises directly out of what Miguel is, and it is what he means by the "difficulty of being Miguel."

The words "I am Miguel" also have significance for the thematic movement of the novel. As Miguel moves toward adulthood, he learns to assume greater responsibility and to act as a member of a social unit. Thus, in the early part of the book the emphasis is always on "me, Miguel"; and although he wants very much to be treated as a "whole man," he does not yet understand all that being a man entails. He moves closer toward growing up in Chapter 5, when he observes that "it would get so sometimes that I would forget what the good of it was. I mean the good that it was for me . . . all that was left was the sheep and what they had to have." Miguel's development becomes especially clear, however, by Chapter 14, when he tells Pedro that his name is neither Miguel nor Twister nor Babaloo, but Chavez. "Me, too," says Pedro. This is the important thing—that Miguel now thinks of himself as a person who is part of a group, who is like others, who is like Pedro, rather than as a completely independent person, different from others, different from both Gabriel and Pedro. Finally, it is significant for the development in Miguel's sense of responsibility that the story ends with his doing a favor for Gabriel and carving the "TTA," instead of his carving his own name, Miguel.

The narrative proceeds essentially in chronological order. Miguel begins by describing how it has been in the past and is still now, at the start of the New Year. He then tells in order everything that happens from the lambing until the day the men in the Chavez family reach their first summer camp in the Sangre de Cristo. His story is of how he gets to go with the others, and, as he explains in Chapter 2, of the two conditions that must be fulfilled—he must be ready, and he must wait until the time comes.

The narrative can be divided into two corresponding sections, with Chapters 1 through 7 telling how he tries to make his father see that he is ready, and Chapters 8 through 14 telling how he finds that being ready is not enough and he must learn to wait as well. As the story begins, we find that Miguel is almost ready: he displays a great deal of knowledge about sheep in his narrative and he is competent at the tasks assigned to him. Later, when his father begins asking him personally for help, as with the swinging gate, Miguel shows that he grasps the basic principles even if he cannot yet execute his ideas perfectly. The problem, then, is to show his father that he is ready. This involves communication, and Miguel frequently has trouble communicating, especially with his father. He finally succeeds, although not as effectively as possible, when he finds the sheep and brings them home. It therefore shocks him to hear his father tell him, "No," he still can't go. It is not enough to know about sheep; he must know about men, too, and he must know how to wait: getting the sheep displayed his knowledge of the former and his lack of knowledge of the latter. It is not until after he has found that he is to go to the mountains, at the point when he decides to make his "new kind of prayer" to San Ysidro, that he learns the true meaning of waiting and reaches the beginning of a man's knowledge and sense of responsibility.

It is in this second half of the book that Miguel approaches the adult world for the first time. The first glimpses of it bring nothing but confusion. At the very beginning of Chapter 11, nothing is simple and straightforward anymore: "And now," he says, "what there is to explain is how the worst thing happened, and then how the best thing happened, and then how everything got mixed up, what was good and what was bad." He gets to go to the Sangre de Cristo, but only because his brother is drafted. How everything gets mixed up and what one must be responsible for form the subject of the important conversation between Gabriel and Miguel on wishes. Miguel begins to understand that in the adult world, to which he has finally gained his long-sought-for admittance, good seldom comes unaccompanied by bad, and if one is going to work for something he wants, he must be prepared to assume responsibility for whatever bad comes with it.

Because Miguel is both narrator and central character, the importance of his narrative style should be readily apparent. He tells his story like a twelve-year-old, at times naïvely reporting things he does not fully understand. This naïveté is evident especially in the humor, as at Miguel's first dinner with the rest of the men or when he falls into the fleece bag. The same sort of honest and faithful reporting of others' remarks is responsible for the occasional points of reference which provide the reader with a certain perspective denied Miguel through the greater part of the book. The reader is given a key to the novel when Miguel's father tells him it is not his job to look for the sheep, or when Gabriel remarks that being Miguel might be easier in a few years. The point of view, however, always remains Miguel's, never shifting to another character or to the author himself, and the occasional points of reference do not invite us to make moral judgments on Miguel.

The language of the book is also well suited to the narrator. Almost any passage in the book read well aloud will sound just as one would expect Miguel to sound if he were speaking, and much of the novel's effectiveness lies in its ability to convince us that we are listening to Miguel himself. The rather simple words, colloquial and informal diction, occasional Spanish words, nonstandard constructions, and freedom of punctuation all succeed very well in creating this effect. We accept the narrator as Miguel, and through him we can understand in his own language and from his own point of view what it means to be Miguel.

STUDY QUESTIONS

CHAPTERS 1-7

1. Why does the author begin his book with the sentence, "I am Miguel"? Who is telling this story? Who is the story about? What is the story about?

Is the narrator someone involved in the story or outside of it? Reread the beginning of Chapter 2. How would the point of view change if, for example, Miguel's father were the narrator? If a person outside the story were the narrator? Be specific. Could the book still begin with the words, "I am Miguel"? How would this affect the novel?

2. Who is Pedro? How old is he? How does Miguel describe him? What does he think it means to be Pedro? Who is Gabriel? How old is he? How does Miguel describe him? What does he think it means to be Gabriel? Miguel contrasts himself with both Pedro and Gabriel. What does being Miguel mean to him? In what ways does he think he is different from his brothers?

3. The following passage is part of a conversation that takes place between Gabriel and Miguel in Chapter 1:

> "But it's not so easy for me—to be Miguel."
> "Maybe not." Gabriel smiled, watching the snow ahead. "It takes a little time. Wait a year or two, and it'll be easier."
> "Only to wait? Isn't there something else I can do. Like—practice?"
> "Being Miguel—it's not like playing basketball. No, it's a hard thing to train for."

Towards the end of the chapter Miguel says: "But to be in between, not so little anymore and not yet nineteen years, to be me, Miguel, and to have a great wish—that is hard." Why does Miguel say that being Miguel is "not so easy" for him? Both of the passages quoted emphasize his age: what does age have to do with its being difficult for him to be Miguel? Do you think it would be any easier for him if he were either older or younger? Why? Why does Gabriel say, "Wait a year or two, and it'll be easier"? Do you think Gabriel ever may have found it a problem to be Gabriel? Why do you think so? Do you think Pedro will ever find it a problem to be Pedro? Why? Have you ever found being you difficult?

4. Miguel says: "In our family there is always one thing, and that is the sheep. . . . Everything comes and goes. Except one thing. The sheep." How does this passage help explain why it becomes so important to Miguel to be allowed to work with the rest as a "pas*tor*"?

Miguel's family is very important to him. In what ways is it important to him? Why? Whom does he regard as his family? What does being a Chavez mean to him?

5. Miguel's great wish is to go to the Sangre de Cristo Mountains. What do the mountains mean to him? Does going there involve only sight-seeing or getting away from home? In Chapter 6, when Miguel is thinking of leaving home, he considers going to the Sangre de Cristo by himself, but then he realizes that that was no good. "It was impossible. There was only one way to go up into the Mountains of the Sangre de Cristo. And that was to make everyone see you were ready, and then you would go." Why does he reach this conclusion? What does going to the mountains involve for him? How do you know? Would going to the Sangre de Cristo mean the same thing to you or someone from your family as it does to Miguel Chavez? Why or why not?

What conditions must be fulfilled before Miguel can go? Fulfilling these conditions becomes very important for him in this story. How does knowing this help us understand what the Sangre de Cristo mean to him?

6. Where does this story take place? What is the land like around Miguel's house? What is it like in the mountains?

7. Miguel tells how once during the lambing he tried to make his father see who he was when he brought some bags. Why is it important to him that his father know that it is Miguel bringing the bags? Is this part of the difficulty of being Miguel? How? Why doesn't his father ask him by name to get the bags? What sort of job is it? Do other people get called by name? What sort of jobs are they doing?

8. Miguel contrasts school with working with his family and the sheep. He feels that in school he, Miguel, gets credit for what he does, but whether he does well or not does not make a great difference from day to day. Working with the sheep, on the other hand, he does not get recognition for what he does, but here it makes a big difference whether a job is well done or not. Which is more important to him, school or the sheep? Why? What would be the ideal situation?

9. The following conversation takes place in Chapter 2:

"And after so many years," like I told Pedro, "it's not enough, just to watch anymore."

"Why?" said Pedro. "This is fine. Nothing to do. No school. What could be better than this?"

Why isn't it enough to watch anymore? One reason Miguel gives is that it is not so lonesome, working with the others. Why should he feel this way?

10. In Chapter 2 Miguel tells us: "But for me, I have the wish to be part of everything that happens, even if it is not happening to me." Why should Miguel have this wish? Is it like his wish to go to the Sangre de Cristo? How?

11. When Miguel tries to go out in the middle of the night to help with the lambing from the start, his mother sends him back to bed, explaining that "even a whole man must learn to wait until his time comes. He can work, and he can prepare, but he must know how to wait, too." Miguel replies, "I've learned how to wait. In twelve years, I've learned." Has he? Why is waiting often necessary?

12. When Miguel gets back to his bedroom he tells Pedro and Faustina about the Sangre de Cristo and his great wish. How does he describe the mountains to them? How does this description differ from that he gives us elsewhere in the book? Do you think he believes everything he tells them? Why does he describe the Sangre de Cristo to them in this way?

13. In this same conversation on the night when the lambing begins, Pedro gives his opinion on how one gets to go to the mountains: "Arrange. That's not the way. . . . First you got to know how to do everything. Then when you get into high school, or sometime like that, then it happens." Is this what is meant by waiting, that one can't "arrange" anything, that when the time comes, it will just "happen"? Why?

14. Working with the numbers, Miguel makes a discovery. He says:

This part is a little hard to say. It was good that I was a part of all the work, and everyone knew that it was me, Miguel. And it is good, too, I didn't have to fool Pedro anymore. All this was good.

But the something else is this. It would get so sometimes that I would forget what the good of it was. I mean the good that it was for me. Or even that what was happening was me, Miguel, doing what had to be done for myself. All that was left was the sheep and what they had to have. . . .

What does Miguel find is happening to him? Is this good? Why do you think it happens?

15. What does the word "pastor" mean? How is it usually used? What does it mean when Padre de Chavez uses it? Why do you think the author has it printed "pas*tor*," with the second syllable in italics?

In talking with Miguel, Padre de Chavez tells him that "that is the real work of a pas*tor*, . . . of a shepherd. To see that in all the flock there is no one that is alone by himself. Everyone together. Only so can all live." How is the job of this kind of pastor, of a shepherd, like that of the other kind of pastor? Why does he say, "Only so can all live"? Is this true for the sheep? Padre de Chavez next draws an analogy between the sheep and men. It is true for men, too, that "only so can all live"? Why? How is this related to Miguel's problem of being Miguel?

16. Why does Padre de Chavez say it is a sin if the "ewe and the child go apart from each other"? He also says, "Whenever something grows and you keep it from growing anymore, that's a sin." Why? If Miguel's father had not given him any opportunity to help with the work, would that have been a sin? Why?

17. Why does Miguel feel that an orphan can never be very happy? How does this help explain Miguel's own feelings and desires? Does he ever feel like an orphan? When?

18. Why does Miguel skip school to look for the sheep? Why doesn't he just send word to the men to tell them where Juby saw the flock? Why is he glad whenever something happens to make the job of finding the sheep more difficult? How hard is it for him to find them? For him to bring them home?

Is his father right when he says that finding the sheep is not a job for Miguel? Why? Is anything changed because Miguel is successful in finding the sheep? Why? Why does his father say, "How you did it was wrong. But for what you did, I want to thank you"?

19. After being thanked by his father for bringing home the

sheep, Miguel decides to ask him whether he can go to the mountains this year. Why does his father say "No"?

20. Reread the first four pages of Chapter 4 through the paragraph ending, "He always goes *borracho* and falls down in a heap." Note the language. Who is telling the story? Does he use words that you didn't know? Which ones? Does he use words which you know but which you would tend not to use in either speaking or writing? Which ones? From what language does the word "borracho" come? Is Miguel trying to impress us with his knowledge of a foreign language, or is this an ordinary part of his vocabulary? Defend your answer.

Such sentences as the following are characteristic of the way Miguel speaks:

> She goes all over the field looking as if for some place to lie down.

> Then happens a remarkable thing.

> For once they look smart, like for instance the ewe was an old man who knew how everything should be and was standing off to one side watching it should happen right and in order.

Does he use any sentence constructions that seem strange to you? Which ones? Does he use constructions which you have heard but which you would not use in speaking? In writing? Which ones?

In what ways does this section at the beginning of Chapter 4 sound like Miguel? Does the language sound like that of an adult or of a child? Defend your answer. Does the language sound like that of writing or of speaking? Defend your answer. Does it add to or detract from the novel to have the book written so that the language sounds like Miguel? Why?

CHAPTERS 8-14

1. Why does Miguel say, "But for anything more important, words get mixed up." What happens to mix things up? Why does Miguel become confused whenever he tries to explain things to his father, as the day at the lambing when he tried to explain about the bags? Why is it important that words not get mixed up?

2. The following passages are from the part of Chapter 8 dealing with the fiesta on San Ysidro Day, Miguel relates:

> I didn't drink anything. I wasn't very thirsty. I sat on a rock and watched Mr. Moreno and Mr. Summers cook.
>
> For myself, I wasn't hungry. I watched how the others ate. . . .
>
> . . . I didn't feel like dancing. I felt more like watching.

Why doesn't he join the others? Why does he feel "more like watching"? Jimmy too is unhappy. What does Miguel think is making Jimmy sad? How does this reflect Miguel's own feelings?

3. Recalling various incidents and the information Miguel gives us on sheep throughout the book, how ready do you think he is to go to the Sangre de Cristo? When his father asks his advice or help, how well qualified is he to give the answer? Does he give the right answer? Cite specific instances.

Miguel's father tells him to figure out how to fix up a swinging gate. What does his father say about the plan he works out? Is Miguel himself pleased with what he has done? His father suggests a few changes in the way he has set things up. How extensive are these changes? What does his father call them? What does Miguel call them? Why does his father proceed as he does? Why doesn't he just tell Miguel that he has figured everything out wrong? Has he? What has he done correctly? How important is this?

4. Referring to the conversation at the tractor, Miguel's father tells Johnny Marquez, "The big thing we decided was that Miguel here should become a regular part of the work this year when school was over." In his narrative Miguel states that what his father "said was the big thing, that wasn't exactly so." What does Miguel think was the big thing? Who do you think is right?

5. At the beginning of Chapter 11 Miguel says:

> And now what there is to explain is how the worst thing happened, and then how the best thing happened, and then how everything got mixed up, what was good and what was bad.

What is the worst thing? Why does it happen? How does Miguel make it worse? What is the best thing? Why does it happen? How does everything get mixed up?

6. After the humiliation of falling in the fleece bag and hearing all the men joke about it, Miguel decides it was all a joke, about his being "a new hand, with a new name, Twister" and about "sitting down first with the men who ate first." He concludes that there wasn't any miracle after all; San Ysidro hadn't heard his wish. Is this true? Was it all a joke? Was there a miracle? Why do you think so?

7. Why does Miguel tell Pedro that his name is neither Twister nor Miguel but Babaloo? What does Twister mean to him? Why doesn't he want to be Miguel anymore? What does Babaloo mean? Who else uses this word in the story? Why does Miguel choose it as his name now?

Later, when Miguel is leaving for the mountains and it comes time for him to say goodbye, the following conversation takes place between him and Pedro:

> "Goodbye," he said, "whatever your name is."
> "That part is settled," I told him.
> "What is it? Twister, Miguel, Babaloo?"
> "Chavez."

Why does Miguel decide that the important name is Chavez?

8. Why does Miguel ask Gabriel to get rid of the letter? Why does he think Gabriel can change things so that he won't have to leave home? Can he? Why? Later Miguel takes the letter and hides it. Does this do any good? Why? What does this indicate that Miguel must learn?

9. Why does Miguel think he is to blame for the letter? Is he? Do you think so? Why or why not? Gabriel tells him that it is partly his own fault, too, because he wished to go away for a while and see the ocean. Do you think this is part of the reason he got the letter? Why? Are either Miguel or Gabriel responsible for what has happened?

What do you think is the conclusion reached in the long conversation Gabriel and Miguel have about wishes? Must one stop wishing? Why? What wishes are good and what ones are bad?

Miguel says he is going to make a new kind of wish to San Ysidro next year, and Gagriel says the new kind of wish he is going to make is like the prayer, "Our Father Who Art in Heaven." How are they similar? Why is this a good "wish"?

10. Why does the story end with Miguel carving the "TTA" for Gabriel and not with him carving his own name? How is this related to the new kind of prayer that he tells Gabriel?

Teaching
The Witch of Blackbird Pond

ENGLISH CURRICULUM
STUDY CENTER STAFF

Kit Tyler arrives at Wethersfield in Puritan New England with values and ideas from her previous life in Barbados. With her fashionable gowns and slippers, her aversion to "the work of servants," and her vivacious impulsive nature, she conflicts with the austere, work-oriented Puritan world. The reader follows Kit as she visits the Quaker woman whom the townspeople call a witch, listens with her to heated political discussions of the colonists, and shares with her a young girl's indecision toward marriage. As Kit tries to meet new situations with a preconceived view of life, the reader sympathizes; and when she is able to expand her world of Barbados values to include New England as well, he is proud.

Elizabeth Speare's novel is interesting and easily accessible for the average junior high school student. Language is no problem and characters and incidents are simply but carefully drawn. The teacher's task is not to remove obstacles to basic reading, then, but to lead students to the implications which, though not essential to the enjoyment of the story, contribute to the most complete understanding. Perhaps the best way to approach meaning without falling prey to an oversimplified study of themes is to examine the way the author manipulates her material—the way she controls events and characters within her story and influences the reader's reaction to them.

Though the person telling the story—the one through whose eyes we view the characters and events—lives outside the story, he mirrors Kit's struggle to reconcile her new life with past experiences. "There were no words to explain grandfather." "Water! For Breakfast!" "Oh! Why had she ever come to this hateful place." These typical comments appear in the novel as narrative, yet they reflect Kit's unspoken reaction and expand the reader's knowledge of both character and situation. The story demands that Kit control much of her spontaneity if she is to survive in her new environment. It also demands some externalization of her internal conflict, which is at the heart of the novel. By incorporating in the narrative Kit's unvoiced responses, the author is able to present the conflict without sacrificing story credibility.

Interwoven in the novel are three centers of tension or conflict, each of which might have been the basis of a separate story. There is the conflict between Kit's former and present ways of life, the love plot involving the six young persons, and the antagonism between colonists and royalists. In the first Kit is at the center, in the second she is a participant, and in the third she merely observes. Movement in all three is toward self-definition and tolerance.

Having experienced two frequently opposing standards, Kit learns to define herself against the social order within which she lives. In Barbados, where her position was determined by that of her grandfather, she did not feel the force of social control. But in the Puritan community, where control is the very essence of life, her spontaneous behavior is continually checked by her neighbors' reactions. When she impulsively goes ashore at Saybrook before arriving at Wethersfield, townspeople stare—"No one on the island had ever presumed to stare like that at Sir Francis Tyler's granddaughter." And when she goes into the water to retrieve Prudence's doll, she is accused of being a witch—because she floats. Swimming was great fun in Barbados, but in New England the water is cold and the sport taboo.

The conflicting values apparent between the Barbados and Puritan worlds are paralleled on a more personal level in Kit's relationships with William, John, and Nat. Her final choice of Nat, who embodies the strength of New England character without the confining Puritan views, is not surprising. The conflict which is not resolved—the British-American conflict—functions mainly as a backdrop for characters and other situations. But in this instance, too, mutually exclusive ways of life collide. Kit is finally able to expand her personal world, but the political dispute, as the students have learned in their history classes, ended in war.

The way the story is told leads the reader to comparisons. Instead of adhering to a strict chronological method in which Kit's past life is summarized early in the book and then dismissed, the author allows information to be revealed gradually as each new experience causes Kit to recall some incident in her past. In Chapter 2 we learn that Kit enjoyed reading plays in Barbados and that plays are scorned in New England. In Chapter 3 we learn that she once had her own Negro slave and that New Englanders cherish freedom. By this method the author is able to control the reader's knowledge of, and reaction to, situations. In a similar way she is able to create an atmosphere of suspense by suggesting questions and withholding their answers until later in the novel. We are told that Hannah has a scar on her forehead, but do not learn why until later. We know that a seaman has been visiting Hannah, but not until he appears during Kit's visit do we realize that the seaman is Nat.

By her storytelling methods, the author also points up some of the inconsistencies with which persons and societies can view themselves and others. The Puritans are rebelling against the British land tax, which they consider a limitation of their freedom, but they impose fines on those who don't attend church meetings. The situations are juxtaposed in such a way that, though the author does not draw the parallel either through narrative or characters, the reader infers her meaning. Somewhat more explicitly stated are the different reactions of Kit and Nat to the horse smell on the Dolphin and the contrasting attitudes of Kit and John toward reading. All of these underline the rigidities of little man-made worlds which exclude opposing points of view.

STUDY QUESTIONS

CHAPTERS 1-5

1. Why does the author tell us in the first sentence of the book when the story is taking place? Can you recall incidents which might be confusing or difficult to understand if we did not know that they were happening in 1687?

2. Why does Kit find her first glimpse of America disappointing? What does this suggest about Colonial America? And what does it suggest about Kit?

3. Kit acts impulsively when she goes ashore at Saybrook and again when she dives into the water to retrieve the child's doll. By whom is her behavior criticized in these particular situations? Are these just reasons for disapproving her actions? Is impulsive action always unwise? Explain your answer.

4. Startled by Kit's behavior on the boat, Goodwife Cruff insists that the girl is a witch. What clue suggests to the reader that this charge will become important later in the book? Though persons on the boat will not believe the accusation and there is no more talk of witches for several chapters, the incident should alert the reader to new possibilities in the action.

5. At the conclusion of Chapter 1 we learn that "there was something strange about this country of America, something that they all seemed to share and understand and she [Kit] did not." What are some of the things that Kit has failed to understand? Is it because she is stupid? Is it because she will not confront new experience with an open mind? Or is it simply because her childhood in Barbados did not prepare her for this kind of life?

6. When Kit first enters her uncle's house, she sees a woman whom she considers "quite plainly a servant," but who is actually her Aunt Rachel. And when her aunt first notices Kit, she cries out "Margaret"—mistaking Kit for her mother. Is the effect serious or comic? What do these responses tell us about the person mis-

taken? What do they tell us about the person who makes the mistake?

7. Kit was born in Barbados, but all of the action takes place in America. Instead of summarizing previous events in the first chapter, the author allows this information to be revealed gradually as each new experience causes Kit to recall some incident in her past. What are the advantages of this method of presentation? In Chapter 2 we learn that Kit enjoyed reading plays in Barbados and that plays are scorned in New England. In Chapter 3 we learn that she once had her own Negro slave and that New Englanders cherish freedom. Not until Chapter 4 do we learn the true reason for her sudden arrival—that she wished to escape the advances of an elderly suitor. How does this gradual introduction of information affect our attitudes toward Kit? How would the contrast between her past and present life be altered if her childhood had been summarized near the beginning of the book and mentioned no more?

8. Note that Kit's responses to her new surroundings are immediate, impulsive, and seldom qualified by reflection. The Connecticut shores strike her as "bare and ugly"; the town of Wethersfield is also "ugly"; the Puritan service seems to her "plain and unlovely." By the end of Chapter 5 she wonders why she ever came to this "hateful place." On the basis of the evidence presented, would you agree that Wethersfield is hateful? Do you share Kit's responses to her new surroundings?

9. Despite their growing up in the same surroundings, Judith and Mercy differ in their attitudes and actions. How does each react when Rachel takes corn bread to Widow Brown? When Matthew Wood finds the girls trying on Kit's clothes? Which of the sisters seems most content with her life?

CHAPTERS 6-10

1. Compare the attitudes toward the English king expressed by Matthew, Kit, William, and John. What do the political debates in Matthew Wood's house suggest about the roots of the American Revolution?

2. The incidents at the Dame School dramatize two approaches

to education. The traditional approach is characterized by strictness, rigid discipline, and attention to the subject. Mercy accepts this approach. Kit seeks to introduce more leniency and imagination—with catastropic results. What are the merits and dangers of each approach? Which do you prefer?

3. The Bible was the most important and sometimes the only book read in a Puritan community. Kit, John Holbrook, and the Reverend Mr. Bulkeley value different things in the Bible. What does each find of most importance? What does each person's preference tell us about what he or she values most in life?

4. After several months in Wethersfield, Kit can no longer tolerate the constant warnings, sermons, and preaching which she encounters at every turn. In this context Hannah's remarks about the African flower are noteworthy:

> "It came all the way from Africa, from the Cape of Good Hope,"
> Hannah told her. "My friend brought the bulb to me, a little brown
> thing like an onion. I doubted it would grow here, but it just
> seemed determined to keep on trying and look what has happened."

> Kit glanced up suspiciously. Was Hannah trying to preach to her?
> But the old woman merely poked gently at the earth. . . .

Hannah's story is a sort of *parable*, a short imaginative story that points, by analogy or comparison, to a moral. What is the moral of this parable? Can you recall other parables from your reading? From the Bible, for example? The African flower seems to "stand for" or represent a specific idea. What do you think it represents? Do you find special significance in the fact that it comes from the Cape of Good Hope? Can you make a distinction between the preaching of Hannah Tupper and the preaching of the Reverend Mr. Bulkeley? Which has a greater effect upon Kit? Why?

5. What reasons do the people of Wethersfield have for supposing that Hannah is a witch? Are these "reasons" a measure of knowledge or ignorance? Explain your answer.

CHAPTERS 11-15

1. Kit speaks of her visits to Blackbird Pond as an entrance into a "secret world." Why must it be secret? In what ways does the

world of Hannah's cottage differ from the world of Wethersfield?

2. Describe the appearance and manner of the Reverend Mr. Gersholm Bulkeley. Why does John Holbrook admire him? Why does Matthew Wood dislike him? What is Kit's opinion of him? One way to learn about a character is to observe the opinions which others hold about him. Which of these opinions do you find most acceptable?

3. The visit of Governor Andros sparks an important political controversy. What are the issues involved? Compare the attitudes of the men and the women to this visit. Can we fairly call these typical masculine and feminine reactions to politics? Defend your answer.

4. In Chapter 7 William Ashby argued for the royalist cause. In Chapter 15 he argues against the king and for the Charter. Why has he changed his position? What reason does Judith have for his changed attitude? Can you think of another reason? What role does William play in the disappearance of the Charter?

5. Kit does not adjust easily to life in Wethersfield. Do you agree with her criticisms of the Puritan character and the Puritan community? Is she always fair?

6. What is a woman's role in Puritan society? Describe woman's status in the family, in the community, in political life. Support your answers by referring specifically to incidents in the novel.

7. Kit sometimes forgets that Nathaniel Eaton is also a New Englander and a Puritan. In what ways is he similar to the people of Wethersfield? In what ways is he different? What are the reasons for these similarities and differences?

CHAPTERS 16-21

1. Some of the words in the novel refer to artifacts, customs, or institutions that were common in Colonial New England but which are now largely unknown. Can you describe each of the following?

taper	The Charter
Meeting House	pillory
Lecture Day	stocks
Dame School	hornbook

2. Why did John Holbrook go to Massachusetts to fight the Indians? Aunt Rachel and Judith offer different explanations. Can you think of another? Why do you think he acted wisely or unwisely?

3. A time of crisis often brings out the best, or worst, in a man's character. For example, the Reverend Mr. Bulkeley is narrow-minded in political debate, but he helps his political enemy when sickness strikes; William Ashby intends to marry Kit, but he fails to appear at her trial; Prudence Cruff is terrorized by her parents, but she is fearless before them when Kit is in danger. Are these people acting "in character"? Can you find incidents in the past behavior of each which look forward to these decisive actions?

4. What are the penalties for practicing witchcraft in Connecticut?

5. When Hannah Tupper is accused of witchcraft, she has to face the fury of a mob. When Kit is accused of being a witch, her neighbors lie and slander her in court. Which is in greater danger? Why is the neighbors' evidence ruled inadmissable in a court of law?

6. How is Kit's dream important to the story?

7. Why has Kit been unable or unwilling to admit her attraction to Nat? Has she been reluctant to admit other things as well? What did she fail to recognize about the Puritans? About her uncle? About America? Support your answers with specific evidence from the novel.

8. Is the ending of the novel entirely satisfactory? Suppose that Hannah had not escaped from the mob, or Mercy had died, or John had failed to return from the war. Would the novel then have been more true to life?

GENERAL QUESTIONS ABOUT THE BOOK

1. Before an author writes a novel he must choose a storyteller, or narrator—a person through whose eyes we see the characters and events. This narrator may be a character within the story or an unidentified person outside. Who is telling the story in *The Witch of Blackbird Pond*? Do we know anything about the nar-

rator as a person? How does this narrator differ from the one who told . . . *and now Miguel?* Would the point of view change if Kit were to tell the story herself?

2. Frequently novels contain two or more situations which might have been told as individual stories. The stories may be used together to reinforce the ideas which they share, to help the reader to see the characters in various situations, or to increase the interest and adventure in the novel. Usually the stories are connected by the characters who appear in both or incidents in which the stories interlock. What separate stories are present in *Witch?* Outline briefly the story line of each. In what ways are they connected? How does each contribute to the reader's understanding of the main characters? Can you think of other ways that the presence of more than one story helps the reader to understand Kit's experiences in Puritan New England?

Teaching *The Light in the Forest**

EDWARD B. JENKINSON

From his forced return to his white family until he betrays his Indian friends, True Son thinks he is a Delaware. He looks at the world from an Indian point of view, criticizing white man's civilization. He sees "the sad, incredible region where the Indian forest has been cut down by the white destroyers and no place left for Indian game to live." Forced to wear his cousin's pants and jacket, "symbols of the lies, thefts, and murders by the white man," he is outraged. The scalped Mohawk, the murdered Conestogo, and the ignorance of his arrogant Uncle Wilse add to his hatred of white men.

True Son and his Indian companions think of the early pioneers as liars, stealers, and murderers. According to Little Crane, white men are preoccupied with material things: "they heap up treasures like a child, although they know they must die and cannot take such things with them." They build a barn to store what they cannot put in their houses. Their desire to add to their wealth only results in stealing.

Cuyloga believes that white men cannot be trusted, that they break promises, that they do not want peace with the Indians. He tells True Son:

> When will the white man learn! He says to the Indian, brother, have peace. The Indian buries the tomahawk. He hides it deep

* Copyright © 1964 by L. W. Singer Company. Reprinted by permission of L. W. Singer Company and of the author.

under a stump. He believes his brother, the white man. He visits his brother, the white man. Then his brother, the white man, murders him, a guest under his roof. He thinks no more of it than killing a snake in his cabin. The white man talks to other Indians. He says, brother, what's the matter? Why do you go to war? Why dig up the tomahawk? *Elkih!* The white man is a strange creature of the Almighty. He is hard to fathom. How can you reason with him? He is like a spoiled child without instruction. He has no understanding of good or evil.

In *The Light in the Forest,* the white men are not all good, not all brave heroes, not all television idols seen in the Western dramas of white men versus Indians. The author presents the other side of the coin in the struggle of the pioneers to win America. He gives us the Indian point of view. He shows, quite vividly, the civilization and beliefs of the Delaware Indians. He paints, in words, pictures of the atrocities committed by both Indians and whites. He shows that neither side was perfectly right nor completely wrong.

In giving us the Indian point of view of white man's civilization, the author does more than simply tell a story based on historical fact. He writes in the *Acknowledgements*: "I thought that perhaps if we understood how these First Americans felt toward us even then and toward our white way of life, we might better understand the adverse, if perverted, view of us by some African, European, and Asian peoples today."

Disputes among people frequently arise from failure to try to see the other man's point of view; to determine how he thinks and why he thinks the way he does; to see what his civilization has to offer before forcing him to change. Myra Butler, Aunt Kate, and Uncle Wilse fail to consider that the Indians had a decent way of life, that they were human, that they had a right to the land. In her first meeting with True Son, Myra Butler says: "Your education has been arrested. You've had to live in heathen darkness and ignorance."

Did Myra Butler know what she was saying? No. She did not know that True Son believed in a Great Spirit, that he had been educated to make his own way in the forest, that his Indian people had a code of life as decent, as moral, and as good as her own. She simply spoke her prejudices. Prejudices that are echoed throughout the novel by Uncle Wilse, Parson Elder, Aunt Kate, and the tailor. Prejudices that stem from a lack of understanding, from an unwillingness to see the other man's point of view.

Angered by True Son's refusal to speak English, Uncle Wilse dismisses the Delaware language as "gibberish." The killer of Little Crane accepts only what he knows. He refuses to tolerate anything else. He will not admit to himself or to anyone else that the Delaware language is rich, that the Indian life, although different from his, is equally good.

Through both the white men and the Indians in this novel, the author points out the prejudices that lead to misunderstanding and sometimes to brutality.

True Son stands in the middle. He sees the prejudices, the evils, the lack of understanding on both sides. Reared as an Indian, he accepts the Indian way of life—but not completely. After living with the Butlers, he shows that he can no longer accept Half Arrow's belief that what belongs to the white man also belongs to the Indian since the white man stole the land from the Indian. He begins to accept, slowly and reluctantly, the white man's ideas of property rights and of right and wrong. He still thinks like an Indian, yet he cannot accept Thitpan's reasons for scalping the little girl. He joins Half Arrow in the half-scalping of Uncle Wilse, but he does so for vengeance—not for the savage joy of killing. Unwilling to help his Indian brothers kill the white party in the boat, he unwittingly commits himself to life as an outcast.

Even as an outsider he is more Indian than white. During his trial he feels more like an Indian than ever before, even though he knows that he will be condemned. He is ready to be burned to death; he is not ready to be driven back to white man's civilization. He knows that life among the whites will be miserable, for he is an Indian.

> Ahead of him ran the rutted road of the whites. It led, he knew, to where men of their own volition constrained themselves with heavy clothing, like harness, where men chose to be slaves to their own or another's property, and followed empty and desolate lives far from the wild beloved freedom of the Indian.

To True Son the wild beloved freedom of the Indian is his life in the forest. He loves nature. Educated as an Indian, he calls the earth his mother, the sun his father, the birds his sisters, and the black squirrel his brother. He knows that the Great Spirit will take care of him in the uncut forest filled with game. There he lives the carefree life of teen-age abandon, unchained, untutored, uninhibited by either the laws of the white men or the code of the Indians. In the forest he is free from cares, free from work, free from adult responsibility. Life in the forest is primitive, but happy. Roaming among the trees with Half Arrow, "no one stood between them and life."

> They passed their days in a kind of primitive deliciousness. The past was buried. There was only the present and tomorrow. By day they lived as happy animals. Moonlight nights in the forest they saw what the deer saw. Swimming under water with open eyes, they knew now what the otter knew.

True Son finds the light in the forest. It is the carefree age of youth. It is the age of happiness, of exploring, of learning about and appreciating nature, of forgetting the responsibilities forced on one by civilization—either white or Indian. The light in the forest is the age of "primitive deliciousness."

In the forest True Son finds the glorious freedom and adventure that almost every boy longs for. In the villages of the white man he finds the slavery that old Bejance describes.

> You eat with a fork and spoon. You sleep in a bed. You own a house and a piece of land and pays taxes. You hoe all day in the cornfield and toil and sweat a diggin' up stumps. Piece by piece you get broke in to livin' in a stall by night, and by day pullin' burdens that mean nothin' to the soul inside of you.

True Son must return to the life that Bejance describes. But he does not fit into it. He has no family. He belongs to neither the whites nor the Indians. He asks: "Then who is my father?" There is no reply. What could the answer be?

Why is True Son homeless? Why is he fatherless? Could the novel have ended differently? Yes, had True Son allowed the scalping party to attack the white men in the boat, the novel would have ended happily. But would it have been realistic? Would it have followed the changes in True Son's attitude as he moved from the Indian world to the white? The answer is no. True Son made his decision when he saw, as he stood in the water calling to the white men in the boat, the little boy who resembled Gordie. True Son could not be a party to such a killing. So he is forced to stand alone.

True Son is a boy of principles, a young man of character. Even in defeat, even during his trial, he shows that he is strong. He is an unforgettable character, clearly drawn by the author in simple words. He is the product of history; yet his story is fictional.

As a boy, Conrad Richter tried to run away to live with the Indians. As a man, the author studied the lives of the Indians and discovered that many white boys and girls who had been captured by the Indians did not want to be returned to their white homes. They enjoyed their lives in the forest. Richter wanted to know why some white children wanted to live with the Indians. He searched for the answer to his question, and the answer is the descriptions of Indian life contained in this book.

Combining his knowledge of Indians with the little-known historical fact of Colonel Bouquet's march through the Pennsylvania and Ohio woods to gather white captives of the Indians, Richter has given us an exciting adventure story. But it is more than a story—more than a tale told to entertain. For Richter has given us a point of view to consider. He has shown us the other side of the white-Indian struggle.

STUDY QUESTIONS

CHAPTER 1-3

1. Learning that his tribe must release all white prisoners, True Son panics, blackens his face, and runs away. Why does he believe that he is an Indian, not a white prisoner? Why does his Indian father take him to the white soldiers?

2. Left alone with the white soldiers, True Son sees a clear and beautiful mental picture of the land of the Tuscarawas. Which sentences show that he is observant, that he loves nature? Where is the land of the Tuscarawas?

3. How does True Son react to Del Hardy? How would you defend his attitude toward the white soldier? Do you think True Son behaves and thinks the way he does because he has been reared as a savage? Or would you call him a savage? Explain your answer.

As you read on, ask yourself: Are True Son's actions realistic? Would he behave the way he does if he did not think he is an Indian? Does he, at times, act more civilized than some of the white men in this novel?

4. By using a device called flashback, the author tells you about important events that occurred before the action of the story begins. What do you learn about Del Hardy in the flashback at the beginning of Chapter 2? Why is this passage more than a flashback?

Why does Del call his mission a "suicide march"? What is his attitude toward Indians? Toward Colonel Bouquet? According to Del, why did the Indians give up their white prisoners? What does Del think of True Son? Why does the white soldier sometimes experience Indian feelings?

5. How does True Son plan to show the Indians that he is not a coward? What does he think his Indian friends will do if he succeeds in his plan?

6. Why does Half Arrow join True Son on the march? When Half Arrow says that he wants to talk of "pleasant and cheerful things," what does he talk about? What is his opinion of white men? What gifts does he bring to True Son? Why does the bearskin have a great effect on the white Indian boy?

7. Knowing the meaning of every word will add to your enjoyment and understanding of this novel. When you read a new word, you will want to look up its meaning in a good dictionary, or you may find the contextual meaning of a new word at the bottom of each page. Sometimes, however, you can tell what a new word means by the way it is used in a sentence. On page 7, for example, you may have known that *overwhelmed* means *overcome completely* or *crushed*. You understand the word by the way it is used in this sentence: "Homesickness *overwhelmed* him, and he sat there and wept." Can you infer the meaning of the underlined words by the way they are used in these sentences?

1. But what *affronted* the boy was that the white guard laughed at him (page 8).
2. It was his first *stint* with the army and his only one with Colonel Bouquet (page 9).
3. And yet the *peace-palavering* Colonel swore he wouldn't halt . . . (page 10).
4. He had to be tied up with strips of buffalo hide, and then he struggled like a panther kit *trussed* up on a pole (page 13).
5. When he went from the council house, the guard kept hold of him like a *haltered* beast (page 19).
6. The boy's eyes found a young Indian in leggins, *breech clout* and *strouding* (page 20).
7. At the same time he made a wry *grimace* over the meat (page 23).
8. So that's why they're so pale and *bandy-legged,* having to eat such old and stringy leather while Indian people have rich *venison* and bear meat (page 23).

CHAPTERS 4 AND 5

1. As they march toward white civilization, Little Crane, Half Arrow, and True Son discuss the ways of the white man. Why does Little Crane think that white men act so strangely? Why did the Great Spirit have to give white men the Good Book? Why didn't He have to give it to the Indians?

According to the Indian trio, what are some of the peculiar traits of white men? Why do the three Indians think white men are nearsighted, hard of hearing, and heedless like children? Do you think they offer good reasons? Explain your answer.

In the last paragraph of the *Acknowledgments* in the front of this book, the author gives you one of his reasons for writing *The Light in the Forest.* After rereading that paragraph, what do you think of the charges that the Indian trio makes against white men? Why do you think that foreigners coming to the United States today could make some of these charges?

2. According to the Indians, who killed the Mohawk? Do you think white men living in Colonial times would have scalped an Indian? Explain your answer.

3. Half Arrow apologizes to the white soldier for True Son's

attempted escape. Which sentence makes you wonder if he is actually apologizing? What do you think is his purpose for the apology?

4. What advice does True Son's Indian father give him? What is the meaning of the story about the bear? Do you think a father today would give his son such advice? What parts of it can you agree with? How does True Son accept the advice?

5. What does True Son think of Fort Pitt? Why does he dislike plowed ground?

True Son is a prisoner of the whites, but he thinks they have made themselves prisoners in their own homes. He wonders how men can live in the confinement of white villages. He looks at civilization from a different point of view. With which of his sentences describing civilization can you agree?

6. What virtue, according to True Son, did the Colonel and his staff learn from the Indians? Why does he refer to the prisoners as a "sacrificial cluster of captives"?

Before he even meets his white father, True Son dislikes him. But why does he dislike Mr. Butler even more when he actually sees him? Why must Del Hardy accompany True Son to the Butler home?

7. To keep you interested in the story, the author gives you clues of events to come. He builds suspense by hinting, for example, that True Son may escape. On page 34 True Son says: "Tell him I will bear my disgrace like an Indian and will wait to strike till the time is in my favor." How did you react to that sentence? What do you think True Son will do?

Find other sentences in Chapters 4 and 5 that are intended to heighten your interest in the story by giving you hints of events to come.

CHAPTERS 6 AND 7

1. True Son disliked the sight of Fort Pitt and civilization; Del Hardy joyfully threw his cap in the air when he saw the fort. True Son saw a "sacrificial cluster of captives" on page 40, while Del thought of the "freed white captives" on page 45. The unhappy boy saw the "gloomy stone" of Fort Pitt, but the white soldier saw "walls of mortared stone" that "bespoke his own people."

Although True Son and Del look at the same marks of civilization, they do not see them in the same way. In giving you these different points of view, Conrad Richter carefully chooses the words for each. What other marks of civilization do True Son and Del see differently? Show how the choice of words reflects the differences in the points of view.

2. Conducting himself as he thinks an Indian should, True Son refuses to speak English to his white father. What does Del think of True Son's refusal to speak his native language? What does True Son say when he hears the name of the river? What do you think of his white father's reply? What provokes True Son to attempt escape?

3. Instead of writing that Mr. Butler is a wealthy man, the author gives you a description of the Butler farm as Del sees it. Why do you think this is more effective than if the author had simply written that Mr. Butler is rich? Why do you think this is a more specific description than one which would have simply used the words *rich, very rich,* or *wealthy*? Write a paragraph in which you describe a man's wealth or poverty without using the words *rich* or *poor*.

4. When she first sees True Son, Myra Butler exclaims: "Why, you look like an Indian, John! You even walk like one. You've had a hard fate, but thank God your life was spared and you're home with us again. Are you happy?"

What do you think of these words from a woman who has not seen her son for eleven years? How would you describe Mrs. Butler after meeting her in Chapter 6? Which of the words in the list below best describe her? Select passages to support your choices.

foolish	vain
weak	compassionate
prejudiced	unsympathetic
persistent	stubborn
self-pitying	temperamental
sensitive	sensible

5. What is the Conestogo story? How does remembering it affect True Son as he lies in the white man's bed? Where does he finally go to sleep? Why does he go to sleep there?

In his first encounter with Uncle Wilse, True Son accuses him of murdering the Conestogo. In which sentences does Uncle Wilse admit his guilt? How would you describe Uncle Wilse? Why do you think True Son will not soon forget the sting of his uncle's hand?

What explanation does Uncle George give for the white man's behavior toward the Indians? What do you think of his reasoning?

6. Early in his conversation with Uncle Wilse, True Son defends the Delaware language. Why does True Son think it is a rich language? Why does Uncle Wilse dislike it? What does Uncle Wilse's refusal to accept another language tell you about him? Are there persons in America today who refuse to accept any language but English? How does this attitude affect our relations with other countries? Can you find, in the *Acknowledgments,* what might be the author's reason for including the passage on the Delaware language?

7. When he is first offered white man's clothing, True Son stares with loathing at the pants and jacket. "They were the symbols of all the lies, thefts, and murders by the white man." What is the meaning of that sentence?

In Chapter 7 True Son believes that he is thrice imprisoned. What are the three confinements?

8. To paint a vivid picture in the mind of the reader, authors frequently compare two unlike objects by using the words *like* or *as.* On page 46 the author has Del mentally describe the Butler boy as "sullen as a young spider." On page 58 True Son thinks that "the white man flourished in the stale sickly air of his house like fleas in his wall and borers in the cabin logs." These comparisons of two unlike objects are called *similes.* What other similes can you find in Chapters 6 and 7? How do similes give you a clearer mental picture of the objects described?

CHAPTERS 8 AND 9

1. After Del leaves, "all the odious and joyless life of the white race, its incomprehensible customs and heavy ways, fell on him [True Son] like a plague." Describe True Son's joyless life. How

does he react to the white man's church? Compare the Delaware Indians' belief in God with the white man's.

2. Bejance tells Gordie that the two Butler boys are slaves although they don't know it yet. What proof does he offer? What do you think of his ideas of slavery? To Bejance, what is freedom? How does his conversation affect True Son?

3. As they ride to see Corn Blade, Gordie asks True Son what he sees and hears. Why can't True Son answer his brother? What does he feel as he sees the woods and the creek?

Why do you think Uncle Wilse immediately accuses True Son of trying to run away? What do you think of the statements of Uncle Wilse and Mr. Butler? What do you learn about the two men from their reactions to True Son's proposed trip to see Corn Blade? How does True Son behave after he is accused of lying? Write a paragraph in which you describe Uncle Wilse.

4. As the sun shines outside, Myra Butler lies in the "welcome dimness" of her room. Why would her shutting out the sun be loathsome to True Son? What does she think about so frequently? Why do you think she has stayed in her room for eleven years?

5. Describe Parson Elder. What do you think of his discussion with True Son? With which of the parson's statements can you agree? With which of True Son's points can you agree? According to the parson, what will change True Son's attitude? What do you think of his advice to Myra Butler?

6. As he introduces an Indian word or a translation of an Indian expression, the author frequently gives you its meaning in the same sentence. On page 78 he writes: "All I recollect now is: *nitschu,* friend, and *auween khackev,* who are you, and *kella,* yes, and *matty,* no." Frequently, the English translation immediately follows each Delaware Indian word or expression.

The author also uses the English translations of the colorful Delaware Indian names for the months of the year. When he first uses them, he gives you the name of the month in the same sentence. Example: "Then it was February, the Month When the First Frog Croaks." Later he does not always give you the English name of the month. What do the Delawares call some of the other months? What effect does the author achieve by occasionally using Indian words or translations of Indian expressions?

1. In Chapter 10 we learn that all Dr. Childeley knows definitely about True Son's illness is that the boy has some "unknown fever, probably the result of his long unhappy captivity." Why does the doctor bleed True Son's foot? Is the doctor's diagnosis correct? Select passages from Chapters 10 and 11 to support your answer.

How does True Son's illness affect his white father? What gives Mr. Butler great pleasure?

2. On page 112 the author writes: "There was provided for him a way of escape. He need not walk or run in it, only yield to the inward voice telling him what to do, let himself sink, permit the light of day to close over him, and the prison cell would be left empty above him." What is the way of escape? Why do you think True Son will not take this way out of white captivity?

3. Parson Elder's son is obviously referring to Little Crane when he says: "Then he started boasting about himself and abusing the whites. There were some cronies with Mr. Owens and they said the Indian told degrading stories on the white people." How does this account differ from Half Arrow's description of the visit to Uncle Wilse's shop? What do you think of Little Crane's "happy stories"? Why did the stories make the white men angry? What change in True Son can you detect as Half Arrow tells him the stories?

4. How was Little Crane killed? Who do you think killed the Indian? Can you find a passage to prove who the murderer is?

What emotion does True Son feel as he bends over the body of Little Crane? Are these emotions peculiar to a savage, or would a civilized man in like circumstances experience them?

5. Do True Son and Half Arrow go to Uncle Wilse with the idea of killing him? Why do they attack the uncle? Why does True Son prevent Half Arrow from cutting out his uncle's heart? As he is being choked by Uncle Wilse, True Son sees Half Arrow

with "the good Indian hate" on his face. What does this mean? Why does the author use the word *good* to describe Indian hate?

6. You can learn a great deal about a man's character from what he says. What do you learn about True Son from his conversation with Half Arrow in Chapter 11?

When he translates their conversation into English, the author has both boys make a few grammatical errors, speak slightly broken English, and sprinkle their sentences with Indian words. In what other way does the language they use differ from that spoken by the white men in this novel?

CHAPTERS 12 AND 13

1. Nature and freedom are the medicines that make True Son strong again. How does the freedom he enjoys differ from the freedom white men have in civilized towns? Although he has little to eat, True Son thrives in the forest. Show how he believes that all nature is his and that he is closely related to it.

2. Why do you think the author called this novel *The Light in the Forest?* Could the word *light* represent the complete enjoyment True Son finds in nature? Could it represent the freedom he feels when he is deep in the forest away from civilization? Or does the title have another meaning? Write a paragraph in which you explain the meaning of *The Light in the Forest.*

Authors frequently include quotations from other authors or poets in the front of their books. Conrad Richter has chosen four lines from William Wordsworth's poem, "Intimations of Immortality from Recollections of Early Childhood." To get a better understanding of the title of this novel, you may want to read Wordsworth's poem.

3. Why does True Son tell Half Arrow that he must be his brother? Do you think True Son will miss his little white brother even after he gets to the Indian camp? Explain your answer.

4. On page 37 Half Arrow tells his cousin that he has been too long among the white men. According to Half Arrow, how has True Son been corrupted in his thinking? What do you think of Half Arrow's reasons for stealing from white men? Why does he

decide to take only one of the trader's boats? How does he steal the boat?

5. Why do the two boys spend so much time camping at the deserted mouth of the creek? Show that both have faith in a Supreme Being.

What is the meaning of this passage?

They passed their days in a kind of primitive deliciousness. The past was buried. There was only the present and tomorrow. By day they lived as happy animals.

6. How do the boys prepare their bodies for their return to their families? Why do they immediately "bathe in the home waters" when they reach the mouth of the Muskingum? How do they behave when they are home at last? Why do they believe they must behave as they do before their people?

7. What Indians do they see as they enter the camp? What similarities can you find between the few Indians described and a group of white men who may live in a small town or in the same neighborhood? In every large group are there persons who are strong, weak, or crippled?

CHAPTERS 14 AND 15

1. Why do Thitpan and his followers talk of war? How could True Son and Half Arrow have prevented Thitpan from going to war?

2. Discuss Cuyloga's speech to True Son about white man's ways. With which of his accusations can you agree? Do you believe that the white man of Cuyloga's time had "no understanding of good and evil"? Or do you believe that the white man and the Indian had different standards of good and evil? Explain your answer.

3. How does the council of war affect True Son? Why does Thitpan choose Disbeliever as guide?

As he sees the first scalps, why does True Son lose some of his fervor for war? Why are the Indians displeased when True Son says, "I did not know we fought children"? Why, according to Thitpan, did the Indians kill the white girl? How does Thitpan plan to make True Son atone for his statement that offended the Indians?

4. What is the significance of True Son's dream? What does the dream tell you about John Butler?

5. Why doesn't True Son lure the boat to shore? How has he changed since he was taken from his Indian family only a year before?

6. Why do the Indians black half of True Son's face and chalk the remaining side? As he waits for the Indians to decide his fate, True Son feels more like an Indian than ever. Why does he decide to accept the fate of Be-Smoke and Heavy Belt?

7. Why does Cuyloga black his own face? How does he prove he is a man of principles? Why does he treat True Son so coldly after they leave the war party? Is Cuyloga cruel, or is he behaving the way he was taught? Explain your answer.

Show that even when he is telling True Son to go, Cuyloga still has great affection for his son. How must the two act toward each other if they ever meet again?

8. True Son cries out in despair, "Then who is my father?" What is your answer to his question? Write a paragraph in which you answer True Son's question. Support your answer by referring to passages in this novel.

9. If you were looking for a happy ending, you may have been disappointed. But what other logical ending could this novel have? Could it have ended in a happy-ever-after flourish? Why not? Why do you think True Son must go back to the white man?

If you have read Elliott Arnold's *White Falcon*, compare the hero of that novel with True Son. Why can White Falcon live happily with the Indians? Why does True Son fail?

Teaching *Shane*

STERLING JACKSON

Teacher of English
New Trier High School
Winnetka, Illinois

Jack Schaefer's story of a young boy who finds a life-sized hero in a stranger called Shane is a novel of quiet honesty, warmth, and power. Young people like the book immediately for two reasons: they are involved in scenes of violent action and they have empathy for the four leading characters. Although the figure of Shane assumes symbolic proportions, students will have little trouble either in identifying with him or in understanding what he represents. His manliness, integrity, and physical prowess set Shane apart from other men—even Joe Starrett—and make him universally appealing. The Starretts are likeable people too, but for full appreciation the teacher will want to call attention to the subtle play of emotions triggered by the dynamic Shane in each person who has contact with him. Bob is strangely fascinated by the assurance, the natural grace, and the aura of mystery surrounding Shane; Marian Starrett is moved by his gentlemanly qualities; and Starrett is impressed by his individuality and an integrity that is apparent in the man's face.

A series of incidents tests and reaffirms the mutual respect these four persons hold for one another. Shane prevents Joe from being swindled by the trader Ledyard, he helps Joe remove the giant tree stump, and he listens sympathetically to Joe's problems with the farm, the other homesteaders, and Fletcher. Thus a bond is formed between the two men. Bob's instant admiration for Shane is increased when Shane refuses to treat him with the condescension most adults proffer a boy. (Note how quickly Bob understands Ledyard's insincerity.) For Marian, Shane is not only a handsome, somewhat romantic stranger; he also represents contact with the civilized world which, as a frontier woman, she sometimes misses.

Throughout the summer, these characters are drawn more closely to the centripetal figure of Shane until at the end, when Shane has killed Wilson and Fletcher and left the valley, the significance of his loss is fully felt. It is a long night, which each member of the family spends with his own kind of sorrow. Bob's sadness is that of a small boy who has outgrown a dream. His mother's grief is for the loss of the only man besides her husband whom she could love. And Joe Starrett's vigil at the corral reflects the ultimate aloneness of man.

As in . . . *and now Miguel* the story is seen through the eyes of a young boy, but in *Shane* the point of view is more complex. It is a straightforward, chronological narrative, and events are described as Bob witnessed them at the time; but there is also a subtle double vision present throughout. When he tries to make Bob understand why it was necessary to fight Chris, Shane talks about a man's self-respect and asks if Bob can "see that." The narrator says,

> And still I could not. But I said I could. He was so earnest and he wanted me to so badly. It was a long, long, time before I did see it and then I was a man myself and Shane was not there for me to tell. . . .

By means of this "mirrored" time effect the reader is able to *see* the events happening as the boy experiences them and, at the same time, to *understand* their significance in the perspective of maturity.

This is a particularly effective point of view for the novel because one of the basic themes certainly is that of maturing. If Bob is too young at the time to comprehend everything that happens, he is, nevertheless, because he is perceptive and sensitive, made aware of complex emotions that without Shane's visit he would not have known until much later. The dangerous arrogance of Wilson and the brutal cowardice of Red Marlin are foils to the calm strength of Marian Starrett and the magnetic power of Shane. These important traits of character the boy comes to recognize. Shane had told him "A gun is just a tool." It's "as good—and as bad— as the man who carries it," and this is a mature concept for a boy to realize.

A second theme which students may need help in exploring is that of "choice and decision." The teacher might introduce this idea by referring to the third paragraph of the novel, where Shane, just before arriving at the Starrett's ranch, comes to a fork in the road. "He hesitated briefly, studying the choice, and moved again steadily on our side." The phrase "studying the choice" is inevitably going to suggest Frost's "The Road Not Taken," and the parallel and implications of that poem could be discussed at this time or used later as a summary. (The teacher will be reminded again of Frost on page 18 in the battle with the stump. Schaefer writes: "The man and the axe seemed to be partners in the work.") By Shane's randomly selecting one trail over another, then, his life and the lives of everyone in the valley are altered.

How many other decisions in the narrative become significant, demand a price, disturb the universe? Shane decides to stay a while to help on the farm. Fletcher decides to take over the valley with a hired gunman. Shane decides to wear his gun again. Marian Starrett, too, meets an emotional turning point; and, in addition, she must force Joe to make the "right" decision: to stay on the ranch they have built together. A chance visit from a passing stranger has set in motion a series of events which changes the course of many lives; and as a result understandings and insights are discovered. Each person must face the reality of himself.

STUDY QUESTIONS

CHAPTER 1

1. The setting is stated on the first page; this is Wyoming in 1889. The reference to "homesteaders" should suggest other

stories and novels dealing with the West. Name some of these. What were the hazards traditionally faced by homesteaders on America's frontiers?

2. Through whose eyes is the story being told? What details are noticed first? Why is the boy struck by a sudden chill? Would a small boy be so observant of the details of the stranger's clothing?

3. What, other than dress, sets this stranger apart and rouses the boy's curiosity? What is the very first reference to the man's "differentness"?

4. "Even in this easiness was a suggestion of tension. It was the easiness of a coiled spring, of a trap set." What kind of tone or mood is suggested by this description of the stranger?

5. The Starrett farm is described in careful detail. The pasture is fenced tight; the barn is solid; they were experimenting with crops. What goals and characteristics of the owners are suggested by such details?

6. What qualities of character or temperament are implied by the stranger's (a) letting the horse drink first, (b) brushing his clothes, (c) picking the petunia?

7. Explain the man's abrupt behavior when the boy's father says, "Don't be in such a hurry, stranger."

8. Why is the art of cooking well important to Mrs. Starrett?

9. Fencing in range land was a long-lived and hard-fought issue for the West. Discuss both sides of the question. What was Joe Starrett's argument?

10. By the end of Chapter 1 the line the story is going to take has been rather well defined. What is the conflict? Is there only one? How do the following incidents contribute to suspense: (a) Shane's care for his saddle roll, (b) his refusal to talk about his past.

CHAPTER 2

1. A keen ear for dialect often enables one to identify the geographic origin of a person. Thus Mrs. Starrett comments on Shane's use of "flannel cakes." What do you call them? What else have you heard them called? What other dialectal differences in names of foods can you think of? (For example, cornbread, hoecakes.)

2. Why does Bob Starrett dislike Ledyard, the trader?

3. On the day the cultivator is bought, some secret, unspoken bargain is sealed between Shane and Starrett. What is it and what is each man's "gift" to the other? (Clue: The stubborn tree stump has foreshadowed this event.)

CHAPTER 3

1. Why was Marian Starrett's "new hat" a mistake? Explain why the men were indifferent and why she could not understand that indifference.

2. During the midday meal the men's "minds were on that old stump and whatever it was that old stump had come to mean to them . . ." What does it stand for at this point? Recall what Starrett said about it when it was first mentioned in the story. If it has now assumed wider implications and has become a symbol, is it an appropriate one for this novel? Why?

3. What recognition or understanding causes Bob's mother to sew back the old ribbon on her hat?

4. When Mrs. Starrett brings the fresh biscuits, her husband lets out a deep sigh. The author says, "There was just something in him too big to be held tight in comfort." What emotions are indirectly expressed in this line?

5. How does Joe react to his wife's suggestion that they use horses to uproot the stump? Why?

6. What do the men do when the stump has been conquered? Why? Where have you seen a similar gesture?

7. When Starrett and Shane compliment Marian on her second pie, Shane says, "Yes. That's the best bit of stump I ever tasted." Explain what he means. How does this remark clear the air and restore harmony to the group?

CHAPTERS 4-6

1. The growth of affection between each of the Starretts and Shane is shown gradually. At the beginning of Chapter 4 Bob's thoughts as he wakens help explain this affection, and their strategems to get Shane to stay emphasize it again. Has there been sufficient motivation for this reaction? In other words, are their mutual feelings realistically prepared for? Consider each one—

Bob, Mr. Starrett, his wife—and decide what each finds in Shane to admire and respect. In what ways do you agree with them?

2. When Starrett asks Shane to help him with the farm, he adds, "Are you running away from anything?" Shane answers, "No . . . Not in the way you mean." What different ways of "running away" might be meant here? What kinds of things do men run away from? Which of these could be appropriate to the story?

3. Why do you think Marian Starrett begins to show reluctance to Shane's staying at the ranch?

4. After he decides to stay, why does Shane take a new seat at the table?

5. Why do you think Shane does not wear his gun? Are there any clues to the answer in the scene where he teaches Bob to draw?

6. Why should Shane rather than one of the homesteaders become Fletcher's prey?

7. How does taking the hay tongs into town affect the flow of action?

8. What is Shane's feeling toward Chris? Why does he refuse to fight Fletcher's cowhand?

CHAPTER 7

1. Schaefer describes Fletcher's foreman, Morgan, as "a broad slab of a man with flattened face and head small in proportion to great sloping shoulders. . . ." Is this a caricature of a villain? What specific traits are suggested by the author's choice of words?

2. Fletcher's men resort to name-calling to bait the homesteaders. What insult is implied by (a) ordering soda pop at Grafton's, (b) pretending they smell pigs in the valley? Why is this means of "fighting" a particularly childish one? What examples of name-calling have you experienced or heard?

3. The account of Shane's fight with Chris is told by Ed Howells, a secondhand narrator. Why is this necessary? What is the significance of the way Shane fought, slapping rather than punching? What evidence is there that Shane punished Chris reluctantly?

4. Why is Marian concerned about the effects of the fight on Shane?

CHAPTER 8

1. Does Shane change after the fight? In what ways? What does his preoccupation with the farm and the soil suggest about his attitude and thoughts? Shane is no farmer, but the farm must represent something that he would like to know or possess. What?

2. At the close of Chapter 8 Marian asks Shane's help in keeping the farm. Why does she do this? Why is it difficult for her to ask him for help? What does the action reveal about her as a person?

CHAPTER 9

1. Despite the familiarity of the fight scene at Grafton's, there is still excitement in watching Shane hold his own against five men. How does the author describe Shane's movements?

2. How are we made aware in this chapter of the closeness which has grown up among Shane, Joe, Marian, and Bob?

3. Sometimes more than brute, physical force is needed to win a battle. How is this demonstrated in the Shane-Morgan conflict?

4. Shane's defeat of Fletcher's men is obviously a turning point or climactic scene in the action. What are some of the choices open to the novelist at this point. In what directions might the narrative turn?

CHAPTER 10

1. Surprisingly, both Mr. Weir and Mr. Grafton want to assume the responsibility for the damages to the saloon. Why does Joe Starrett insist on paying?

2. Marian registers several emotions following the fight. Try to define them, citing evidence from her reactions and comments.

3. At the end of Chapter 10, when Joe comforts his wife, he says, "Do you think I don't know, Marian?" What is he referring to? Although unstated, what has been resolved by Marian's last words?

CHAPTER 11

1. The answer you gave to question 4 under Chapter 9 can now be checked. Did you suspect that the final showdown would be between Shane and a skilled, deadly gunman? What clues led you to such anticipation?

2. What actually caused Ernie Wright's death—short temper, pride, foolhardiness, courage? Shipstead says, "Wilson badgered Ernie into getting himself in a spot where he had to go for his gun." How did Wilson do this? Of the following words which ones can most appropriately be substituted for *badgered* in the context of the sentence: bait, provoke, vex, arouse, incite, harass, lure, entice?

3. The decision of whether to stay or to leave before Wilson challenges the Starretts is finally made by Marian: "But I just know that we're bound up in something bigger than any one of us, and that running away is the one thing that would be worse than whatever might happen to us. There wouldn't be anything real ahead for us, any of us, maybe even for Bob, all the rest of our lives." Notice the vagueness of what's being expressed. What do you think she means by the pronouns *something, whatever, anything*?

CHAPTER 12

1. Note the contrast between the pleasant weather and serenity of the farm and the brewing hate and violence represented by those outside the farm. Examine the openings of Chapters 9 and 12. Where else have you seen this contrast?

CHAPTER 13

1. Describe the change which occurs when Shane makes his decision to ride into town in place of Joe Starrett. What dominating quality impresses Bob most?

2. Why does Marian not interfere when Shane hits Joe on the head? "She was watching Shane, her throat curving in a lovely proud line, her eyes wide with a sweet shining in them." How do you interpret her look? For whom is the "warmth"?

CHAPTER 14

1. When does Bob first realize that Shane is leaving for good?

2. In this chapter the author provides some clues to the symbol which Shane becomes. "He was the symbol of all the dim, formless imaginings of danger and terror in the untested realm of human potentialities beyond my understanding." Can you explain in your own words what the speaker is saying?

3. Bob continues to follow Shane into town because "the call was too strong." What urgencies and emotions composed this "call"?

4. What is unusual about Grafton's on this particular evening, and how does this difference make the scene more effective?

5. The scene, it is written, "was stilled in a hush more impressive than any noise could be." In what situations can silence be more impressive or dramatic than noise?

CHAPTER 15

1. How does each person—Joe, Marian, and Bob—react to Shane's leaving? Who feels the loss most keenly?

2. What is the meaning of the scene in which Marian asks her husband to pull down the corner post of the corral?

CHAPTER 16

1. In what ways is Shane's presence felt by the Starretts? Why doesn't Bob join the kids who spin wild tales about Shane?

2. Do you like the ending of the story? Would you have preferred Shane to stay on with the Starretts? What problems would such an ending pose?

GENERAL QUESTIONS FOR DISCUSSION, WRITING, OR TESTING

1. Through whose eyes do we experience the story? How old is Bob when he tells the story? Why, if the story is being told by an adult in retrospect, does the narrator respond with the naïveté

of a boy to certain incidents, looks, and conversations in the story? What are the advantages of this storytelling method?

2. Not all the characters in the story are fully developed. They are useful for background realism but they remain "flat" characters. A famous novelist and critic has clarified the distinction between "flat" and "round" characters by saying that "round" characters are "capable of surprising in a convincing way." Distinguish between flat and round characters among the following, and be prepared to defend your classification: Will Atkey, Marian Starrett, Fletcher, Chris, Bob Starrett.

3. For everyone names carry emotional overtones, and an author chooses his characters' names with care. As a rather obvious example, why is Stark an appropriate first name for Wilson? (Consider meaning, brevity, and sound.) Joe and Bob are extremely common names, but Shane is not. What might have been the author's purpose here? Why are we not told Shane's last name?

4. In 1953 *Shane* was made into a movie by Paramount, starring Van Heflin as Joe, Jean Arthur as Marian, Alan Ladd as Shane, and Brandon de Wilde as Bob. Among today's actors on film or television, whom would you choose to play these roles? Why? Assume that you are to direct *Shane* as a film; choose a favorite scene and describe in detail the set, the lighting, the costumes, and the action you would demand.

5. "A man is what he is, Bob," says Shane, "and there's no breaking the mold. I tried that and I've lost." Do you agree with this statement? What is meant by "breaking the mold"? How has Shane tried to? In what way has he lost?

6. Why did Shane become a legend in the valley? Could this have happened if he had stayed in the community? Why? Can you find examples of such legend-making in real life?

7. What rules for living well does Shane leave with Bob? Which do you think is the most important? Which would probably have the greatest influence on Bob's life?

Teaching *The Red Pony*

VIRGINIA OLSEN BUSH

The Red Pony is not a novel in the same way as the other books in the novel sequence. Most of the novels familiar to students are characterized by a causally connected story line running from the beginning of the book to the end. In *The Red Pony*, however, there is no significant causal connection among the four sections. "The Gift," "The Great Mountains," "The Promise," and "The Leader of the People" are four separate stories and may be read as such; but Steinbeck has also structured them as a unit, through patterned repetition, interrelationship of characters, and thematic rhythm. As the result, the four sections of the book, when considered as a whole, take on added shades of meaning.

At the heart of the novel, as Arnold L. Goldsmith has pointed out, is the thematic rhythm of the life-death cycle, "an organic theory of life ending in death which in turn produces new life."[1] This theme can be seen in the life and death of the red pony, the buzzards eating on the corpse, and Jody killing the buzzard; in the dying life in old Gitano and Easter; in the birth of the new colt only with the slaying of the mare; and in the contrast of age and youth in grandfather and grandson, the old "leader of the people" and the new. These and other elements of the book, such as the cycle of the seasons, fall into a rhythmic pattern in which life and death are continually juxtaposed, with one evolving naturally out of the other.

Such a juxtaposition is fundamental to Steinbeck's use of the water-tub and the black cypress tree: the water-tub is a place of "cool green grass" and "singing water," a place of life, while the cypress tree is a "fascinating" yet "repulsive" place associated with pig slaughter. "The water-tub and the black cypress were opposites and enemies,"[2] but both represent facts of existence that must be accepted. Jody himself, the "little boy" who is growing, is representative of life continually coming into contact with death and dying things. Each experience forming one of the stories of this book is an encounter of "opposites and enemies."

It is the contrast of these two opposites, of life and death, that gives the book its poignancy. Jody feels this contrast in the antipathy between the water-tub and the black cypress. His consciousness of coexistent life and death, inextricably mixed, is the cause of his lashing out at the buzzard at the end of "The Gift," of the "nameless sorrow" at the end of "The Great Mountains," of the aching, horror-struck, stupefied stare in "The Promise," and finally of the compassionate pity shown in the offer of the lemonade at the end of "The Leader of the People."

Details of the stories emphasize the poignant sadness of life in death and death in life. The horse that dies in the first section of the book is not an old beast for which Jody had conceived an affection, but a fine, spirited young pony at just the age when it could be broken to riding. This pattern of the death of vigorous life is repeated in the third section, "The Promise": the mare Nellie was young and useful; she could have borne other colts. The other two sections of the book, "The Great Mountains" and "The Leader of the People," present the complementary pattern of lingering life. Both Gitano and Grandfather have finished their useful life, they are old and dying, but they are still alive. The hint of vivid life remains in Gitano's eyes and in the rapier, as it does in Grandfather's "merry eyes," in his chuckling over the mouse hunt, and in his memories of and belief in westering. Details such as these help to convey to the reader how sad it is, both for the lusty young to die and for the useless old to live.

Steinbeck's use of nature reinforces the tension he has set up between coexisting life and death. In "The Gift," the same rain that is fatal to the pony causes the moss that had been all summer "as gray as lizards" to turn a brilliant yellow-green and makes "little new grass" appear. Later, Jody walks to the barn in a "cold sunny morning" through the "young grass" and the "new green crop of volunteer," only to enter the barn and find his pony very much worse. In "The Great Mountains," the paragraph telling how Jody kills the bird concentrates also on describing the bustling, restless life found in the sagebrush. Jody himself shivers at the contrast between the "jolly" Gabilans and the forbidding Great Ones. In "The Promise," the day is just dawning as the mare is killed and the colt is born.

The second major element unifying the book is the patterned repetition of plot. The four stories are patterned to bring out similarities and differences. As we have already noted, each section of the book tells a story of Jody's encounter with death and dying things. During the course of the novel, however, about three years elapse and Jody grows from a boy of ten to one of twelve or thirteen, so that each succeeding encounter portrays his increasing maturity. This is the basic pattern of the book. Each story presents near the beginning a picture of the "little boy Jody." These initial pictures of Jody's behavior do show some slight increase in maturity, in that by the time of "The Leader of the People" he does at least recognize that the mouse hunt is only play, while there is no such recognition that the march of the army is only make-believe in "The Promise."

Then, in the course of each story something happens—Jody is given a pony, an old man comes to die, a mare becomes pregnant, Grandfather comes for a visit—and in each case events lead Jody to an encounter with death. If the novel may be seen as an encounter of "opposites and enemies," then we may regard Jody's reactions as steps in his learning to accept and love his enemy; for Jody progresses from blindly lashing out, to "nameless sorrow," to a horrified stare, to compassionate pity. By the end of "The Leader of the People" Jody is still a "little boy," but he has learned a great deal, and this is evident in the sort of response of which he is capable.

The stories are patterned in other ways as well. The first and third deal with the death of the young; the second and fourth with the lingering life and approaching death of the old. In the former stories, the victims are horses; in the latter, they are men. The first and third are violent; the second and fourth quiet. These and other patterns which tie the first story with the third and the second with the fourth give a rhythm to the book as a whole and, by the variations which they introduce, avoid the monotony which four stories on the same theme might have produced.

The third major element of the book is characterization. The four principal characters—Jody, his father, his mother, and Billy Buck—appear in each section of the book, and each is well drawn. Carl Tiflin emerges as a "stern disciplinarian," a man who "has good sense sometimes," but nevertheless is too strict and stern to develop and express the emotions of love and pity. He does not know how to be kind, and he is frequently cruel. He can communicate with neither his wife nor his son. In "The Leader of the People," when he uses "a tone of apology Jody himself might have used," we find that Carl Tiflin is often less mature than his son. Billy Buck on the other hand has the understanding that Jody's father so often lacks. Billy is not a hero, he is not a "leader of the people," but he is an honorable representative of ordinary human kind. Billy Buck and Carl Tiflin are in many respects opposites, and each is defined to a certain extent against the other.

Jody's relationship with the two men helps to define his own character. Jody's emotions are not atrophied as are his father's, and his sensitivities are perhaps more refined and his capabilities greater than Billy Buck's. When Billy says furiously to Mr. Tiflin, after Jody has killed the buzzard, "Jesus Christ! man, can't you see how he'd feel about it?", we understand that Jody has just experienced something completely foreign to his father, and this tells us a great deal about Jody's response. In the same way, Billy Buck provides a standard against which we can measure Jody's action in "The Leader of the People," when we find that even Billy is clearly bored by Grandfather's story, while Jody is the only one to "arise to heroism" and ask his grandfather to tell about Indians.

Because *The Red Pony* lacks the strong central plot that is usual with novels, the other structural devices—such as theme, story patterns, and characterization—assume greater importance, and the ways in which they function become more apparent. The teacher may wish to emphasize characterization since this is especially well done and may perhaps be easier for students to understand. But much of the art of *The Red Pony* lies in the rhythms of theme and plot, and the novel provides an excellent opportunity for showing students how these devices work.

STUDY QUESTIONS

"THE GIFT"

1. What do you learn about Billy Buck from the opening description of him? What words used to describe him seem especially effective? The description concentrates on Billy's physical appearance. Can you tell anything about his character from this description? What would you name as his main character traits?

2. The first pages of "The Gift" also introduce the other main characters in the story. Does the author give us our first impression of Jody through description, action, or conversation? What do we learn of him through each of the methods of character development used? Why do you think Steinbeck chose to introduce Jody in this way?

3. How does the author introduce Jody's mother? How does this method differ from the one he used with Jody? Is our initial impression of Mrs. Tiflin more, or less, vivid than our impression of Jody? What in the author's method accounts for this difference? Why do you think he develops his characters as he does?

4. What do we learn of Jody's father in these first pages? How does Steinbeck develop his character? How is his development of Mr. Tiflin's character different from that of Jody's? Why?

5. What does the conversation at the breakfast table reveal about the characters involved? Does the conversation support the descriptions that the author has already given us of the characters? How?

6. Steinbeck sometimes uses certain words as clues to a character's personality. In this manner he frequently applies the words "shy" to Jody and "stern" to Carl Tiflin. How may "shy" be con-

sidered a clue to Jody's personality? How may "stern" be considered a clue to Carl Tiflin's? How effective do you think this method
is in each case? Does conversation or action reinforce the impression Steinbeck is trying to create?

7. What method does Steinbeck use to provide the reader with
a description of the setting? From whose point of view do we see
the setting? Does this method give you a mental picture of the
ranch? What kind of atmosphere does the following passage
create?

> He felt an uncertainty in the air, a feeling of change and of loss
> and of the gain of new and unfamiliar things. Over the hillside
> two big black buzzards sailed low to the ground and their shadows
> slipped smoothly and quickly ahead of them. Some animal had
> died in the vicinity. Jody knew it. It might be a cow or it might be
> the remains of a rabbit. The buzzards overlooked nothing. Jody
> hated them as all decent things hate them, but they could not be
> hurt because they made away with carrion (p. 90).

What seems to be the importance of this passage? The mood created here is carried into the next paragraph, in the uneasiness
Jody feels when he smashes the muskmelon. "It was a bad thing
to do, he knew perfectly well" (p. 91). Why does he smash the
muskmelon? How does the atmosphere reflect Jody's attitudes and
feelings? Is this same sort of atmosphere present elsewhere in this
section of the book? Where?

8. On page 92, as Jody thinks of the consequences of his pointing his empty rifle in the direction of the house, we are told that
"Nearly all of his father's presents were given with reservations
which hampered their value somewhat. It was good discipline."
Does this passage add anything to our impressions of Jody's father?
Does it tell us anything more about Jody? What? How is this description of Jody's father consistent with the way he treats Jody
when the men return from Salinas? Does this treatment continue
the following morning?

9. Is the gift of the red pony given with "reservations" on the
father's part? Why do you think so? What does Jody's father intend to develop in his son by his "good discipline"? Does he succeed? What in the story suggests that he does? Do you consider

Mr. Tiflin's approach valuable? What does the story suggest is its principal disadvantage? How is this related to Mr. Tiflin's leaving the barn "embarrassed"? Does the story indicate that the advantages outweigh the disadvantages?

10. How does Jody feel about the gift? How do the boys from Jody's school feel about him? Explain the following passage: "Out of a thousand centuries they drew the ancient admiration of the footman for the horseman. They knew instinctively that a man on a horse is spiritually as well as physically bigger than a man on foot." How does this make Jody feel?

11. Why do you think Jody liked to torture himself with "delicious little self-induced pains" on his journey from the house to the barn each morning?

12. On page 99 Steinbeck tells us a good deal about Billy Buck's knowledge of horses and his skill in handling them. What is the context of these remarks? What does this passage reveal about the relationship between Billy and Jody? How does it do this? Does this relationship change at all after the incident in which the pony is left in the rain (pp. 105-108)? How does Billy Buck feel about the incident?

13. The following passage is found on page 113:

> On the way to the barn, Jody noticed how the young grass was up and how the stubble was melting day by day into the new green crop of volunteer. It was a cold sunny morning.

How does this scene compare with the one that Jody finds when he enters the barn? What contrast is presented by the two scenes? What meaning is contained in this contrast? Why do you think Steinbeck presented the two scenes in this way? Do you think that the contrast is effective? Why?

14. On page 108 we are told that "Carl Tiflin hated weakness . . ." and yet later (p. 116), when the pony has become much worse, he wants to take Jody away from the barn, presumably to spare him the pain of watching the pony die. How is this incident like the earlier one when Mr. Tiflin is telling stories? Is his action in trying to spare Jody consistent with the way he usually acts? Why do you think so? Why does this action on the father's

part make Billy Buck angry? How do you explain his angry remark to Jody's father? Why does Jody's father feel hurt by Billy's
remark?

15. Why does the place seem "familiar, but curiously changed"
(p. 118) to Jody? Why has it become merely "a frame for things
that were happening"? Why does Steinbeck again call attention
to growing things: "little arms of new weeds spreading out over
the ground"?

16. The final scene is a vivid one and very important to our
understanding of both Jody and his father. What does this scene
reveal about Mr. Tiflin? Why does Billy Buck again become angry
with him? What does this scene reveal about Jody? Why does he
kill the buzzard? How do you account for the difference between
Jody's and Mr. Tiflin's responses to this incident? Is it merely
because the pony belonged to Jody, or is the cause perhaps related
to a difference in the characters?

17. On page 112 we are told about something Jody sees one
evening after Gabilan has become sick:

> The sky above the hills was still light. He saw a hawk flying so high
> that it caught the sun on its breast and shone like a spark. Two
> blackbirds were driving him down the sky, glittering as they at-
> tacked their enemy. In the west, the clouds were moving in to rain
> again.

In what ways can this passage be considered symbolic? Upon
what details does its effectiveness depend?

18. Reread the passage quoted in question 7. Does the passage
now seem more important to you? Can you now explain the expressions "uncertainty in the air," "a feeling of change and of loss
and of the gain of new and unfamiliar things"? Does the description of the buzzards and Jody's thoughts about them now mean
more to you? What?

19. The weather and aspects of nature are important to the
effective development of this chapter. Question 13 asked you to
notice and analyze the contrast between the description of things
that Jody notices on the way to the barn ("the young grass" and
the "sunny morning") and what Jody finds in the barn itself. In
question 15 you were again asked to analyze the importance of

Jody's noticing the "little arms of new weeds spreading out over the ground." Look back through this chapter carefully and find other examples of this use of weather and things of nature to present a contrast or set the atmosphere for something that happens.

In a short, well-organized theme, discuss Steinbeck's use of weather and nature to make his telling of the story more effective. In the theme, you might want to express your own opinion on the effectiveness of such a method. If you do this, however, be certain that your argument is well supported by actual examples from the book itself.

"THE GREAT MOUNTAINS"

1. At the beginning of this section, Jody is throwing rocks, setting traps, and killing birds: what explanation can you give for this behavior? How is it related to the action in the rest of this story?

2. How does Jody feel about "the great mountains"? Why? How are these mountains different from the Gabilans? What words does the author use to make the reader feel this difference between the mountains? Why does Jody shiver at the contrast?

3. How does Jody's father try to make old Gitano feel unwanted? Why does he do this? On page 131, after Mr. Tiflin makes his "joke" about "if ham and eggs grew on a side-hill," Steinbeck tells us that "Jody knew how his father was probing for a place to hurt in Gitano. He had been probed often. His father knew every place in the boy where a word would fester." What makes Mr. Tiflin "probe" both Jody and Gitano? Does Jody resent his father's treatment? Why?

4. What is the significance of Gitano's riding off toward the "great mountains" on Easter? Why do you think Steinbeck has named the old horse "Easter"? Is the name perhaps symbolic? Of what?

5. After Jody has visited Gitano and seen his rapier (p. 135), we are told that

As he went back toward the house, Jody knew one thing more sharply than he had ever known anything. He must never tell anyone about the rapier. It would be a dreadful thing to tell anyone about it, for it would destroy some fragile structure of truth. It was a truth that might be shattered by division.

Explain why Steinbeck uses the following words and phrases in this passage: "sharply," "dreadful," "fragile structure of truth," "shattered by division." This is a key paragraph for understanding the rest of what happens in this story. How does it help us understand what actually has happened when Gitano leaves? How does it help us understand Jody's reaction to this incident?

6. What is the significance of the final passage in this section?

And he thought of the great mountains. A longing caressed him, and it was so sharp that he wanted to cry to get it out of his breast. He lay down in the green grass near the round tub at the brush line. He covered his eyes with his crossed arms and lay there a long time, and he was full of a nameless sorrow.

What is the "nameless sorrow"? What causes it? Why is it nameless? How is it related to the "fragile structure of truth"? How is Jody's response to this incident similar to his response to Gabilan's death? How are the two different?

"THE PROMISE"

1. While he is questioning Billy Buck about the colt, Jody asks miserably, "Billy, you won't let anything happen to the colt, will you?" What effect does this question have on Billy? What does this incident reveal about the relationship between Jody and Billy? Has it changed at all since "The Gift"? How important does this relationship seem to Billy? How would you describe the relationship? Compare it to that between Jody and his father. How do you account for the difference between the two?

2. Explain this statement on page 151: "The water-tub and the black cypress were opposites and enemies." How does the author use this contrast in the paragraph that follows? How does he use it elsewhere in the novel?

3. Why is Jody "tight with pride" after his father tells him that he has done a good job taking care of Nellie?

4. Give several reasons for Jody's restlessness when the colt is not born on the predicted date. Why does Billy "growl" at Jody

when Jody asks, "You won't let anything happen, Billy, you're sure you won't?" How does Jody react to this incident (p. 157)? Why?

5. Jody learns (p. 144) that he must wait nearly a year until the colt is born, and later (p. 149) he cries out in despair, "I'll be grown up," when Billy tells him that it will be another two years after that before he will be able to ride. Is this another of Mr. Tiflin's gifts "with reservations"? He tells Jody that "Billy says the best way for you to be a good hand with horses is to raise a colt" (p. 142); Jess Taylor says that it's a "good thing" and "Carl has good sense sometimes" (p. 146). Why is it a good plan? What does this add to our impression of Mr. Tiflin? Why is waiting important?

"THE LEADER OF THE PEOPLE"

1. On page 164 Jody speaks of "those damn mice" and then looks "to see whether Billy had noticed the mature profanity"; but "Billy worked on without comment." Why does Jody use the "mature profanity"? Is this a true sign of being grown up? Why do you think so? Why doesn't Billy say anything? What in this section does Jody do that indicates more truly how much he has grown up since the beginning of the book?

2. At the start of this section of the book, Jody's parents call him "Big-Britches." Has he been called this before? Why is he given the name? How is it related to his new use of "mature profanity"? Why does the name embarrass him?

3. Why isn't Jody's father very happy that the grandfather is coming for a visit? How is his attitude toward the grandfather like that he showed toward Gitano? Is Mr. Tiflin justified in feeling as he does about the grandfather? Why do you think so?

4. When Jody's mother challenges his father's attitude toward Grandfather, Steinbeck emphasizes that "in his explanation there was a tone of apology Jody himself might have used." Why does the author draw our attention to this similarity? In what ways are Jody and his father alike? In what ways are they different.

5. As Jody goes to meet his grandfather, why does he drop his "unseemly running" and approach "at a dignified walk"?

6. What does the description of the grandfather on page 169 reveal about him?

About the whole face and figure there was a granite dignity, so that every motion seemed an impossible thing. Once at rest, it seemed the old man would be stone, would never move again. His steps were slow and certain. Once made, no step could ever be retraced; once headed in a direction, the path would never bend nor the pace increase nor slow.

Notice that Steinbeck not only describes his features and physical movements but comments on what he describes. Why do you think Steinbeck does this? Does this give the reader a fuller picture of the grandfather? How? What does the term "granite dignity" mean? Is its connotation good, bad, or ambivalent? Why do you think so?

7. What does the grandfather mean when he tells Jody that hunting mice is like "when the troops were hunting Indians and shooting children and burning teepees. . ."?

8. How does Steinbeck make the reader, although he has not heard the grandfather's story as often as the Tiflins have, feel that it is boring and has been told many times before? Why does Grandfather tell his stories? On page 180 he admits: "I tell those old stories, but they're not what I want to tell. I only know how I want people to feel when I tell them." How does he want people to feel? Why don't they feel this way when he speaks, instead of becoming bored? Why does he keep repeating that "it was a job for men but only little boys like to hear about it"? Why does it happen that only little boys like to hear about it? Why is it that even Billy Buck is clearly bored while the story is being told?

9. What is "westering"? Is actually traveling west the only significant action for a leader of the people? Why?

10. Why won't the grandfather come with Jody to hunt the mice? Why is Jody then no longer interested in killing them?

11. Why does Jody feel "very sad" after talking to Grandfather (p. 181)? Why does he ask him if he would like a lemonade? At first Grandfather is about to refuse, but he changes his mind when he sees Jody's face. Why?

12. Earlier, Billy Buck had offered to show Grandfather an old powder horn and pistol, saying "Did I ever show them to you?" (p. 174), in just the same way that Grandfather would try to in-

troduce a story by saying "Did I ever tell you that one?"; but Grandfather had told Billy, "Yes, I think you did, Billy." Why did Grandfather refuse Billy's offer? In what ways is the grandfather's behavior like Carl Tiflin's? In what ways is it different?

13. Compare the incident between Grandfather and Billy Buck and the later one between Grandfather and Jody about the lemonade. In what ways are the feelings of the persons involved similar? In what ways are they different? How are their actions similar? How are they different? What do these comparisons tell us about the grandfather? What do they reveal about Jody?

14. Who is the real "leader of the people" in this section? Why?

GENERAL QUESTIONS

1. Compare Jody as he is presented at the start of each section. In all four sections Steinbeck brings Jody into the story, calling him a "little boy." In what ways is Jody's behavior at the beginning of each section that of a little boy? Does this initial behavior continue throughout the story to the end in each section? How does it change? Approximately how many years does the whole of *The Red Pony* cover? Does the "little boy" behavior that Jody displays at the beginning of each section become progressively more mature as Jody grows older, or does each section present merely a different manifestation of basically the same sort of immature behavior? Defend your answer.

2. Explain the passage at the end of "The Promise":

> Then Jody turned and trotted out of the barn into the dawn. He ached from his throat to his stomach. His legs were stiff and heavy. He tried to be glad because of the colt, but the bloody face, and the haunted, tired eyes of Billy Buck hung in the air ahead of him.

Compare Jody's reaction to the death of the mare with his reaction to the death of Gabilan; with his reaction at the end of "The Great Mountains." When you have finished the whole of *The Red Pony*, compare these three responses with Jody's response to the central incident in "The Leader of the People." How are the incidents involved in all four sections similar? How are Jody's responses all similar? Do the responses become progressively more mature as Jody grows older? How? Question 1 on "The Great Mountains" asked you to make this same sort of comparison for Jody's behavior at the beginning of each section: now compare these two progressions, that of initial behavior and that of final response. In which progression is the increase in maturity more marked? What is the significance of this finding?

3. A number of repetitions and contrasts link the sections of The Red Pony. Examine as many of these links as you can find and discuss the three which you consider most important. What elements tend to split the stories apart and break down the recognizable relationships that exist between them? How effective is Steinbeck's organizational structure in this book?

4. The red pony Gabilan figures in only the first section, "The Gift." Why did Steinbeck entitle the book as a whole *The Red Pony?* Explain the significance of the titles of the four sections with respect to the structure of the book as a whole.

NOTES

1. Arnold L. Goldsmith, "Thematic Rhythm in *The Red Pony*," *College English*, XXVI (1965), p. 392.

2. John Steinbeck, *The Pearl and The Red Pony* (New York: Viking, 1965), p. 151. All page references are to this edition.

Teaching
The Adventures of Tom Sawyer

VIRGINIA OLSEN BUSH

Mark Twain was a humorist and satirist—a writer concerned with pointing out the weaknesses and faults which society could improve. Although his purpose in *The Adventures of Tom Sawyer* was avowedly to entertain boys and girls and to "pleasantly remind adults of what they once were themselves,"[1] the book also contains a large share of criticism and opinions about people. The wonderful thing about Mark Twain is that he is so easily able to persuade us to accept his views and insights. Any reader, upon opening the book, will look through Twain's eyes at Aunt Polly and her spectacles and will agree with him in a gentle chuckle, scarcely aware that he has been using Twain's eyes at all. By the end of the novel we have accepted, even if only temporarily, a whole multitude of Twain's opinions, from the most general—such as the goodness of childhood—to the most specific—such as the schoolmaster's vanity. Because the author's personality and beliefs are so deeply a part of this book, one method of teaching it might be to explore the ideas which it contains and to discover why they are so persuasive.

The goodness of childhood is certainly one of the major themes of the book. The world of the novel is for the most part a child's world, in which actual evil is lacking. Evil appears only when the adult world intrudes, as it does when Tom and Huck become involved with Injun Joe. The boys are not angels, of course; rather, they are typical of the nineteenth-century "bad boy," a cleverly mischievous sort whose behavior was more or less expected by society and thus, in a sense, sanctioned by it. Tom's pranks are considered as evidence more of high spirits than of an evil nature. Even more culpable behavior, like Tom's thoughtlessness, is excused by the fact that he is a child. We often see that behavior which is innocent enough in the children is repeated "with grotesque reality"[2] by the adults. When Tom and Huck swear not to accuse Injun Joe of the murder, we can excuse them, for they are only children and we understand the fear that motivates them; but we do not so easily excuse the cowardice and moral laxity of the grown citizens of the town in failing to prosecute Injun Joe for grave-robbing. Similarly, when Tom and Huck go digging for buried treasure, we think nothing of it, for it is only play; but later, when troops of grown men rush to dig at every haunted house in the area, the reality of their intentions produces a grotesque effect. In the end, of course, the "good" boys triumph over the evil adults, and the nostalgic picture of childhood is held intact.

Twain's attitude toward society as a whole can be deduced in part from an analysis of Tom's character. Twain appears to have been extremely sympathetic to his hero, in spite of the fun he sometimes pokes at his histrionic tendencies and his taste for the melodramatically romantic. Tom is an ideal of what everyone should be. He is the "rightly constructed boy." He is high-spirited, happy, and remarkably in harmony with the world around him. One critic, James M. Cox, remarks on Tom's latent respectability:

> The discovery of the treasure, significantly hidden under Injun Joe's cross, enables Tom to enter heroically the ranks of the respectable. Of course, he has been slyly respectable all along. Even when he breaks the law he does so with the intimate knowledge that he is expected to break it. His acute dramatic sense enables him to see the part he is to play, and he is constantly aware of his participation in sacred social rites. This awareness results in a kind of compulsive badness in his nature; he achieves the Frommian ideal of wanting to do what society expects him to do.[3]

His willingness to conform is evidenced not only in his cheerful acceptance of the role of "bad boy," but also in numerous snatches of conversation which indicate his conception of life and society, of how things actually are. In Chapter 13, for example, while he is explaining to Huck the life of a hermit, he says dogmatically:

> ". . . And a hermit's got to sleep on the hardest place he can find, and put sackcloth and ashes on his head, and stand out in the rain, and—"
>
> "What does he put sackcloth and ashes on his head for?" inquired Huck.
>
> "*I* dono. But they've *got* to do it. Hermits always do. You'd have to do that if you was a hermit."
>
> "Dern'd if I would," said Huck (p. 70).

Similar discussions are held over almost everything else the boys think of doing. Both Tom and Huck accept, without knowledge and on faith, that the way things are always done is the way they *must* be done; but Tom goes one step further than Huck in conforming by believing that this way of doing things is good and accepting it as his own: Huck merely says laconically, "Dern'd if I would." Surely, Twain is poking some fun at dogmatic belief here, and we sense that if it were an adult talking as Tom talks, he would be vigorously attacked, whereas such statements coming from Tom are only amusing since he is not expected to know any better. But it is nevertheless significant that Tom's basic attitude is one of conformity to society, one of wanting to belong.

Society is something of a given quantity for Twain, at least in this book: one must work with it and do the best he can. A man who is going to work with satire must believe that those persons satirized are capable of improving themselves, for there is a strong didactic element in the use of humor to point out weaknesses and follies in such a way that people will accept the criticism. Twain must believe that society is capable of correcting its faults, and so he elects to work within the structure of the community; his criticisms in *Tom Sawyer* are not so devastating as to require its destruction.

The faults which Twain points out are numerous and diverse.

They range from absurd behavior as a group to the private follies of individuals. He notes the eagerness of the townspeople to come and stare at the murder site or at Widow Douglas's stile; the enjoyment they derive from Injun Joe's funeral; the uncritical appreciation of the minister's poetry reading or the young ladies' compositions on "Examination Day"; the sudden, factually unwarranted change in their opinion of Tom and the other boys when they are believed drowned or of Tom and Huck when they become heroes; the oversentimentality which motivates the people to circulate a petition for Injun Joe's pardon. Mindlessness, where use of the mind is required and is pretended, is always a target for Twain's wit.

Similarly, the petty follies of individual men, faults which are widespread throughout humanity, come under attack. Twain has us notice Aunt Polly's vanity and the harshness which she assumes toward Tom because she feels it is her "duty"; Judge Thatcher's "showing off" and his fine, empty words; the change in the Sunday-school superintendent's way of speaking from Sunday to weekday. When the fault occurs in an otherwise kind and well-intentioned person, Twain uses a combination of humor and satire to bring it out. An occasional minor character, such as Mary, is good enough to escape satirization and is not pictured with even the small follies to make her amusing (although she is a pleasant character and is treated by Twain with good humor). At the other extreme, the few really vicious persons in the book are treated with a total lack of humor, for there is no hope that they can change: both Injun Joe and Sid (who meanly tells everyone the Welshman's big secret) are such persons, and Twain attacks them directly, without satire.

Humor, however, is Twain's most powerful weapon. He creates his satire through a skillful manipulation of words which leads us to agree with him. The paragraph telling how Tom falls in love parodies second-rate romantic fiction by applying its extravagant and precious language to a small boy's passion: "As he was passing by the house where Jeff Thatcher lived, he saw a new girl in the garden—a lovely little blue-eyed creature with yellow hair plaited into two long tails, white summer frock and embroidered panta-

lettes. The fresh-crowned hero fell without firing a shot . . ."
(p. 14). The language is all the more successful because this is
undoubtedly the way the dramatically romantic Tom Sawyer saw
himself.

Twain commonly produces in us a sense of the ridiculous by
combining elegant and inelegant language, the diction of formal
prose and colloquialisms. At the end of Chapter 1, Twain tells us
that Tom

> . . . got home pretty late, that night, and when he climbed cau-
> tiously in at the window, he uncovered an ambuscade in the per-
> son of his aunt; and when she saw the state his clothes were in her
> resolution to turn his Saturday holiday into captivity at hard labor
> became adamantine in its firmness (p. 7).

The inappropriateness of words and phrases like "ambuscade,"
"captivity at hard labor," and "adamantine" in this otherwise
simple paragraph causes them to stand out. We sense that this is
the way Aunt Polly views her own activity, though she may not
think of it in precisely these terms, and the inappropriateness of
the feeling to the situation makes the incident ridiculous and
amusing to us.

This same principle is applied in longer passages of alternating
dialogue and narration, where Twain is at his best. His dialogue
is always realistic, with colloquial expressions and the suggestion
of dialectal pronunciation. In contrast, the diction in the narrative
passages is often formal and stilted, as in the paragraph quoted
above. At one point in Chapter 1, the conversation in which Aunt
Polly intends to trap Tom into revealing that he has played hooky
is introduced by a paragraph of narration which lets the reader
know exactly how she sees herself: she is asking questions that
are "full of guile, and very deep," "marvels of low cunning" (p. 3).
When we go on to read the conversation itself and the simple
questions she asks, we laugh at the contrast between what she
thinks she is doing and what she actually does. Yet the conversation is so ordinary that, without the narrative as preparation for
it, it would be not even faintly amusing.

By exploring these and many other ideas which Twain expresses
through plot, character, and language, one can begin to arrive at

an understanding of the way he thought: what he felt people must correct in themselves, what he thought was good, what he liked or disliked, why his attitude toward society was so equivocal. It is through his satiric humor, however, that we can come to know him best, for it is in the satire that his personality is most evident. Twain's virtuosity in manipulating language into humor is fascinating to watch, and a detailed examination of it will acquaint the student with the best part of the book.

STUDY QUESTIONS

CHAPTERS 1-5

1. From what is said about Aunt Polly and her spectacles, what do you think is Mark Twain's attitude toward her? What makes you think he likes her or dislikes her?

2. The following passage is found in Chapter 1:

> While Tom was eating his supper, and stealing sugar as opportunity offered, Aunt Polly asked him questions that were full of guile, and very deep—for she wanted to trap him into damaging revealments. Like many other simple-hearted souls, it was her pet vanity to believe she was endowed with a talent for dark and mysterious diplomacy, and she loved to contemplate her most transparent devices as marvels of low cunning (p. 3).

Why do you think the author has chosen such words and phrases as the following: full of guile, very deep, revealments, simple-hearted souls, transparent devices, low cunning? What is the general effect of this paragraph? How is it created? How effective is it? Reread the conversation between Tom and Aunt Polly that immediately follows this paragraph, imagining that the conversation stands by itself without introductory narration. What would the tone of the conversation then be? Would the passage be amusing? Why? How does the paragraph quoted above prepare for the humor and make it possible?

3. We learn a good deal about Tom, even before he actually appears in the book, from Aunt Polly's remarks as she looks for him. What do these remarks tell us about him? Is this first im-

pression reinforced by the rest of the chapter? What else do we learn about Tom's character in Chapter 1?

4. Consider the dialogue in Chapter 1. How realistic is it? Compare the diction used in dialogue with that used in narration. Which contains the more colloquial expressions? Which uses the more elegant and formal language? What is the effect of the contrast between the language used in dialogue and that in narration? Why do you think Twain created this contrast?

5. What bothers Tom most about having to spend Saturday whitewashing the fence?

6. Returning from the Saturday afternoon war games in Chapter 3, Tom sees Becky and falls in love. The event is described in the paragraph beginning, "As he was passing by the house where Jeff Thatcher lived, he saw a new girl in the garden . . ." (p. 14). What are the characteristics of this description? What is its tone? What is the point of view? Is this the way Tom saw what happened? Are these the words he would have used to describe it? Why do you think Mark Twain wrote this paragraph as he did?

7. Becky throws a pansy, and Tom disappears around a corner, "But only for a minute—only while he could button the flower inside his jacket, next to his heart—or next to his stomach, possibly, for he was not much posted in anatomy, and not hypercritical, anyway" (p. 15). What makes this passage amusing? Would the effect have been the same if it had ended, ". . . for he did not know much about anatomy, and he was not too critical anyway"? Why?

8. What sort of a person is Mary? In what ways are she and Sid alike? In what ways are they different? Does Twain satirize her at all? Why? Does he poke fun at most of the characters in the book? Which ones escape satirization and why?

9. What motivation to study is used in the Sunday school? How consistent is this method with what the school is supposedly trying to teach? How effective is it? What do you think of the system? What do you think Twain thought of it? What in Chapter 4 indicates Twain's attitude? In light of the nature of the ticket system, how would you evaluate Tom's method of procuring a Bible?

10. In his speech Judge Thatcher calls Tom's "very plainly bound," forty-cent prize "a beautiful Bible—a splendid elegant Bible" (p. 26). Is it? Why does Judge Thatcher describe it as he does? What reflection does this cast on all the rest he says?

11. Why does Tom take out the pinch-bug? Is it only the children who become interested in the bug and the poodle? Why? What do you think Twain thought of the church service? How does he satirize it? Cite specific details.

CHAPTERS 6-11

1. Why do all the mothers "cordially hate and dread" Huckleberry Finn? Why do all the boys admire him?

2. In Chapter 7, Twain calls a "glow of gratitude" that lights up Tom's face "prayer" (p. 41). Why can this glow be considered prayer? How is it different from the minister's prayer in church? Which do you think Twain feels is more truly a prayer? Why?

3. Why does Tom become melancholy in Chapter 8 and want to die? Why does he only want to die "temporarily"? What makes him decide to run away and be a pirate? Did he really want to die? What does he actually want?

4. In Chapter 8, one of Tom's magic spells fails to work, and his "whole structure of faith was shaken to its foundations" (p. 47). Why? Why do you think he believes in such things as magic and ghosts?

5. Why do Tom and Huck solemnly swear to keep quiet about the murder? Why don't the townspeople try Injun Joe for graverobbing? Compare the boys' behavior with that of the adults. In whom is this sort of action more excusable? Why?

CHAPTERS 12-24

1. In Chapter 12, when Tom is growing more and more melancholy and pale, Aunt Polly tries to cure him with patent medicines. Finally, when she uses pain-killer, Twain relates that

> Tom felt that it was time to wake up; this sort of life might be romantic enough, in his blighted condition, but it was getting to have too little sentiment and too much distracting variety about it (p. 66).

What does this passage tell us about Tom? What is romantic about the sort of life he has been leading? Why does a romantic life appeal to him? Is Tom really a romantic?

2. Why does Tom finally go off to be a pirate? What aspects of piracy appeal to him? Why does he sob at the sound of the schoolbell as he leaves? Had he ever really been that fond of school? To what extent is his emotion real and to what extent is it acted?

3. Going off to be a pirate, Tom comes across Joe Harper, and "plainly here were 'two souls with but a single thought'" (p. 69). Why, then, if Tom may suspect that Joe's intentions are similar to his own, does he tell him that he is going away never to return and that he hopes Joe won't forget him?

4. Why does Tom come down the bluff the hard way (Chapter 13, p. 70)?

5. The following conversation takes place between Tom and Huck in Chapter 13:

> ". . . And a hermit's got to sleep on the hardest place he can find, and put sackcloth and ashes on his head, and stand out in the rain, and—"
>
> "What does he put sackcloth and ashes on his head for?" inquired Huck.
>
> "*I* dono. But they've *got* to do it. Hermits always do. You'd have to do that if you was a hermit."
>
> "Dern'd if I would," said Huck.

What does this conversation tell us about Tom? About Huck? Is this difference between the two boys important in other places in the book? Where?

6. What in the thought of attending his own funeral appeals to Tom so much? Why is the moment when Old Hundred is being sung in praise of the boys' safe return (p. 94) the "proudest" in Tom's life?

7. Why does Tom tell Aunt Polly about his "dream"? Why do you think Sid suspects it is not a true dream? Why does Aunt Polly accept it unquestioningly?

8. What makes Tom see "a new aspect of the thing" he had done in making his aunt believe in his dream (p. 102)? What

makes him lighthearted and happy again when he kisses Aunt Polly (p. 104)?

9. Why does Tom deny spilling the ink? What other things does he do for the sake of "custom"?

10. Why does Tom take Becky's flogging?

11. What are the "Examination Day" exercises like? What do the townspeople think of them? What do you think Twain thinks of them? What in the story suggests his attitude? What is a "declamatory gem" (p. 110)? What is Twain satirizing in the young ladies' compositions?

12. Why does Tom finally tell the secret about the murder? Is this act consistent with the rest of his behavior? Defend your answer.

CHAPTERS 25-35

1. What do Huck's questions and Tom's answers in the conversation about buried treasure in Chapter 25 (pp. 123-25) tell us about each boy?

2. At the end of Chapter 28 (p. 141) Huck tells Tom about his friendship with the Negro Uncle Jake. Does he like or dislike Uncle Jake, or is he indifferent to him? Why does he say, "A body's got to do things when he's awful hungry he wouldn't want to do as a steady thing"?

3. At several points in the book virtually the whole town turns out to see something sensational: the scene of the murder (Chapter 11, p. 61); the stile in front of Widow Douglas's house (Chapter 30, p. 152); Injun Joe's funeral (Chapter 33, p. 167). What does this tell us about the community? What sort of community is it? What good does Twain find in it? What would he like to see improved? Cite specific details.

4. When Tom, Joe, and Huck are off being pirates, we are given only brief glimpses of the search efforts from the boys' viewpoint on the island. When Becky and Tom are lost in the cave, however, we are told a great deal about rescue operations, and we observe them first hand. How do you account for this difference in narration? What is the effect of each type?

5. What qualities in Tom are brought out during the episode

in the cave? How does Becky act? Why doesn't Tom tell her that he saw Injun Joe?

6. How does Tom react to Injun Joe's fate? Why?

7. Why had a petition been circulated for Injun Joe's pardon? What do you think Twain thinks about this petition and the feelings that motivated the people to circulate it?

8. What made Sid give away the Welshman's big secret? What does this tell us about him? Does Twain satirize Sid? Is Sid an amusing character? Why?

9. What effect is produced by the sudden rush of grown men to dig up treasure in haunted houses? Compare and contrast this effect with that produced when Tom and Huck went looking for treasure. What accounts for the difference?

10. What do you think of the town's revised opinion of the boys (Chapter 35, p. 177)? Why has the opinion changed?

11. How does Tom convince Huck to stay with the widow? Why must Huck be "respectable" in order to join the gang?

12. In the "Conclusion," Twain says:

> . . . When one writes a novel about grown people, he knows exactly where to stop—that is, with a marriage; but when he writes of juveniles, he must stop where he best can (p. 181).

What does he mean? Has he ended his book well? Why do you think so?

13. From whose point of view has this story been told—a child's, an adult's, or neither? Explain. Who is the narrator?

NOTES

1. Mark Twain, *The Adventures of Tom Sawyer* (New York: Macmillan, 1961), p. ix. All page references are to this edition.

2. This phrase is used by James M. Cox in discussing this device in "Remarks on the Sad Initiation of Huckleberry Finn," *Sewanee Review,* LXII (1954), p. 390.

3. Cox, pp. 392-93.

Teaching *The Pearl*

MARILYN JODY

Assistant Professor of English
Western Carolina College

The plot of *The Pearl* is simple; it is "the story of the great pearl —how it was found and how it was lost again." Interest is generated in part by what happens to the pearl and to some extent through the fate of the characters. But the chief value of the novel—the aspect which dominates the whole—is the author's masterful style. Through a variety of structural, stylistic devices, Steinbeck fashions a parable, the meaning of which is less significant than the technique which reveals it.

A brief prologue to *The Pearl* announces the plot, main characters, setting, and point of view. We are prepared by this introduction to accept the novel on special terms, in a form which may sacrifice probability and characterization for theme. This controlling theme emerges from and is reinforced by the setting.

> The uncertain air that magnified some things and blotted out others hung over the whole Gulf so that all sights were unreal and vision could not be trusted; so that sea and land had the sharp clarities and the vagueness of a dream. Thus it might be that the people of the Gulf trust things of the spirit and of the imagination, but they do not trust their eyes to show them distance or clear outline or any optical exactness. . . . There was no certainty in seeing, no proof that what you saw was there or was not there. And the people of the Gulf expected all places were that way, and it was not strange to them.

The novel focuses on the quality of illusion. The pearl fishermen live with a dream of the great pearl, the Pearl That Might Be. For them, exemplified in Kino, this is the great possibility, the hope that gives purpose to their lives. The doctor dreams, too, of Paris and youth; the priest dreams of a rich church; the pearl buyers dream of succeeding the patron. Their fantasies parallel Kino's dreams of the great pearl. Kino is afraid to open the large oyster shell, fearing that what he had glimpsed might be "a reflection, a piece of flat shell accidentally drifted in or a complete illusion. In this Gulf of uncertain light there were more illusions than realities." Juana fears that "perhaps the dealers were right and the pearl has no value. Perhaps this has all been an illusion." The doctor's beautiful Parisian mistress is a dream that would vanish should he ever return to Paris. It is Kino's great "misfortune" to discover that the promise of the pearl is also only a dream.

Music functions structurally in the novel. The interplay of theme and mood and the movement of the novel from harmony to discord to resolution are suggested throughout by what the author calls "songs." So that the songs will appear natural to their setting, Steinbeck explains that Kino's people "had sung of everything that happened or existed . . . and the songs were all in Kino and in his people—every song that had ever been made, even the ones forgotten." When Kino is in harmony with his world, the song is melodic and sweet; when that harmony is threatened, the song becomes discordant and shrill. The "Song of the Undersea" and its "counter-melody," the "Song of the Pearl That Might Be," express Kino's and his community's relationship to their environment, their work, and their dreams: life is tied to the sea, to the oyster pearl, and to the hope of the Pearl That Might Be. But these people are unable to formulate an abstract thought; thus "songs" express the vague, powerful, inarticulate forces in their village culture.

In the first scene Kino's world is shown to consist of fire and dawn and the earth; of Juana, the baby, and a brush hut; of superstition and fear, expressed in the simple act of covering his nose with a blanket to keep out the evil night air. These make up Kino's Song of the Family. For him, "this is safety, this is warmth, this is the *Whole.*" The Song of Evil grows out of any threat to this basic harmony and is a composite of helplessness, terror, and rage.

We are prepared by this use of song as symbol to accept Kino and Juana as characters whose responses will be essentially primitive—physical, emotional, nonrational. Theirs is a world of simplicity and survival, of serenity and violence, as subject to destruction as any animal world, in which only the strong or the clever survive.

Several images reinforce the survival theme. Kino watched "with the detachment of a God" while an ant "frantically tried to escape the sand trap an ant lion had dug for him." Night hawks silently hunt for mice, and schools of large fish devour smaller fish while the human predators of the town prepare to devour Kino and his pearl. Kino's attempt to escape the town has all the savage suspense of the hunt as the trackers whine with eagerness "like excited dogs on a warming trail," and Kino runs for high ground "as nearly all animals do when they are pursued." The theme is most powerfully communicated at the pool of water in the mountains, where "the cats took their prey . . . and lapped water through their bloody teeth." Here the Song of the Family becomes "as fierce and sharp and feline as the snarl of a female puma," and Kino kills to defend the family. In this highly theatrical scene one of the trackers is shot between the eyes after he has fallen into the pool, and Coyotito—little coyote—his cry mistaken for that of a coyote pup, is killed by the hunter.

Images foreshadow action, as in the "vision" of a mountain described in the opening paragraphs of Chapter 4, "a great stone peak . . . above the timber line." Various objects function symbolically to reveal half-developed themes or subtle characterizations. The pearl buyer's coin becomes an index of his greed. Juana's shawl is her badge of womanliness and maternity. She uses it to heal and comfort both Kino and Coyotito and as a bond between herself and her child. The shawl becomes the baby's shroud, bloodstained, and symbolic of the destruction of Juana's world as she returns to the town with it "slung like a sack over her shoulder," carrying the dead child.

The pearl itself is the central image of the novel, carrying with it suggestions of purity and perfection as well as material wealth. Steinbeck describes the pearl as an accident of nature which brings the finder "luck, a little pat on the back by God or the gods or both." But it is an evil kind of luck that Kino finds, and the reaction of the gods is swift and predictable. Kino has found "the Pearl of the World," and he finds that he must live by the savage laws of that world if he is to preserve the pearl and his own life. He has found the Pearl of the World—this world—but not "the Pearl of Great Price." The first pearls to appear in the story are "ugly and gray as little ulcers," valueless to buy the doctor's services. The Pearl of the World proves just as valueless to Kino, and in the end it, too, is "gray and ulcerous."

The scene in which Kino finds the pearl illustrates Steinbeck's masterful prose. The language captures in a sort of breathless effect the hope, reticence, and wonder of the characters:

> She pretended to look away. It is not good to want a thing too much. It sometimes drives the luck away. You must want it just enough and you must be very tactful with God or the gods. But Juana stopped breathing.

Here the storyteller has manipulated the point of view, capturing Juana's hopeful yet superstitious approach to the Pearl That Might Be. The couple's growing realization of their great fortune is conveyed in the measured understatement of the lines: "Kino lifted the flesh, and there it lay, the great pearl, perfect as the moon."

The author moves closer, into the eyes and minds of the characters, seeing the pearl before them: "It captured the light and refined it and gave it back in silver incandescence. It was as large as a sea-gull's egg."

And finally the reality their minds must strain to accept: "It was the greatest pearl in the world." The tension of the scene begins with Juana holding her breath and builds steadily to an explosive release in Kino's howl of total exultation. It is a cry of victory over all the frustration and terror and rage of a lifetime.

Steinbeck imitates the style of a folk tale to give *The Pearl* what he once described as a "set-aside, raised-up feeling." He uses formal, almost Biblical patterns to approximate the "old language" spoken by the Indians. His descriptions are intensely visual, sensory, poetic. Narrative usually imitates village expression, though meaning is sometimes conveyed by subtle shifts in tone. For example, Kino's boat is described by one who shares the values of the community and speaks the spare, simple language of its people: "It was at once property and source of food, *for a man with a boat can guarantee a woman that she will eat something*" (emphasis added). The tone changes when the point of view moves from that of the community to that of a narrator who stands between the reader and the legend:

> She had not prayed directly for the recovery of the baby—she had prayed that they might find a pearl with which to hire the doctor to cure the baby, *for the minds of people are as unsubstantial as the mirage of the Gulf* (emphasis added).

The tone changes again when Steinbeck interrupts the storyteller: "That was the only breakfast he [Kino] had ever known outside of feast days *and one incredible fiesta on cookies that had nearly killed him*" (emphasis added). The statement is not meant to be understood literally and is clearly inappropriate to either the village-tone or the narrator-tone. Intrusions such as these flaw the narrative and damage the illusion. If it were not for Steinbeck's careful control of tone, the story could quickly become a farce, a parody of second-rate Western fiction, in which all the Indians speak in monosyllables or give noble speeches in pidgin English.

STUDY QUESTIONS

1. How might we account for the formal tone of the language that Steinbeck has his characters speak?

2. Why do the pearl buyers remain loyal to the patron rather than become independent buyers?

3. Why does Juana repeat ancient "magics" along with her Hail Mary's? Is the expression "Go with God" used in this novel to express religious belief or superstition?

4. How does the priest gain control over the people? How does the doctor conquer Kino?

5. What significance does the broken boat have for Kino? For the community? Why doesn't Kino steal a boat to replace his broken one?

6. What do the "songs" represent? What do they tell us about the characters?

7. Outside this novel, what does a pearl commonly represent? Read the reference to the "pearl of great price" in the Bible (Matthew 13:45-46). What value do these associations have for the novel?

8. What does throwing away the pearl mean to Juana when she first attempts it? Why does Kino offer to let Juana destroy the pearl at the end? Why does she refuse?

9. What duties belong to Kino as man of the family? What is Juana's role? Why does Juana walk beside rather than behind Kino when they return to the village?

10. Why do Kino and Juana return to the village after Kino has killed the trackers?

11. Why does Steinbeck leave the identity of Kino's attackers a mystery?

12. In what ways is this story a protest against contemporary society? What is Steinbeck protesting? Does he think man should live in a primitive and ignorant state? Explain.

13. Are there characters in the novel who are neither heroes nor villains? If so, who and why? If not, why not?

14. Why does the author tell us the plot before the story begins? What else does he tell us in the prologue? Why?

15. Who tells the story? Do all the judgments expressed in the novel belong to the narrator? If not, whose are they? Are we expected to believe that the narrator heard rather than invented the legend? What effect does this point of view have on the story?

16. Does the setting seem real? How would you describe it? How does the setting explain and reinforce the meaning of the story?

17. Steinbeck says of *The Pearl* that it is a "strange piece of work, full of curious figures. A folk tale, I hope. A black-and-white

story like a parable. . . . I tried to write it as folklore, to give it that set-aside, raised-up feeling that all folk stories have." What does he mean by the "feeling that all folk stories have"? Does he succeed in creating that feeling? If so, how? If not, why not?

18. The legend of the pearl as Steinbeck heard it and reported it in *The Sea of Cortez* was a simple story of a boy who found a pearl, dreamed of the wealth and pleasure it would bring him, but was cheated and beaten when he tried to sell it and finally threw the pearl away. Does Steinbeck change the meaning of this tale? If so, in what ways?

SUPPLEMENTARY READING

"Flight" by John Steinbeck. In this short story Steinbeck presents a character similar to Kino in a situation which previews the pursuit scene of *The Pearl*.

"The Ministers Black Veil" and "Young Goodman Brown" by Nathaniel Hawthorne. Like *The Pearl*, both of these short stories have controlling central images which dominate incident and character.

The Old Man and the Sea by Ernest Hemingway. This short novel of the sea has a setting similar to, and shares some of the dominant themes of, *The Pearl*.

The Sea of Cortez by John Steinbeck. Containing the legend of the pearl as he first learned it, this is a travelogue of Steinbeck's trip to the Gulf of California. It also contains Steinbeck's first description of La Paz, the setting of *The Pearl*.

Teaching *Great Expectations*

THOMAS E. WALKER

Teacher of English
Culver Military Academy

Plot, character, and theme are so brilliantly interrelated in *Great Expectations* that each leads inevitably to the other two. The plot concerns Pip's involvement with various people in situations which affect him and bring about significant changes in his character. During the course of the novel Pip moves through three stages of development—from innocence through guilt to redemption. These stages also reveal the structure of the novel: the end of Chapter 19, after Pip has learned of his expectations and just before his journey to London, marks "the first stage of Pip's expectations"; Chapter 39, in which Pip learns the identity of his benefactor, ends "the second stage of Pip's expectations"; and from there to the end of the book Pip works out his redemption. These changes in Pip point up the theme of the novel, that the pursuit of the Victorian ideal of gentlemanly living at the expense of others is dehumanizing.

In accepting from an anonymous benefactor the idle life of a "gentleman" with great expectations, Pip rejects his state of innocence with Joe Gargery, who believes in honest labor as a way of life, and substitutes for love and natural morality a selfish, snobbish, but socially approved cruelty. Only after he forgoes his great expectations and gives himself to Magwitch in an act of complete self-surrender can he return to Joe and the forge, al-

though guiltily and incompletely. The fact that Pip has partici-
pated in the guilt of the world and its institutions precludes the
possibility of his staying permanently with Joe, but necessitates
his going back into the world, where he can hope to do only the
least possible harm.[1]

Pip's guilt stems not only from his treatment of Joe but from
his realization of the guilt of all men and institutions. The same
all-powerful class prejudice which shames Pip into preferring the
empty meaninglessness of Satis House and all it holds to the vital,
loving innocence of Joe also leads to double standards in the law
courts, where social standing affects both judge and jury. It leads,
with its emphasis upon property, to prison ships, to Newgate
prison, and to heartless child labor. Certainly we have in *Great
Expectations* Dickens' dramatic presentation of these evils of Victorian society at their worst.

Pip's development toward mature understanding of himself is
easily followed because Dickens has let him tell his own story.
But the student should distinguish carefully between the narrator
and the boy he describes. The narrator, an adult, writes skillfully
and dramatically, humorously and sympathetically. Throughout
the story the narrator reveals himself a better person now for having learned from the earlier experiences which he recounts. Although he can re-create vividly the drama, the mood, the feelings,
the motives for acting or reacting as he did at a particular time,
the narrator comments upon the action far more sagely than the
boy Pip could ever have done. He often compresses repeated action into a single sentence without the loss of dramatic effect. He
brings mature thought to bear upon incidents which happened
too long ago for full or accurate remembrance (p. 296).[2] He makes
the reader aware of the passage of time from event to telling, time
necessary for objective analysis of motive (pp. 297-98).[3] The narrator then looks back upon characters and events which shaped
him into the man he is.

In a brilliant combination of character and action and theme,
Dickens first shows Pip in the graveyard, a small boy sniveling,
not from grief over the death of his family, whom he never knew,
but from the fear of the wilderness and the savagery of the world,

which he, "the small bundle of shivers growing afraid of it all" (p. 2), somehow seems to sense that he cannot escape. It is interesting that Dickens has the narrator comment that this particular afternoon was his "first most vivid and broad impression of the identity of things" (p. 1), and that as Magwitch talks to Pip, he tilts him little by little until finally "the church jumped over its own weathercock" (p. 3). Little does Pip realize on that afternoon how symbolic that physical action is to become and what a significant part Magwitch will play in his realization that the world of which he has this day become aware is indeed an upside-down one, full of paradoxes and ironies. The student should have little trouble finding examples of upside-downness: guilty innocence and innocent guilt, great expectations which destroy man's potential to fulfill himself, loveless and malignant "gentlemanliness" and Christianity without social standing, selfless criminality and greedy respectability, the ability to find oneself by losing oneself.[4]

Dickens' ironic approach to his society demands not only finely drawn portraits of the types he hopes to satirize but of character foils against which the reader can measure and judge. For this reason Dickens carefully interrelates his characters and their effects upon one another. Throughout the novel the reader is aware of the lasting effect upon Pip of his association with Joe Gargery. Even at the peak of Pip's snobbery, he suffers when he treats Joe badly. He could not retain the reader's sympathy if he did not. Joe contrasts drastically to the frigid Estella and to Pip when he makes Estella's ideals his own. The heart of this peace-loving workman contains more than can be expressed in words. Joe's patient courage and selflessness make themselves felt better through gesture and deeds than through speech. The fact that Joe dedicates his life to work is in itself a criticism of Pip's ideal of living in ease at the expense of others, and it is against Joe's belief in the spiritual rewards of honest labor that Pip's membership in The Finches of the Grove must be measured. Joe fills his place in the social order respectfully and uncomplainingly.

In the scene between Miss Havisham and Joe, Dickens has shown the utter impossibility of real communication between the Joe Gargery's and the cold, cheerless, selfish manipulators of men.

In the scene with Pip in his London rooms Joe, likewise, has trouble communicating. He constantly addresses Pip as "Sir" and indicates by his nervousness that he is not at home with "gentlemen." Joe ends the interview by stating that he and Pip are wrong together in London except someplace "private and beknown and understood among friends" (p. 215). Pip, although he had done little to make Joe's visit easier, remarks

> I had not been mistaken in my fancy that there was a simple dignity in him. The fashion of his dress could no more come in its way when he spoke those words, than it could come in its way in Heaven. He touched me gently on the forehead, and went out. As soon as I could recover myself sufficiently, I hurried out after him and looked for him in the neighboring streets; but he was gone (pp. 215-16).

At the end of the novel there is no less acceptance or love shown to Pip upon his return than before he left. Pip refers to himself as a brazen pretender, as arrogant and untrue, as thankless, and ungenerous, and unjust. But he does not need to deserve his return to Joe and Biddy. It is against Joe's constant goodness and true gentlemanliness that Pip measures himself and finds himself wanting. Surely Dickens shows throughout the book that without the Joe Gargery's society would crumble and that the society which places its values solely in property dehumanizes the men who comprise it.

To Magwitch, Pip must also relate. Even their backgrounds are similar. Just as Pip's first sense of identity began with feelings of helplessness in his encounter with Magwitch and of guilt in stealing for him, Magwitch's first memories are of "thieving turnips" (p. 331). Both are "helpless, repressed, and tortured by established society, and both rebel against its incomprehensible authority."[5] Pip by his act of mercy kept Magwitch alive to be further brutalized by society, and his realization and acceptance of his own guilt allow him to forget self in order to help Magwitch.

Like Pip in the graveyard, Magwitch throughout the novel is dominated by fear—fear for his daughter, whom he loves dearly, and fear of Compeyson begin his struggle with society. The increased control of Compeyson finally leads to the life of the prison ship, chains, escapes, and hiding. Magwitch displays his gratitude for what Pip has done for him; his loyalty to and sacrifice for the small boy, who, out of fear, procured his freedom; and, in the closing chapters of the novel, real love. Even though he uses Pip to achieve vicariously the place in society which he himself would have liked to reach (not unlike Miss Havisham's use of Estella to achieve vicariously her revenge upon all men), his love for Pip in the final chapters obviously transcends his hatred of society.

That Pip would have knowingly put himself into the hands of Magwitch is unthinkable, but certainly he encourages the grotesque Miss Havisham to shape his destiny. Because he believes that she can put Estella within his reach, Pip willingly exchanges the honest workaday world of Joe Gargery for the life of Satis House, warped, paralyzed, decayed, cold, and insincere. Miss Havisham is inseparable from her home, now devoid of any kind of life-giving force. As long as Pip feels that Miss Havisham intends that he marry Estella, he is happy, no matter how much suffering he must undergo; but after he discovers that Magwitch is his benefactor, and even after he has spoken forgiveness of Miss Havisham, he feels, perhaps subconsciously, such a profound sense of injustice that he once again experiences the hallucination of her hanging from the beam of the brewery.[6]

Miss Havisham has brought Pip and Estella together not for companionship but to use them to avenge her own broken heart. Miss Havisham has befriended Pip only to cause him pain, and for years she has cultivated Estella as an instrument of her own resentment and wounded pride. She has "stolen her heart away and put ice in its place." (p. 383). But even Miss Havisham is not simply a caricature. We may wonder at the *degree* to which Miss Havisham has reacted to her fiancé's jilting her, but when we realize the reason for her mental deterioration, we understand sympathetically as does Pip (pp. 382-83). Her appeal to Pip for forgiveness and his granting it help to raise Miss Havisham a point above a two-dimensional caricature, even though her realization of her guilt seems contrived, coming as it does just before the accident which leads to her death.

Miss Havisham, even after her death, lives in Estella, whose jewels sparkle like her name. Dickens presents his opposition to the Victorian sense of values in this bane of Pip's existence. The irony of Estella's birth, her appeal in completely material terms, her guilt in the suffering she inflicts for no other reason than to inflict pain are all comments upon the surface values of Dickens' time. Too often Estella is interpreted as a flat character without the complexity of human feelings and motivations which real people show. Certainly a literary character who has been trained from early childhood to think only of hurting others can be no more "well-rounded" than its real-life counterpart, but we do get hints occasionally that Estella's lessons from Miss Havisham have not succeeded completely in overcoming a very natural reaction to an attractive member of the opposite sex. The blush which crosses her face when she allows Pip to kiss her after his first encounter with Herbert Pocket does not suggest a total lack of feeling.

The minor characters also help to advance the plot and contribute to the development of the theme. Apart from their relation to the main character, which we expect, they are also related to each other. Jaggers and Wemmick emphasize Dickens' belief that success in business "can be won only at the expense of everything nobly generous, elevating, sympathetic, and humane."[7] After Jaggers' clients leave, Jaggers washes his hands with soap; and after a particularly nasty criminal case he washes his face, gargles, and, as Pip says "scrapes the case out of his nails before he puts his coat on" (p. 202). In these actions Jaggers serves Dickens' symbolic purposes; in his ability to manipulate he also represents a limited control over the sinful world in which he operates. In Chapter 20 his rejection of a "witness" is at once a participation in the corruption of the Victorian legal and penal system and a ray of hope for a victim led to crime by a guilty society. This paradoxical position of Jaggers is perhaps best reflected in the contrast between his professional callousness and his private concern for Molly and Estella. Yet, if it were not for Pip's unthinking revelation to Jaggers of Wemmick's private character, the reader might never have seen the real Jaggers.

Wemmick, who works with Jaggers, also reflects the necessity of separating a personal life from professional obligations. Professionally an extension of Jaggers, Wemmick is described on the job in inanimate terms—his mouth is a "post office." At home, however, he surrounds himself with quaintness and shows deep personal concern for his aged father. His heart-to-heart talks with Pip cannot take place at the office but only at his home. How appropriate that Wemmick's house, although the smallest house Pip had ever seen, should be provided with a drawbridge "to cut off the communication" and that the "top of it was cut out and painted like a battery mounted with guns" (p. 197). How appropriate, too, that even Wemmick's marriage plans should be hidden from the world of business.

Although Jaggers and Wemmick have worked together for years, neither dares show the other his private side. When Pip in the presence of Jaggers refers to Wemmick's pleasant home, his old father, his "innocent cheerful playful ways with which you refresh your business life" (p. 395), Jaggers and Wemmick stare at each other in such a way that Pip fears Wemmick might be dismissed, "but it melted as I saw Mr. Jaggers relax into something like a smile, and Wemmick become bolder."

> "What's all this?" said Mr. Jaggers. "You with an old father, and you with pleasant and playful ways?"
>
> "Well!" returned Wemmick. "If I don't bring 'em here, what does it matter?"
>
> "Pip," said Mr. Jaggers, laying his hand upon my arm, and smiling openly, "this man must be the most cunning impostor in all London."
>
> "Not a bit of it," returned Wemmick, growing bolder and bolder. "I think you're another" (p. 395).

Only after this encounter does Jaggers dare show himself human enough to tell Pip of Estella's background.

The three real villains of *Great Expectations*, those with absolutely nothing to recommend them to the reader's sympathy, make an interesting study in character relationships. Compeyson we meet only a few times in very short scenes, and in all but one of these he remains nameless. Yet he has had a profound influence upon most of the major characters and has provided, sometimes indirectly, the motivation for all the major actions of the novel. He has caused Magwitch's constant fear and his several imprisonments. He has caused Miss Havisham's derangement and her subsequent dehumanization of Estella. Dickens constantly shows us the effects of Compeyson's evil upon other characters, but only shortly before the final dispositions of Magwitch and Miss Havisham, in revelations which increase the reader's sympathy for his victims, does he reveal Compeyson as the cause.

In some ways Orlick and Drummle, the other villains, relate far more closely to Pip than do any other characters in the novel. They do more than merely create incident or provide motivation. They are, in effect, character supplements. Dorothy Van Ghent (in *The English Novel: Form and Function*) comments upon Dickens' superimposing one flat character upon another "to form the representative human complexity of good-in-evil and evil-in-good."[8] Orlick and Drummle actually represent the evil side of Pip's character. The student should carefully trace the parallels in the careers of Pip and the villains. Julian Moynahan has pointed out that both Pip and Orlick work for Joe. When Orlick attacks Mrs. Joe, Pip takes upon himself the blame for his guilty thoughts about his sister and for unknowingly supplying the weapon. Both work for Miss Havisham, and both are associated intimately with an ex-convict. Orlick in robbing Pumblechook suffers a punishment in direct proportion to the seriousness of the annoyance which Pumblechook has been to Pip. In the scene at the limekiln Orlick, who is guilty, accuses Pip, who is innocent, but as Orlick interprets Pip's character, he really describes himself. As Pip moves up the social scale, Drummle replaces Orlick but serves the same dramatic purpose.

> Drummle, like Orlick, is a criminal psychopath. . . . To an extraordinary degree, these two physically powerful, inarticulate, and dark-complexioned villains are presented to the reader in terms more often identical than similar. Orlick, again and again, is one who lurks and lounges, Drummle is one who lolls and lurks.[9]

Both are often described as "creeping" and as amphibious creatures. Drummle functions as Pip's instrument of punishment toward Estella in the same way in which Orlick functioned against Mrs. Joe. Both villains leave the action of the novel suddenly after they have performed their functions as Pip's avengers.

Mrs. Joe, Pumblechook, Wopsle, and Trabb's boy are worthy of mention as they relate to the main character, but their functions in the novel are not difficult to perceive. Their significance in the novel is explored in the appended study questions.

Because of the close interrelation of plot, character, and theme in *Great Expectations*, it does not matter a great deal which the teacher takes hold of as an approach to the novel as long as he does not neglect the other two. In this guide the main emphasis has been upon character, but the study questions are meant to lead the student to see how character, plot, and theme work together.

STUDY QUESTIONS

Part I

CHAPTERS 1-4

1. In these chapters how does Dickens show that cruelties and injustices are performed by pillars as well as by outcasts of society?

2. In what way is the convict's appearance from among the graves symbolic? Is our reaction anything but one of horror? How does the convict's attitude toward Pip change throughout these four chapters?

3. Pip describes Joe as a "Hercules in strength, and also in weakness." What does he mean by a "Hercules in weakness"?

4. What devices does Dickens use to characterize Mrs. Joe? Why is so much made of her apron? Do Pip's clothes reflect his life with Mrs. Joe in any way?

5. How does nature reflect Pip's state of mind at the beginning of Chapter 3? Why does Dickens use this device at this point in the story?

6. Notice the animal imagery in these chapters. It plays an important part throughout the novel. Can you determine why Dickens uses it?

CHAPTERS 5-8

1. Does it seem strange that Joe should side with the convicts against the law? What does the scene at the end of Chapter 5 reveal about both Joe and the convict?

2. How does Pip's guilt affect his relationship with Joe? Why?

3. How do Joe's attitudes toward his father and toward Mrs. Joe reveal his character and further endear him to Pip?

4. What is the significance of the name Satis House? (*Satis* means "enough.")

5. How does Estella's treatment of Pip affect his relationship with Joe?

6. How do you account for Pip's vision of Miss Havisham hanging from a beam?

CHAPTERS 9-12

1. Why would Pip willingly lie to Pumblechook and Mrs. Joe but not to Joe? How does Joe's untutored wisdom help Pip? How are the characters of Mrs. Joe and Pumblechook furthered in this chapter?

2. Is it Pip the character or Pip the narrator who speaks in the last paragraph of Chapter 9? How can you tell? Examine the paragraph in Chapter 12 beginning "Perhaps I might have told Joe about the pale young gentleman. . . ." Have you been able to separate Pip the character and Pip the narrator in these first few chapters?

3. In Chapter 11 why would Pip's answer to Estella's question cause her to slap him?

4. In Chapter 11 who is the "him" to whom Miss Havisham refers when she says, ". . . and which will be the finished curse upon him" (p. 85)?

5. Is there anything in these chapters to make you think that Estella is capable of any kind of human feeling? How do you account for the advice which Miss Havisham whispers into her ear?

CHAPTERS 13-16

1. Why would Dickens have Joe speak to Miss Havisham only through Pip?

2. How does Pip feel about the change which has come over him? By whose standard is Pip measuring his position in life?

3. Why does Miss Havisham ask Pip, "Do you feel that you have lost her?" How does this fit her whispered words to Estella in Chapter 12?

4. What are some foreshadowings of impending tragedy in Chapter 15?

5. Why does Pip think of himself as the legitimate object of suspicion and feel particularly guilty when the weapon is discovered? How does Mrs. Joe finally communicate who the attacker is?

CHAPTERS 17-19

1. How does Biddy reveal the kind of person she is? Can you answer Pip's question as to why he prefers Estella to Biddy?

2. What is Dickens trying to suggest by Orlick's appearing from "the ooze"? What would cause Mrs. Joe to take a "fancy" to her attacker?

3. How does Joe in this chapter show that he is not part of the money-grubbing society about him? Why does he at one point suddenly lapse into the language of a boxer?

4. How are Jaggers' business attitudes reflected?

5. What in Pip's character is revealed by his reaction to Joe's and Biddy's comments upon his becoming a gentleman? What is shown by his remark that "Joe wanted comforting for some reason or other"? Which Pip is speaking, the character or the narrator? How does Biddy react to Pip's comments about Joe?

6. Why does Dickens remind us now of the story about the rich man and the kingdom of Heaven?

7. Why does Pip desire to walk away from Joe's alone? What does he mean by "if I had cried before, I should have had Joe with me then"?

Part II

CHAPTERS 20-23

1. How does Dickens establish the character and reputation of Jaggers?

2. Why does Dickens describe Wemmick in terms of wood? Why not paste or clay or iron?

3. How does Wemmick's description of murder and robbery as merely for selfish gains reflect upon Pip?

4. What has been the effect of "great expectations" upon Mrs. Pocket?

CHAPTERS 24-27

1. What other character besides Mr. Wemmick seems also concerned with "portable property"? (See the beginning of Chapter 13.) Why has Mr. Wemmick built his home as he has?

2. Drummle is described "like some uncomfortable amphibious creature." Who in Part I is described in similar terms? Why would Jaggers be more interested in Drummle than in any of his other guests?

3. Dickens frequently describes Wemmick's mouth as a post office. When and why?

4. How can Pip tell when Jaggers has been working on a case involving a greater degree of crime than usual?

5. Why does Pip most fear Joe's being seen by Drummle, a person he despises?

6. Joe says that it is right for Pip and him to be together only under certain conditions. What does Joe mean by this?

CHAPTERS 28-31

1. What does Pip's remark that he cheats himself by rationalizing his staying at the Blue Boar instead of at Joe's show about his true character? What persuades him not to visit Joe on this trip? What has happened to Pip in his trying to become a "gentleman."?

2. What example do we have in these chapters of "honor among thieves"? Have we had any other examples?

3. In Pip's speaking of his love for Estella, is there anything which leads us to believe that his is an ideal kind of selfless love? What different meanings does the word "love" take on as Miss Havisham repeats it again and again? What relationship is there between this scene and Miss Havisham's questions in Chapters 12 and 15?

4. What does Pip mean by the last five words of Chapter 29?

5. Do you sympathize with or are you antagonistic toward Trabb's boy? Why?

CHAPTERS 32-35

1. Why does Dickens use the "greenhouse" imagery in describing Newgate Prison?

2. Why would Dickens want to treat the funeral scene humorously?

3. Why is Pip hurt by the way Biddy has talked to him? Was Biddy wrong in talking to him in such a way?

CHAPTERS 36-39

1. Toward the end of Chapter 36 we have an interesting medley of Wemmick's trademarks. What are some of them?

2. What is implied in the relationship between Estella and Pip in Chapter 38?

3. How does Dickens establish an atmosphere appropriate to the entrance of Magwitch?

4. How does Pip's leaving Joe now become ironic?

Part III
CHAPTERS 40-43

1. Is all that Magwitch is doing for Pip solely to pay him back for his kindness, or is there another motive? Why does he enjoy hearing Pip read a foreign language?

2. Why does Pip say that he now has no expectations?

3. How do Magwitch's and Pip's early lives parallel each other? Is this just coincidence or is it important to Dickens? Why?

4. Does Magwitch's explanation of the difference in penalties given to Compeyson and himself fit in with any previous social criticism in the novel?

CHAPTERS 44-47

1. In the scene in which Pip objects to Estella's marriage to Drummle, does Estella show any hostility toward Pip? Does she

evidence any ability to feel or to make moral distinctions? Why does she look at Pip in "incredulous wonder"? How do you account for the difference between Estella's and Miss Havisham's reactions?

2. Why do you suppose Dickens describes the furnishings of the room at the Hummums in animate terms?

3. What pastime of Pip's at Mr. Pocket's now begins to take on practical value?

4. What is happening to Pip's attitude toward Magwitch?

5. How does Dickens keep his satire upon the theater from being a digression?

CHAPTERS 48-51

1. What do we find out about Molly? What details which earlier seemed insignificant now take on added importance?

2. How does Miss Havisham's question to Pip about whether or not he is unhappy differ from the way in which she has asked it before? What does she say that reminds you of what Estella said in Chapter 38?

3. What in this visit would cause a recurrence of Pip's hallucination? Can you account for his not having seen this vision during the time he thought Miss Havisham was his benefactor?

4. Why at this point of the novel is it necessary to dispose of Miss Havisham?

5. What do Wemmick and Jaggers mean when they call each other "imposters"? Why does Jaggers find it easier to tell of Estella's background after he finds out about Wemmick's home life? Why at the close of Chapter 51 are the words of Wemmick and Jaggers to Mike particularly effective?

CHAPTERS 52-55

1. What is Pip's first good deed on his way to redemption?

2. How do Pumblechook's actions help reveal the character of Joe to the reader?

3. How is the meeting between Pip and Orlick ironic? How have the careers of these two paralleled each other? Have the guilts of Orlick been to any extent the guilts of Pip? Explain. Has Pip ruined any of Orlick's "expectations"?

4. Is there any foreshadowing in the scene at the inn of a successful or unsuccessful conclusion to the venture?

5. In the battle between Compeyson and Magwitch, what does Dickens gain in suspense by not having Pip able to see everything which takes place?

6. Can you point to the paragraph in which it is made quite clear that Pip redeems himself through love? Why is it fitting that in this same paragraph his "great expectations" should perish?

7. Does Pip's reminding Wemmick of the difference between the portable property and the owner of the property help point up the theme of the novel? How?

CHAPTERS 56-59

1. Do the descriptions of the court take on any added significance from our knowing Magwitch as well as we do?

2. What meaning can you find in the dreams of Pip during his illness, particularly his seeing himself as a brick in the wall and as a steel beam of a vast engine?

3. Why, in terms of the theme of the novel, is it necessary for Pip to be reunited with Joe? Why is it necessary for them to leave London and return to the forge? Why doesn't Dickens allow Pip to stay with Joe and Biddy for a longer time?

4. Can you trace in the novel the various attitudes toward work? How does Pip's statement that "we . . . worked for our profits, and did very well" fit into the theme?

5. The novel began with Magwitch turning Pip upside down. Does this take on signifiance now as you finish the novel? Explain.

NOTES

1. For discussion of theme, I would particularly suggest three articles reprinted in *Assessing Great Expectations*, ed. Richard Lettis and William E. Morris (San Francisco: Chandler, 1960). These are John Lindberg's "Individual Conscience and Social Injustice in *Great Expectations*," *College English* XXIII, 2 (November, 1961), pp. 118-22; Julian Moynahan, "The Hero's Guilt: The Case of *Great Expectations*," *Essays in Criticism*, X. I. (January, 1960), pp. 60-79; and G. Robert Stange, "Expectations Well Lost: Dickens' Fable for His Time," *College English*, XVI, I (October 1954), pp. 9-17.

2. Page numbers of all quotations from the novel refer to the following edition: Charles Dickens, *Great Expectations* (New York: Washington Square Press, 1964).

3. For a more detailed discussion of point of view in *Great Expectations* read Robert B. Partlow, Jr., "The Moving I: A Study of the Point of View in *Great Expectations*," *College English* XXIII, 2 (November 1961), pp. 122-26, 131. This article is reprinted on pages 194-201 of Lettis and Morris.

4. The idea of upside-downness is discussed by Stange in the article referred to in footnote 1 and by Dorothy Van Ghent in *The English Novel: Form and Function* (New York, Holt, Rinehart and Winston, 1953), pp. 125-38, reprinted in Lettis and Morris, pp. 57-71.

5. Stange in Lettis and Morris, p. 77.

6. For a discussion of the two hallucinations, see Moynahan in Lettis and Morris, pp. 163-65.

7. Edgar Johnson, *Charles Dickens, His Tragedy and Triumph*, 2 vols., (New York: Simon and Schuster, 1952), II, 990.

8. Van Ghent in Lettis and Morris, p. 67.

9. Moynahan in Lettis and Morris, p. 162.

10. The material dealing with Orlick and Drummle draws heavily upon Moynahan's article reprinted in Lettis and Morris, pp. 149-68.

BIBLIOGRAPHY

Dickens, Charles. *Great Expectations*. (New York: Washington Square Press, 1964).

Johnson, Edgar. *Charles Dickens, His Tragedy and Triumph*, 2 vols. (New York: Simon and Schuster, 1952).

Lettis, Richard and William E. Harris, eds. *Assessing Great Expectations*. (San Francisco: Chandler, 1960).

Pearson, Hesketh. *Dickens: His Character, Comedy and Career*. (New York: Harper, 1949).

Teaching *To Kill a Mockingbird*

MARILYN JODY

Most of all, *To Kill a Mockingbird* is a thoroughly readable book, entertaining in the best tradition of the novel. And it is a good book for the same reasons it is entertaining. It is superbly made. The structure is sound; the writing is skillful; the characterizations are convincing; the theme is valid. Craftsmanship is the sole and sufficient explanation for this novel's substantial virtues.

To Kill a Mockingbird is the story of Atticus Finch, his values, and his children's growing awareness of the meaning of those values in their own lives. The core of his philosophy is the right of each man to a fair trial before he is judged—in or out of court. He teaches Scout and Jem that "you never really understand a person until you consider things from his point of view . . . until you climb into his skin and walk around in it." Atticus (whose name is significant—*Atticus*: Athenian, marked by simplicity, purity, and refinement; *Finch*: a type of songbird) shows them that the strong and the good must take the responsibility for protecting the world's cripples and "mockingbirds," as well as for destroying "mad dogs." He lives that philosophy for his children and his community. As Miss Maudie says: "We're so rarely called on to be Christians, but when we are, we've got men like Atticus to go for us."

The particular cause in which Atticus must "go for" the people of Maycomb is Tom Robinson's trial, which provides the novel's main plot. The subplot, the mystery of Boo Radley, parallels the main action, underlining it thematically. Part of the novel's genius lies in this neatly woven interplay of action between a child's world and that of the adult community.

The narrator is Scout, grown up; but the point of view is essentially that of Scout as a child. The adult Scout, as narrator, establishes setting, provides summary between scenes, and occasionally adds explanatory comment:

> Although Maycomb was ignored during the War Between the States, Reconstruction rule and economic ruin forced the town to grow. It grew inward. New people so rarely settled there, the same families married the same families until the members of the community looked faintly alike. Occasionally someone would return from Montgomery or Mobile with an outsider, but the result caused only a ripple in the quiet stream of family resemblance. Things were more or less the same during my early years.

But most of the novel consists of action seen through the clear eyes of a bright and curious child:

> Atticus suddenly grew serious. In his lawyer's voice, without a shade of inflection, he said: "Your aunt has asked me to try and impress on you and Jean Louise that you are not from run-of-the-mill people, that you are the product of several generations of gentle breeding—" Atticus paused, watching me locate an elusive redbug on my leg.
> "Gentle breeding," he continued, when I had found and scratched it, "and that you should try to live up to your name—"

The effect is a sense of immediacy that gives the novel life and high humor, as Scout's honesty reveals the absurdities of adult hypocrisy. The author maintains the difficult balance of a double view throughout. Only rarely does the narrator-Scout disrupt the dramatic illusion by stepping into a scene with character-Scout.

Atticus is the only other fully drawn character. The rest are character sketches with a vividness derived from one or two strong identifying traits and a consistent function in the plot. Mrs. Dubose, for example, is a parallel for Atticus. Her courage illustrates Atticus' own in defending Tom Robinson: "It's when you know you're licked before you begin but you begin anyway and you see it through no matter what." Miss Maudie provides reliable commentary on Atticus and Maycomb as she explains the adult world to Scout and Jem. Calpurnia serves a similar purpose, as an interpreter within the Finch household and as a source of information about the Negro community. All of the characters function within Scout's range of vision, adding depth and flexibility to the carefully limited point of view.

The opening paragraphs of the novel suggest its two-part structure:

> When he was nearly thirteen, my brother Jem got his arm badly broken at the elbow. . . . When enough years had gone by to enable us to look back on them, we sometimes discussed the events leading to his accident. I maintain that the Ewells started it all, but Jem, who was four years my senior, said it started long before that. He said it began the summer Dill came to us, when Dill first gave us the idea of making Boo Radley come out.

Boo is the subject of Part I; Tom Robinson's trial dominates Part II. The two stories come together when Boo Radley does "come out" to save Jem from the revenge of Bob Ewell. Jem's crippled left arm, a permanent reminder of Tom Robinson, is the link between the two plots, as Jem himself is the bridge between the worlds of childhood and maturity.

Both Tom Robinson and Boo Radley are "cripples," both social outcasts. Tom has a shriveled arm; he is a Negro in a small Alabama town of the 1930's. Boo has a shriveled spirit; he is an eccentric recluse in a world of social conformity. They are both "mockingbirds," harmless and vulnerable in a dangerous world. When Tom is killed, Mr. Underwood's editorial "likened Tom's death to the senseless slaughter of songbirds by hunters and children." He "didn't talk about miscarriages of justice, he was writing so children could understand. Mr. Underwood simply figured it was a sin to kill cripples."

Boo Radley is the victim in Scout's and Jem's world—misrepresented, ridiculed, and tormented by unthinking children who lack knowledge and understanding. But children, unlike the adults of Maycomb, are willing to learn. When Tom is unfairly convicted, Jem cries; and Atticus says it "seems that only children weep" at the world's injustices. Boo is saved from the community, as Tom could not be; and Scout, too, understands at last what Atticus has taught her and Jem, if not the town—that hurting an innocent man is "sort of like shootin' a mockingbird."

STUDY QUESTIONS

CHAPTERS 1-8

1. As the novel opens, the author arouses curiosity by suggesting that there is a story in the series of events that led to the breaking of Jem's arm. What references in these opening paragraphs are the most mysterious? What does the reader want to know immediately?

2. A long discussion of Maycomb County and the Finch family background grows naturally out of the novel's opening statement. When, in relation to the events of the novel, is the story told? How does the author make the story seem to be happening before your eyes?

3. Why was there "nothing to buy and no money to buy it with" in the Maycomb of Scout's childhood? What is the narrator referring to in the statement that "Maycomb County had recently been told that it had nothing to fear but fear itself"? Why does the author establish the year in this way rather than by stating it directly?

4. The author frequently moves from background description to dramatic situation much as a motion picture camera moves in for a closeup: "We lived on the main residential street in town . . . Calpurnia . . . had been with us ever since Jem was born . . . our summertime boundaries were . . . That was the summer Dill came . . . Early one morning as we were beginning our day's play . . . We stared at him until he spoke: 'Hey'" (Popular Library paperback, pp. 10-11). Compare the scenic introduction of Dill with the summary introduction of Atticus (pp. 8-9). What purpose does a summary introduction serve? What does scene accomplish that summary cannot?

5. The first word spoken is "hey," a Southern expression for "hello," equivalent to the Northern "hi." What other regional expressions occur in this first exchange of dialogue? What effect

does the use of colloquial language have on characterization? Why does the author give the ages of the children ᵤs "almost six," "nearly ten," and "goin' on seven" (pp. 10-11)?

6. Before the first scene opens, we have been told a number of significant facts. We know, for example, that the narrator's brother has a crippled left arm; that the narrator belongs to an old Alabama family; that her father is a lawyer; that her mother died when she was a baby; that Calpurnia, the Finch family cook, takes care of her and her brother. How many characters are introduced before the first scene opens? At what point do we discover that the narrator is a girl? How do we learn her name?

7. How old is Scout when she gives the opening summary? What details cause you to reach this conclusion? How does the narrator's point of view change as the novel moves from summary to scene? Through whose eyes do we view the action?

8. Although we are expected to believe that the narrator reports accurately when Jem says to Dill about Boo Radley, "Boo was about six-and-a-half feet tall, judging from his tracks; he dined on raw squirrels and any cats he could catch, that's why his hands were bloodstained—" (p. 17), we are not expected to believe the description. We know that it is only the product of Jem's imagination. Why, then, does the narrator say that Jem gave a "reasonable description of Boo"? Whose point of view accounts for the word "reasonable"? What makes this passage humorous?

9. Why does the author choose *Dracula* as the movie for Dill to describe? What kind of books provide the plots for the children's games of make-believe? How do these details contribute to the interest of the Boo Radley mystery? To the realism of the characterizations?

10. Compare the attitudes of Stephanie Crawford, Atticus, Miss Maudie, and Calpurnia toward Boo Radley. What elements in the Radley story particularly attract the children? As Jem and Scout tell Dill the story of Boo Radley, they draw different conclusions about him than the reader does. How does the author accomplish this double view?

11. The first chapter ends as it began—by suggesting a question. What does the reader want to know at the end?

12. Why does Walter Cunningham refuse the quarter Miss

Caroline offers him? What does the Cunningham incident reveal about Maycomb's economy? About Atticus' position in the community?

13. Why is Burris Ewell allowed to leave school? Why isn't little Chuck Little afraid to tell Burris to leave? What is the lesson that Atticus wants Scout to learn from her first day at school?

14. What do Scout and Jem find in the hole in the tree? Does either of them know how the objects got there? Do they know who filled the hole with cement? Why does Jem cry about it?

15. Why does Dill spend his summers in Maycomb? Why do you think he tells false tales about his father?

16. What does Miss Maudie mean when she says, "Sometimes the Bible in the hand of one man is worse than a whiskey bottle in the hand of—oh, your father" (p. 49)? Can we accept Miss Maudie's judgments as true? How do you know? What is Scout's opinion of Miss Maudie? What is Atticus' opinion of her?

17. The night visit to the Radley Place has a quality of high suspense. What are some of the details that help to make this childhood adventure seem real? By what methods does the author create tension in the scene?

18. When Jem goes back to retrieve his pants, he finds them folded across the fence and "sewed up . . . all crooked." Who do you think repaired them for him? Why is Jem frightened at the thought that someone seemed to know what he was going to do? Does this incident suggest something about Boo?

19. After the fire at Miss Maudie's, when Jem suspects that Boo Radley has put a blanket around Scout during the night's excitement, he tells Atticus the whole story of their association with the Radleys. In what ways does this revelation mark a turning point in the story? In Jem and Scout's relationship?

CHAPTERS 9-11

1. When Scout asks Atticus if he defends "niggers," Atticus says, "Don't say nigger, Scout. That's common." What does he mean by "common"? Immediately following this passage is an account of how Scout rubbed her head against the head of Miss Rachel's cook's son in an effort to catch ringworm from him and

thus avoid school. What do these two incidents taken together tell us about Scout's understanding of the word "nigger"? What does her use of the term tell us about Maycomb? About Atticus?

2. When Scout asks Atticus why he is going to defend Tom Robinson if he knows he can't win, Atticus replies: "Simply because we were licked a hundred years before we started is no reason for us not to try to win" (p. 80). What does he mean?

3. Why does Cousin Francis call Atticus a "nigger-lover"? Why does he say that Atticus is "ruining the family" by defending Tom? What does Atticus reveal of himself when he tells Uncle Jack that he had "hoped to get through life without a case of this kind"?

4. Who explains to Scout what Atticus means by saying "It's a sin to kill a mockingbird"? How does this passage help you to interpret the meaning of the novel's title?

5. Atticus reveals his ability with a rifle when he shoots a mad dog. Why has he kept that ability a secret from his children? Why had he given up hunting? What does Jem mean when he says, following the mad dog incident, that he wouldn't care if Atticus couldn't do a thing?

6. Why does Atticus have Jem read to Mrs. Dubose? Is there any indication, at this point, how the sessions with Mrs. Dubose contribute to the dominant themes of the novel?

CHAPTERS 12-22

1. Why does Calpurnia use "colored-folks talk" at the church instead of the language she uses in the Finch household? How does the church visit help to advance the Tom Robinson plot?

2. Aunt Alexandra is particularly concerned with "background." What does she mean by the term? What is Atticus' attitude toward family pride?

3. How does Dill's arrival after running away from home help to explain what the author is saying about Atticus as a father? In what way might we compare Dill with Boo Radley? Why, according to Dill, hasn't Boo run away?

4. What does Link Deas mean when he tells Atticus, "You've got everything to lose from this, Atticus. I mean everything" (p.

148)? Why is Jem afraid for Atticus' safety after this meeting in the front yard?

5. What events preceding this chapter have prepared us for Scout's comments to Mr. Cunningham?

6. What two events does Scout associate in the following passage: "I was very tired, and was drifting into sleep when the memory of Atticus calmly folding his newspaper and pushing back his hat became Atticus standing in the middle of an empty waiting street, pushing up his glasses. The full meaning of the night's events hit me and I began crying" (p. 158)? What is the "full meaning" that hits her?

7. Atticus says that Mr. Underwood "despises Negroes, won't have one near him" (p. 158). Why then does he help Atticus guard Tom?

8. What explanation does Jem give for Dolphus Raymond's drinking from a paper bag? What is the real reason? Why does Mr. Raymond reveal his secret to Scout and Dill? Explain Mr. Raymond's comment about Dill: "Things haven't caught up with that one's instinct yet. Let him get a little older and he won't get sick and cry" (p. 203).

9. Where do the children sit to watch the trial? Who takes them there? Where did they first meet him? Why do you think the author places them there?

10. What habit does Judge Taylor have that fascinates Scout? What unusual physical characteristic does Mr. Gilmer have? How do these details add to the story?

11. When do we first hear of Bob Ewell? When does he first appear? What do we know of his appearance? What facts do we have about him before the trial? How do these details help to determine our attitude toward the trial? What evidence is there for believing Ewell's story?

12. Why does Mayella object to being called "Miss Mayella"? Do you feel sorry for her? Why, or why not? How does her characterization affect your opinion of Tom?

13. Why does Mr. Gilmer call Tom "boy"? Why does Mr. Gilmer so strongly emphasize Tom's comment that he felt sorry for Mayella? Does the prosecutor prove Tom's guilt?

14. How does the author make Tom's story seem more believ-

able than the Ewells' account? Does Atticus prove Tom's innocence?

15. What does Atticus mean in his speech to the jury when he
says, "Thomas Jefferson once said that all men are created equal.
. . . There is a tendency in this year of grace, 1935, for certain people to use this phrase out of context" (p. 207)? Does his discussion
of equality (pp. 207-208) offend his listeners? Does it change
their attitude toward Negroes? Is it meant to?

16. Why does Atticus, who, according to Scout, "never loosened
a scrap of clothing until he undressed at bedtime," unbutton his
vest and collar, loosen his tie, and take off his coat during his
speech to the jury (p. 205)?

17. While the crowd waits for the jury to return with its ver-
dict, Scout is reminded for the second time of a "deserted, waiting,
empty street" (p. 213). What is the reason for the association in
her mind of these two events? Why do you think the author refers to mockingbirds in both of these scenes?

18. Why does Reverend Sykes ask Scout to stand up as her
father leaves the courtroom? Why do the Negroes send food to
Atticus the morning after the trial? What does Miss Maudie mean
when she tells the children, "We're the safest folks in the world.
. . . We're so rarely called on to be Christians, but when we are,
we've got men like Atticus to go for us" (p. 218)? Do the children
understand what she means?

CHAPTERS 23-31

1. Why, though Atticus lost the case, does Bob Ewell spit in
Atticus' face and tell him "he'd get him if it took the rest of his
life" (p. 219)? What is Atticus' reaction? How does Aunty respond to the threat? What is the effect on the reader?

2. Why does Scout conclude that Aunty has come to live with
them "to help us choose our friends" (p. 227)? On what does Aunty
base her choice? How does her choice differ from Scout's?

3. How does Jem define "background"? How does his definition
differ from Aunty's? Compare both with Miss Maudie's use of the
word: "The handful of people in this town with background" (p.
239).

4. What does the missionary society tea tell us about the Chris-

tian ladies of Maycomb? Scout says that "if Aunty could be a lady at a time like this, so could I" (p. 240). What does Scout mean by "lady"? Compare this statement with Jem's comment about his father (p. 103): "Atticus is a gentleman, just like me."

5. When Scout wants to "mash" a "roly-poly," Jem stops her because, he says, "they don't bother you" (p. 241). How does this image relate to Helen Robinson's reaction when she hears of Tom's death (p. 243)? How do both relate to what Mr. Underwood says in his editorial about Tom's death (p. 243)? What do these images suggest about the meaning of the mockingbird image? The mad dog scene? Tom's crippled arm?

6. When Scout returns to school for the third grade, why is she no longer afraid of the Radley Place? Why does she feel remorse when she passes the house? What has helped her to develop an understanding of Boo's feelings? How has her fantasy about Boo Radley changed?

7. How does Aunty's "pinprick of apprehension" (p. 256) affect the mood of the story? What does Scout mean in the closing sentence of Chapter 27 by "longest journey"? How do details such as these contribute to the suspense of the novel?

8. As Scout and Jem leave for the Hollowe'en pageant, they hear a mockingbird at the Radley Place. Jem says, "Boo must not be at home" (p. 257). What does he mean? In terms of all that the mockingbird image has come to represent in this novel, what reason do you think the author has for this reference?

9. What devices does the author use to build tension and excitement before the scene of Bob Ewell's attack? The attack is seen only from Scout's limited perspective. What effect does this point of view have on our reaction to the scene?

10. Why doesn't Sheriff Heck Tate arrest Ewell's killer? Who does Atticus first think Sheriff Tate is protecting? Why does Atticus change his mind and allow the sheriff to lie about the killing? How does Scout explain to her father that she understands his decision?

11. Why does Boo want Scout to walk him home? Scout realizes, as she stands on the Radley front porch, that "Atticus was right" (p. 282). Right about what? How does another reference to *The Gray Ghost* (p. 283), the book first mentioned in Chapter 1, contribute to our understanding of the novel?

12. In what way is Jem's broken arm—the image that opens and closes the novel—connected to the Tom Robinson story? The Boo Radley story? How are the two stories related to each other? How are the stories brought together in the working out of the plot? In what way does the mockingbird image serve as a link between them?

13. What connection is there between the name *Finch* and the title of the story? What does the name *Atticus* mean? Is there any significance for the novel in Jem's being named "Jeremy Atticus Finch"?

14. A character serving as narrator may be a reliable guide to the values intended by the author. Or the author may create an unreliable narrator and another character whose values and re-actions are closer to those intended. Who supplies the facts in this novel? Who provides judgments of the meaning of those facts? Who speaks for the values of the novel itself? What are these values in *To Kill a Mockingbird?*

Additional Novels for Class Reading

Teachers may wish to have entire classes read and discuss one or more of the following novels in addition to, or in place of, one or more of the novels in the suggested novel sequence. The novels listed here were recommended by pilot-school teachers, members of the state-appointed committee on literature, or the staff of the English Curriculum Study Center because their literary merit and their appeal to students could justify their being taught to entire classes.

No attempt has been made to group the novels according to grade level or reading difficulty, for the writers of this volume realize that teachers who are familiar with the novels on this list and with their own classes know exactly where any work should be taught.

Annixter, Paul. *Swiftwater*. New York: Hill and Wang, 1950. (Paperback editions—Houghton Mifflin's Riverside Literature Series and Paperback Library).

Barrett, William E. *The Lilies of the Field*. Garden City, New York: Doubleday, 1962. (Paperback edition—Popular Library).

Bradbury, Ray. *Dandelion Wine*. Garden City, New York: Doubleday, 1957. (Paperback edition—Bantam Books).

Cather, Willa. *My Ántonia*. Boston: Houghton Mifflin, 1918. (Paperback edition—Houghton Mifflin's Riverside Literature Series).

Dickens, Charles. *David Copperfield*. (Paperback editions—Airmont, Dell, Modern Library College Editions, Penguin Books, Houghton Mifflin's Riverside Literature Series, Signet Classics, L. W. Singer, and Washington Square Press).

Dickens, Charles. *Oliver Twist*. (Paperback editions—Airmont, Dolphin

Books, Holt, Rinehart & Winston, Perennial Library, Signet Classics, and Washington Square Press).

Fast, Howard. *April Morning.* New York: Crown, 1961. (Paperback edition—Bantam Books).

Forbes, Esther. *Johnny Tremain.* Boston: Houghton Mifflin, 1943. (Paperback edition—Houghton Mifflin's Riverside Literature Series).

Forester, C. S. *Beat to Quarters.* Boston: Little, Brown, 1937. (Paperback editions—Bantam Books, and Houghton Mifflin's Riverside Literature Series).

Hersey, John. *A Single Pebble.* New York: Knopf, 1956. (Paperback edition—Bantam Books).

Kessel, Joseph. *The Lion.* New York: Knopf, 1959.

Kipling, Rudyard. *"Captains Courageous."* (Paperback editions—Airmont, and Signet Classics).

Krumgold, Joseph. *Onion John.* New York: Crowell, 1959.

Rawlings, Marjorie Kinnan. *The Yearling.* New York: Scribner, 1938. (Paperback edition—Scribner Library).

Shotwell, Louisa R. *Roosevelt Grady.* New York: World, 1963. (Paperback edition—Grossett & Dunlap).

Sperry, Armstrong. *Call It Courage.* New York: Macmillan, 1940. (Paperback edition—Scholastic Book Services).

Stevenson, Robert Louis. *Kidnapped.* (Paperback editions—Airmont, Collier Books, Dell, Penguin Books, Perennial Library, Pyramid Books, Scholastic Book Services, Signet Classics, and Washington Square Press).

Stevenson, Robert Louis. *Treasure Island.* (Paperback editions—Airmont, Collier Books, Dell, Macmillan's Literary Heritage Edition, Penguin Books, Perennial Library, Pyramid Books, Houghton Mifflin's Riverside Literature Series, L. W. Singer, Signet Classics, and Washington Square Press).

Stolz, Mary. *The Sea Gulls Woke Me.* New York: Harper, 1951. (Paperback edition—Scholastic Book Services).

Part IV
BACKGROUNDS FOR ALLUSION AND SYMBOL

To be a sensitive reader of literature, a student needs some knowledge of classical mythology and of Biblical story. The units on mythology and the *Odyssey* in this section give eighth grade students some of the background they need to understand allusion and symbol in literature. The extensive unit on teaching the Bible as literature will be published in a separate volume in this English Curriculum Study Series.

No attempt has been made to provide the teacher with day-to-day lesson plans for the unit on mythology or for the unit on the *Odyssey*. Instead, the writers of the units provided the teachers with a critical and pedagogical basis for the development of units of instruction. The role of the teacher in forming the materials for his own class is crucial. The aims of sound courses of study can be realized only by qualified teachers in their classes.

Classical Mythology

ROY L. FELSHER

Suggested texts

Edith Hamilton's *Mythology* (Mentor Books) is recommended for average to talented students. The headnotes and critical observations are valuable and the style is lucid. As this is a "retelling" rather than an actual translation, students may want to compare it with other versions (see bibliography). For less able students, the teacher may prefer Olivia Coolidge's *Greek Myths* (Houghton Mifflin). The stories as retold by Miss Coolidge are more accessible, though less complete, than those in Miss Hamilton's book.

A book for teachers

Robert Graves' *The Greek Myths* (Penguin, 2 volumes) is a useful reference work. Graves has assembled most of the extant versions of the Greek myths and added valuable historical and critical notes. He also summarizes recent contributions to the study of myths from psychologists, anthropologists, and historians. Other important studies are listed in the bibliography at the end of the unit.

Stages of mythology

Mythology is, at first, a simple and primitive effort of the imagination to come to terms with a hostile environment—to make what is nonhuman comprehensible in human terms. The typical product of this effort is a story about a god. At this stage, myths are closely identified with primitive ritual and religious belief. Later on, mythology begins to merge with history, and battles, dynasties, or great heroes are celebrated within this traditional frame. Still later, myth comes to be accepted as literature. It provides an accumulated body of fiction that writers can draw upon for the plots, characters, or details which go into their stories. In classical Greece and Rome there were poets of genius contributing to every stage of this development, and the result is a system of mythology that commands our attention to this day.

This unit aims to acquaint students with a representative selection of classical myths; to suggest ways that mythology may preserve the ideals, perceptions, and values of a civilization; and to indicate the importance of these myths to subsequent literature. The remarks which follow deal primarily with the myths as literature. Questions direct the students to significant details in each story, and the notes for the teacher are written as guidelines for further class discussion.

I. MYTHS OF THE CREATION

Myths of the creation were never completely systematized or reduced to a single dogma. This may explain why there are unaccountable gaps in the story or even contrasting versions of a single event. Miss Hamilton groups the best-known stories into one fairly continuous narrative (pp. 63-75); but teachers may also want to consult Graves (I, 27-50) for supplementary material.

A. QUESTIONS FOR CREATION OF THE COSMOS

1. What were the first existing things?

2. Is the universe described in Greek mythology merely inert matter, or is it from the first comprised of living things? Explain your answer.

3. What are the human characteristics of Night and Erebus, or Earth and Heaven?

4. When writers give human qualities to inanimate objects, we say that the objects are personified. As we progress through the

various "stages" of the creation, do we find more or less personification? Support your answer by citing specific passages.

5. Describe the first creatures who lived on earth. Were they beautiful or ugly? Peace-loving or ferocious? Intelligent or stupid? What finally became of them?

6. Who were the Titans? Are they presented as vague and impersonal beings, or are we told enough about them to form a definite picture of their character and temperament? What are the main characteristics of each of the following: Cronus, Rhea, Prometheus, Atlas? How are these qualities apparent in their actions?

7. How did Cronus attempt to evade what fate had decreed for him? Was he successful?

8. Who were the Olympians? How were they able to triumph over the Titans?

Notes for the teacher

(a) One way to view this mythological account of the creation is to see a gradual movement from chaos to order, from ugliness to beauty, from brute force to force that is exercised and regulated by intelligent beings. In each case the movement is from circumstances hostile to humanity toward circumstances which reflect human (and especially Greek) ideals: order, beauty, intelligence, and the reign of law. In other words, it is a myth of progress, depicting the gradual betterment of the world to a point where it is able to sustain human life.

(b) Personification, a basic literary device, is quite important to this account of the creation. Note that the first existing things—Night and Erebus, Earth and Heaven—have only a few human attributes. They couple and beget children, they know harmony and war, but they remain shadowy and indistinct. As we ascend the scale of creation, however, the personification becomes fuller and more precise; in fact, the later stages of the creation are more advanced precisely because they exhibit more distinct (and more desirable) human qualities. The Giants and the Hundred-headed Monsters are deplorably ugly and antisocial. These are to be replaced by divine beings in whom beauty replaces ugliness and intelligence governs strength. But it is not simply a change from Ugliness to Beauty, from Force to Law. The speculative imagination which created these myths does not rest comfortably in abstractions. It was through the device of personification that the Greek poets were able to humanize these abstractions and so make the nonhuman world comprehensible in human terms.

(c) Is there a governing intelligence behind the creation? Clearly, there is not. In this account there is no omniscient and omnipotent God who creates the universe by divine fiat. At best there is an inscrutable Fate which merely ratifies what is certain to occur. The Greeks had another story of the creation (retold by Graves, I, 34) in which the God Of All Things deliberately designs and constructs the universe. This is quite unlike the story told by Hamilton—resembling instead the account in the Old Testament. Perhaps the teacher will want to read this version to the class. That two such contradictory accounts of the creation could exist side by side is a testimony to the tolerance and lack of dogmatism which characterized the Greeks.

B.   THE CREATION OF MAN

There are several myths which describe the creation of man. In one story Prometheus and Epimetheus are asked by the gods to create mankind. In another version man is created by the gods, not once but several times, as each of the great races of man disappeared and had to be replaced. These two accounts are not so much contradictory as simply independent of each other. They illustrate once more that Greek mythology had an unsystematic development and was never unified into a single body.

Questions

1. What is the meaning of the name Epimetheus? What is the meaning of Prometheus? How do the two Titans justify these names? In this story man is the last of earth's creatures to be created; is he the most fortunate or the least fortunate of earth's inhabitants?

2. What were the "five ages of man"? What qualities do you associate with gold (wealth, splendor, value)? What qualities do

you associate with silver, brass, or iron? Why is each metal appropriate to the age which it symbolizes? According to the myth, is the final age of iron—in which we presumably live—a good one, or is it inferior to those which preceded it?

Notes for the teacher

(a) Prometheus means "forethought"; Epimetheus means "afterthought." In this myth Prometheus showers man with gifts which enable him to stand forth as the apex of creation, the last and best of earth's creatures. In the second version, the men of iron are clearly inferior to the races which have passed away, history is a record of decline, and men yearn for the lost splendors of the golden age.

(b) The two stories, therefore, convey opposite attitudes toward history. In one version we find a myth of progress, because each stage of the creation has been an improvement on what came before. The second version is a myth of decline, as each stage of the creation is somewhat worse than the one which preceded it. The first will appeal to those who view history as a record of achievement; the second will probably appeal to those who look back with nostalgia to "the good old days" when things were better. The popularity of these stories may be due in part to the way that they capture and preserve these two deep-seated views of history.

II. NATURE MYTHS

A great many nature myths tell about the death and rebirth, or disappearance and return, of a god. This divine activity is often associated with some common cyclical process in nature. The god may be a sun-god, dying at night and being reborn at dawn; or he may be a god of vegetation, dying in autumn and reviving in the spring. Perhaps this death-and-rebirth theme is derived from a simple analogy with these changes in the natural world; or perhaps, as anthropologists believe, the stories are more directly related to primitive religious rituals. In either case, the myths of Demeter and Persephone, Dionysus, and the so-called Flower

Myths clearly share this common theme. The questions which follow direct attention to specific aspects of each story; the notes may suggest additional topics for discussion.

A.   QUESTIONS FOR DEMETER AND PERSEPHONE (PP. 47-54)

1. What was Demeter's chief function as a goddess?
2. How was Persephone abducted?
3. Is the fate of Persephone merely a personal tragedy, or does it have larger consequences for the gods and for mankind?
4. By what means does Demeter finally win the return of her daughter?
5. What trick forces Persephone to return to the underworld? How much time must she spend away from her mother?
6. How does Demeter greet the return of her daughter? What benefits does she perform for mankind?
7. Persephone is often depicted on Greek vases surrounded by fruits or flowers. Why are these associations appropriate? How do flowers figure in her abduction? How does a pomegranate mar her escape from the underworld? Why is she associated with the season of spring?
8. How does this myth account for the season of winter? How does it account for the location of Demeter's shrine at Eleusis?

Note for the teacher

The story of Demeter and Persephone is possibly related to primitive rituals that sought to insure good harvests. These rituals at one time called for a human sacrifice. The victim's blood would be sprinkled upon the barren fields in the hope that this might promote fertility. Later, the human sacrifice was replaced by a puppet-like figure composed of vegetable matter. Descriptions of this ceremony may have been the original source for the Demeter-Persephone story, which was changed as it was reinterpreted for each new generation. Graves believes that "the myth accounts for the winter burial of a female corn-puppet, which was uncovered in the early spring and found to be sprouting; this pre-Hellenic custom survived in the countryside in Classical times . . ." (I, 93).

B.   QUESTIONS FOR DIONYSUS (PP. 54-62)

1. What did Dionysus give to men?

2. Describe the early wanderings of Dionysus. How was the god received when he returned to Greece?

3. What is the fate of those who strive with the gods? Consider the punishment administered to a) the band of pirates, b) Lycurgus, c) Pentheus. In each case is the punishment just? Defend your answer.

4. In what way did Dionysus demonstrate his love for his mother?

5. Why was the worship of Dionysus associated with ecstatic reverie? Is such ecstasy always the result of wine-drinking, or may it have a different cause? Explain.

6. How did the worship of Dionysus give man hope of an afterlife?

7. What was the festival of Dionysus and what took place there? Why should the worship of Dionysus, rather than some other god, find expression in theater?

8. Compare the myths of Dionysus and Demeter. You may want to consider the following themes: a) the descent into the underworld, b) the cycle of death and rebirth, c) the association of the god with fertility, d) the changing seasons. How might one account for the parallels?

Notes for the teacher

(a)   Parallels between the myths of Demeter and Dionysus are usually attributed to the fact that both have a common origin in primitive ritual. The annual cycle of the seasons would be represented by a divine figure which dies in the autumn or is killed with the gathering of the harvest and the vintage and returns again in the spring. The community would have special ceremonies to observe this death and rebirth, and perhaps it was a description of this ceremony which in time gave rise to these nature myths. The divine figure might be male (Dionysus) or female (Persephone), but the basic symbolism of death-and-rebirth or sterility-and-fertility would remain constant despite other changes. In this way a single ritual might give rise to a great number of related myths.

(b) Why is the childhood of Dionysus spent outside Greece? Why does he travel to Libya and Crete? And why does he encounter so much resistance on his journey home? "The main clue to Dionysus' mystic history is the spread of the vine cult over Europe. Wine was not invented by the Greeks; it seems to have been first imported in jars from Crete. Grapes grew wild on the southern coast of the Black Sea, whence their cultivation spread to Mount Nysa in Libya, by way of Palestine, and so to Crete. . . . Dionysus' triumph was that wine everywhere superseded other intoxicants" (Graves, I, 107).

C. QUESTIONS FOR THE FLOWER MYTHS (PP. 85-91)

1. Miss Hamilton tells two different stories about Narcissus, each of which attempts to explain the origin of a flower. Which of the two myths do you prefer? Why? Which offers a more convincing explanation? Which is more dramatic? Does one offer better characterizations? Support your answers with illustrations from the text.

2. There are also two stories about Hyacinth. One story makes his death seem accidental, the other makes it a deliberate murder. Which is more dramatic? Which is more believable? Why do you think so?

3. What qualities would you expect to find in a person who was described as "an Adonis"? Is this a compliment? How does the story of Adonis illustrate these qualities?

4. What qualities would you expect to find in a person who was described as "a Narcissus"? Is this a compliment?

5. Compare these Flower Myths with the stories of Demeter and Dionysus. You will want to consider the following themes: a) the theme of death and rebirth, b) the association of the slain youth with fertility. What might account for these parallels?

Note for the teacher

The parallel themes in each of these nature myths could be explained by a common ritual origin. Miss Hamilton examines the ritual behind the Narcissus-Hyacinth-Adonis myth (p. 89); teachers may want to consult Graves (I, 72) for additional information.

III. MYTHS OF HEROES

The first myths are always stories about the gods. In time, however, the focus of mythology begins to shift from religion to history, from stories about the gods to stories about men. In the myths of Perseus or Theseus, it is the human hero who occupies the center of interest; and the gods, when they do appear, assume supporting roles in which they either advance or retard the hero's progress. Of course, the attributes of the hero often correspond more to human wishes than to human reality. The typical mythic hero performs deeds of courage and endurance far beyond the powers of ordinary men. Yet he is still bound by human limitation, capacity for error, and eventual death. The gods are superior to men in kind; the heroes are superior only in degree.

The questions which follow direct attention to important details in each story. The notes discuss the relation between myth and history and examine certain recurrent themes in heroic myth.

A. QUESTIONS FOR PERSEUS (PP. 141-48)

1. Why did King Acrisius have reason to fear his daughter?
2. Whose child did this daughter bear?
3. How did the king try to dispose of Perseus? Why was he unsuccessful?
4. Describe the Gorgons. Who was Medusa?
5. Why does Perseus undertake to slay Medusa?
6. Can Perseus accomplish this feat unaided? What assistance does Hermes provide? What gift does Perseus receive from Athena?
7. Does Perseus have less heroic stature because he has to turn to the gods for help? Will the gods come to the assistance of ordinary men? What qualities in Perseus have proved him worthy of divine favor?
8. Describe the Gray Women. What must Perseus receive from them?

9. How does Perseus overcome Medusa? What happens to those who look upon the Gorgon's head?

10. What happens to King Acrisius? Is his death accidental, or is it the fulfillment of a prophecy?

B.   QUESTIONS FOR THESEUS (PP. 149-58)

1. How does King Aegeus provide for his son?

2. What qualities does Theseus display on his journey to Athens? How does he benefit the countryside? How does he demonstrate his concern for justice?

3. Who prompts King Aegeus to murder his son? For what reason? Why does the plot fail?

4. Describe the Minotaur. Why must Athenian youths be sacrificed to this monster?

5. What was the Labyrinth? Who constructed it? Why were the Athenian youths placed within the maze?

6. How did Theseus find his way out of the Labyrinth? Who assisted him?

7. How did the Aegean Sea get its name?

8. What sort of government did Theseus establish at Athens?

9. Did Theseus perform his greatest deeds unaided, or did he rely upon the help of others? Give examples.

10. Do the heroes of myth act entirely from self-interest, or do they act in behalf of a larger community? In what way do the heroic deeds of Theseus symbolize the ideals of the Athenian democracy?

C.   QUESTIONS FOR HERCULES (PP. 159-72)

1. What incidents in his childhood indicate that Hercules will be a great hero?

2. How did Hercules express his dislike for music lessons?

3. Does Hercules act on the basis of intellect or emotion? How does this lead him into difficulties? Give examples.

4. Why did Hera dislike Hercules? How does she punish him?

5. How did Hercules slay his family? Is he guilty of murder, or can he plead innocence because of temporary insanity? What is Theseus' opinion? What is Hercules' own judgment?

6. What are the twelve labors of Hercules?

7. Who was Antaeus? What was the source of his strength? How did Hercules manage to overcome him?

8. What great sacrifice did Alcestis make for her husband? Do you think he deserved such loyalty? How did Hercules' behavior on this occasion reveal both his characteristic virtues and his limitations?

9. Is there such a thing as heroic suffering? What evidence is there that Hercules suffered more than other men or for better reasons?

10. Compare the stories of Hercules with those of Theseus. How do such myths enable us to compare the ideals and values of the Athenians with those of other Greeks? Give examples that might form the basis for such comparison.

D.   QUESTIONS FOR JASON (PP. 118-30)

1. What was the Golden Fleece?

2. Why does Jason undertake his journey? Do Perseus, Theseus, and Hercules also take long journeys? For what purpose? Is it merely to arrive at a destination? Or does it provide the hero with new opportunities for adventure? Can you think of other myths in which the journey is an important literary theme?

3. Who were the Argonauts?

4. Among Jason's crew are men like Hercules, Peleus, Orpheus, and the brothers Castor and Pollux. Where have you encountered these heroes before? Do you think that the original audience for this story would have recognized such names? Can you see advantages in the storyteller's being able to draw his characters from a great system of mythology?

5. Why does Hercules abandon the quest of the Golden Fleece? Is his reaction to the death of Hylas consistent with what you know about him from other stories? Give another example of his immoderate grief.

6. What are the Harpies? Why were the sons of Boreas the only men who could destroy them?

7. Who was Talus? In which myth have you already encountered an "age of bronze men"? How is Talus overcome?

8. Why does Medea decide to aid Jason? Is the decision her own, or is she governed by the will of Aphrodite?

9. What deed must Jason perform before he can win the Golden Fleece? How is the deed accomplished?

10. What further assistance does Medea lend Jason? How does she help him to escape from Colchis? How does she dispose of Pelias?

11. Is Jason guilty of ingratitude? What explanation does he offer in defense of his second marriage? Can you accept this?

12. Do you condemn Jason for his conduct? Do you condemn Medea for her revenge? Or do you condemn Aphrodite for prompting their union? Is it possible to place the blame solely on one character?

Notes for the Teacher

(a)   The heroic myths allow students to examine the relation between myth and history. Stories about the gods may not yield much historical information, but the heroes are men, and their struggles are always set within a historical frame.

Though historians of Greece and Rome did not accept the literal truth of each story, they did believe that many heroic myths had a historical basis. We know, for example, that Plutarch, the Roman historian, thought that the myths of Theseus were based on fact. Plutarch believed that Crete, the land of King Minos, had once ruled Athens; that it exacted hostages from the Athenians to insure good behavior; that Theseus was able to invade and conquer Cnossus, the capital of Crete; and that this conquest enabled him to achieve a peace treaty between the two powers which was cemented by the marriage of the Athenian king to Ariadne, a princess of Crete. These events are clearly paralleled in the Theseus myths.

In 1902, in an excavation on the island of Crete, Sir Arthur Evans discovered the buried palace of King Minos and the ancient city of Cnossus. The palace was huge. It had a floor plan of more than 8,000 square feet, and the structure itself was as large as Buckingham Palace. Moreover, the palace had an unusually complex arrangement of rooms and corridors (could this be the origin of the story about the Labyrinth?) while on the palace walls there were many paintings of bulls, which were apparently worshiped at Cnossus (and which may explain the story of the Minotaur). Perhaps it is not surprising, then, that Theseus' victory over King Minos should be celebrated in the myth as a symbolic victory over the Minotaur (which means literally the "Bull of Minos"). It is generally acknowledged today that there is at least this core of historical fact behind the myth. (Ceram offers an exciting account of the discovery of Cnossus and its relation to the myths of Theseus in his *Gods, Graves and Scholars*, which is listed in "Further Reading for Students.")

Another myth which appears to have some historical basis is the story of Jason and the Golden Fleece. As Robert Graves tells this story, the voyage of the Argonauts is based upon some risky trading ventures that the Greeks undertook when they first became a sea power. These were, in fact, piratical raids along the shores of the Black Sea—raids which were designed to open up that region to Greek trade. The object of the voyage was not a Golden Fleece but perhaps amber, which was much in demand at that time, or, what is even more probable, gold. There were large quantities of alluvial gold in the Black Sea region which the natives would collect by spreading great fleeces in the waters of a river bed. From here it is but a short step to the notion of a "golden fleece." It is also worth mentioning that the crew of Jason's ship varies considerably from one version of the myth to another. The reason would seem to be that "every city needed a representative Argonaut to justify its trading rights on the Black Sea, and traveling minstrels were always willing to introduce another name or two. . . . Not even the most hardened skeptic seems to have doubted that the legend was in the main historical, or that the voyage took place . . ." (Graves, II, 223). One should not assume, then, that heroic myth is wholly fictitious. Teachers interested in pursuing these historical backgrounds should consult the notes to Graves's edition of *The Greek Myths*.

(b) The historical interest of these stories is, for our purposes, secondary to their literary interest. Our main concern is with the way imagination acts upon the raw materials. It is worth noting, for example, that heroic myths are strikingly similar to each other in form and content. In his study of *The Hero*, Lord Raglan has called attention to this "heroic pattern" and summarized some of its recurrent themes:

> The hero's mother is a royal virgin; his father is a king and often a near relative of his mother, but the circumstances of his conception are unusual, and he is also reputed to be the son of a god. At birth an attempt is made, usually by his father or his maternal grandfather, to kill him, but he is spirited away, and reared by foster parents in a far country. We are told none of his childhood, but on reaching manhood he returns to or goes to his future kingdom. After a victory over the king and/or giant, dragon, or wild beast, he marries a princess, often the daughter of his predecessor, and becomes king (pp. 174-75).

Eighth grade students cannot be expected to arrive unaided at this heroic pattern; but with some assistance from the teacher they should be able to recognize basic similarities in the myths of Perseus, Theseus, Hercules, and Jason.

Perhaps the best approach is to ask a few simple questions about each of these heroic myths, allowing the students to infer a common pattern. For example:

1. Who are the hero's parents? Are they great and powerful or poor and insignificant?
2. What is the relationship between the hero and the ruler of the land?
3. What journey, voyage, or quest must the hero undertake?
4. What dangers does he encounter on these travels?
5. What happens to the hero when he returns home?

By their responses to these questions, students should recognize a basic pattern in the myths. The next series of questions should help them to explore the significance of the pattern.

1. Why is the ancestry of the hero always stressed in these stories?
2. What is the significance of the hero's exile from his native

land? Do young people today sometimes undergo a period of estrangement from parents, home, or society? Why is such "exile" sometimes a necessary step toward fuller maturity?

3. What is symbolized by the hero's journey? Could an ordinary man undertake this journey? Does modern society admire the man who acts with prudence or the man who takes great risks for the sake of an important goal?

4. What evils or terrors might be symbolized by the monsters that the hero slays? Are these necessarily physical evils, or could they be psychological and social evils as well? What "monsters" might an individual have to confront today?

5. Does the hero act entirely from self-interest, or does he serve the interests of a larger community? Why is it significant that the hero becomes a king?

Class discussion will probably conclude that the hero is not a self-absorbed egoist—that he acts in behalf of a community. In fact, the hero performs the role of a savior, for he alone can enter into unknown regions, confront the monsters which threaten civilized life, slay them, and return to become the new king. On this social plane, heroic myth describes a struggle between generations (the new king frequently murders the old), but in the end the struggle always benefits society.

(c) This kind of investigation need not be limited to classical myth. The "heroic pattern" appears with slight modification in other great works. For example: Where does a pattern of exile-adventure-return appear in the Bible? (Consider the stories of Jacob, Joseph, and Moses.) Which Biblical characters must perform tasks or labors in order to achieve their goals? (Consider Abraham, Jacob, and Jonah.) How does such comparison of Greek and Biblical heroes illustrate the qualities that were most admired in each culture? How do the virtues and limitations of Hercules compare with those of Samson? How does Theseus compare to Solomon as an ideal ruler? Discussion of the heroic pattern thus takes us beyond formal considerations to an account of the changing values of Western civilization as they are revealed in its greatest heroes.

IV. MYTHOLOGY AND LITERATURE

The classical myths were told and retold many times without losing their freshness. The earliest writers told these stories with sincere religious piety; the later writers offered them as entertaining fictions. The stories which appear below have all achieved popularity in their late versions, when myth was no longer identified with religion but was clearly recognized as a form of literature. The questions direct attention to their characteristic features: precise delineation of character, functional symbolism, and a tendency to moral allegory.

A. QUESTIONS FOR PHÄETHON (PP. 131-34)

1. Why does Phäethon feel that he has to prove his identity?

2. Why does Helios let the boy drive his chariot, even when he knows that it will be dangerous?

3. What does it mean to promise something "by the river Styx"?

4. What will happpen to the world should the sun-chariot stray from its course?

5. Why does Zeus intervene? What punishment does he administer to Phäethon? Is it just? Defend your answer.

6. Is Phäethon a hero, or a fool? Explain.

7. Is there a moral to this story? Try to state it in your own words.

B. QUESTIONS FOR DAEDALUS AND ICARUS (PP. 139-40)

1. For what cause have Daedalus and Icarus been imprisoned?

2. How do they plan to escape?

3. What advice does Daedalus offer his son? Is it good advice? Why does Icarus disregard it?

4. Icarus (a) deserves his fate because he disobeyed his father,

   (b) is foolish because he follows impulse instead of reason,

   (c) is to be admired because he was prepared to risk much for a thrilling experience.

5. What is meant by the phrase, "an Icarian adventure"?

C. QUESTIONS FOR BELLEROPHON (PP. 134-37)

1. Describe the great horse Pegasus.
2. Why does Bellerophon seek to ride him?
3. Which goddess comes to his aid?
4. Why is Bellerophon sent to kill the Chimaera? How does he overcome this monster?
5. What is the reason for Bellerophon's downfall?
6. In what way does Bellerophon's wish to ride Pegasus resemble Phäethon's desire to ride the sun-chariot? Why does one succeed where the other failed?
7. How does Bellerophon's journey to Olympus resemble Icarus' flight to the heavens? Why do both meet with disaster?

D. QUESTIONS FOR MIDAS (PP. 278-79)

1. What service does Midas perform for the god Bacchus?
2. What is his reward? What is meant by the phrase, "a Midas touch"?
3. Why must he implore the god to take back his gift?
4. What service does Midas perform for Apollo and Pan?
5. How is he rewarded?
6. What is Midas' dominant character trait in each story?

E. QUESTIONS FOR ARACHNE (PP. 288-89)

1. Which goddess was renowned for her skill at the loom?
2. Why does Arachne claim that her own work is superior?
3. Describe the contest between Arachne and Minerva. What was the outcome?

F. QUESTIONS FOR PYGMALION AND GALATEA (PP. 108-11)

1. Why had Pygmalion remained a bachelor?
2. What motive did he have for attempting a statue of the ideal woman? Do you agree that such ideals are more often found in art than in life? Explain.
3. What happened to Pygmalion after he completed his statue?
4. Why did Pygmalion consider his passion hopeless? Was this

an appropriate punishment for a man who had scorned women? Defend your answer.

5. How did Pygmalion indulge his love for the statue? What did Venus think of such behavior?

6. What sign did Venus send to Pygmalion? What had he asked for? What did he receive?

7. Does the story represent Pygmalion as a man to be admired or as a figure of fun? Explain.

G.   QUESTIONS FOR BAUCIS AND PHILEMON (PP. 111-13)

1. Why is hospitality of special importance to Hermes?

2. Why do he and Jupiter take on the appearance of poor wayfarers?

3. How do they "test" the townspeople? Do you think it is a fair test?

4. The house of Baucis and Philemon is described in some detail. Is this description irrelevant, or does it contribute to our understanding of the old couple? Why?

5. How do the gods reveal their true identity? Why is this sign more effective dramatically than a simple declaration?

6. How were the inhospitable townspeople punished?

7. How were Baucis and Philemon rewarded?

Notes for the teacher

(a)   The stories noted above have become popular in their later versions—when myth ceased to be regarded as an agent of religious belief and was frankly accepted as literature. It is often forgotten, however, that each of these stories has a long history. The version that we read was not invented by a single poet, but is rather the end result of a long line of poets.

The myth of Bellerophon, for example, was told by Homer, Hesiod, Pindar, Pausanias, Apollodorus, Ovid, and many others. It is not important for students to remember those names, but they should know that the story which appears in their anthology is only one of many versions of the same myth. The classical poet felt free to borrow his story from earlier writers when he thought that he could tell it better. He might even borrow elements from several different stories and fuse them into a single narrative. Thus, a myth told by a late Roman poet might contain elements borrowed from an early Greek poet, and even this Greek poet might have taken the elements of his story from some still earlier source. As a result, even the latest myths will contain episodes which have an origin far back in time.

The story of Bellerophon provides a good example of this process. In the version told by Miss Hamilton (p. 134) the myth has been shaped into a moral allegory which advises us against foolish pride; Bellerophon's downfall results from his rash attempt to scale Mt. Olympus, which was reserved for the gods. This much is clear. But there are other aspects of this story which do not contribute to the allegory and which may require explanation. What is the origin of the Chimaera? And how did this monster—part lion, part goat, part serpent—become associated with Bellerophon? The problem takes us far back into ancient history. According to Graves, the Chimaera is actually a symbol for a primitive nature goddess who was once worshiped throughout the Mediterranean region. Relics of this cult have been found in ancient Hittite dwellings in Crete and in Greece itself. The goddess frequently assumes a grotesque shape intended to symbolize the seasons of the year—lion for spring, goat for summer, serpent for winter. Eventually, this primitive cult was superseded by the Olympian gods, and the victory of Bellerophon over the Chimaera may once have symbolized this suppression of the old nature cult (Graves, I, 255). Of course, the poets who told and retold this story probably had little notion of its primitive origins. For them it was simply a good story—too good to dispense with, even if it did not contribute directly to the moral allegory that had become prominent in late versions of this myth.

The myth of Bellerophon is not necessarily a better story because it contains such primitive survivals; but attention to these factors should provide students with a better understanding of the way classical myth developed. Any late myth will contain elements which can be traced back in this way, either to an earlier poet or to an aspect of primitive belief. For further information teachers should consult the notes to Graves' edition of *The Greek Myths*.

(b) The writers of classical myth demonstrated that a great literature could emerge from conscious imitation. Each new generation of poets would retell the old stories, elaborating on familiar themes, inventing new episodes, adding new interpretations. At its best this was a process of creative imitation, for the writer would be judged upon how skillfully he could tell the old story or what new meanings he could bring to it. Classical mythology is still important to writers. It is an accumulated body of fiction that they can draw on for the plots, characters, or incidental details which enliven their work. Such imitation and adaptation demonstrates the continuing relevance of classical myth to our times.

Topics for written composition

1. Write a theme in which you compare a hero of myth with a hero from the Bible. You might want to compare Hercules and Samson, Perseus and David, or Theseus and Solomon. Your paper should make note of the differences as well as the similarities between these characters.

2. Many of the Olympian gods appear in more than one story. Write a theme in which you trace the character and behavior of a god through several myths. Does he remain the same sort of "person," or does he undergo important changes?

BIBLIOGRAPHY

A.   GENERAL REFERENCE WORKS

Kirkwood, G. *A Short Guide to Classical Mythology.* New York: Rinehart, 1959. Persons, places, and gods (with guides to pronunciation) are listed in a dictionary format.
LaRousse Encyclopedia of Mythology. New York: Prometheus, 1959. This includes detailed information and many illustrations.
Rose, H. J. *Handbook of Greek Mythology.* London: Metheun, 1928. Included in this standard work are an historical introduction and retellings of the myths.

B.   HISTORICAL BACKGROUND

Ceram, C. W. *Gods, Graves and Scholars.* New York: Knopf, 1952. Chapter 4 of this popular study of archeology investigates the background of myths about the Trojan War; Chapter 6 provides background for the myths of Perseus on Crete. These chapters may be recommended to students.

Finley, M. I. *The World of Odysseus*. New York: Viking, 1954. Reprinted in paperback by Meridian Books, 1961. As Mark Van Doren says in his preface to the Viking edition, this is an attempt to "sketch the human society of which Homer conceived his heroes to be a part."

C. MORE SPECIALIZED SCHOLARSHIP

Campbell, Joseph. *The Hero With A Thousand Faces*. New York: Pantheon, 1949. This is a study of heroic myths in Greek and other cultures.

Gaster, T. H. *Thespis*. Anchor Paperback, Ad30, 1960. The relationship between myth and ritual in the ancient Near East is explored in this book.

Lord Raglan. *The Hero*. New York: Oxford University Press, 1937. New York: Vintage Books, 1956. This is an introduction to the study of heroic myths.

Murray, Henry A., ed., *Myth and Mythmaking*. New York: George Braziller, 1960. In this anthology of modern critical essays, contributors discuss the historical development of mythology and evaluate the importance of myths to modern literature, politics, and religion.

FURTHER READING FOR STUDENTS

Each of the following is a popular retelling of classical myth:

Bulfinch, Thomas. *Bulfinch's Mythology*. New York: Dell, 1845.

Rouse, W. H. D. *Gods, Heroes and Men of Ancient Greece*. New York: Mentor, 1960.

Schwab, Gustave. *Gods and Heroes*. New York: Pantheon, 1946.

For students interested in an important and readable classical source —a translation rather than retelling of the original—the teacher might suggest Horace Gregory's translation of Ovid's *Metamorphoses* (Viking, 1938).

Teaching the *Odyssey**

ENGLISH CURRICULUM
STUDY CENTER STAFF

The *Odyssey* is one of the world's great books. From its own day to ours it has influenced poets (e.g., Virgil, Dante, Tennyson, and T. S. Eliot) and storytellers so profoundly that Western literature is permeated with references and allusions to it. For these reasons students should become acquainted with the *Odyssey* as early as possible. By the ninth grade students should be able to read the *Odyssey* with pleasure and profit, especially after having studied Greek mythology in the eighth grade.

There is no single, best approach to the *Odyssey*; the book is so rich that it can be read and enjoyed, and therefore taught, on many levels, and it is up to each ninth grade teacher to decide which approach or combination of approaches will be best for his students.

THE *ODYSSEY* AS AN ADVENTURE STORY

The first and most basic appeal of the *Odyssey* is as a superb adventure story. The strong and simple plot line—a man's struggle to get home after a long and terrible war—will keep students reading without any prodding from the teacher. The forces that conspire to keep Odysseus from getting home are so varied, so fascinating, and so frightening that they will easily sustain the stu-

* *Suggested Text:* Homer, The *Odyssey*, trans. E. V. Rieu, Penguin Classics, Baltimore, 95¢.

dents' interest; and the many tricks and stratagems that Odysseus employs in order to overcome these forces are so bold and clever that they will delight every reader. The central character, Odysseus, is especially appealing because of his humanity: he is neither a puppet in the hands of malignant gods nor an impossibly virtuous hero, but rather a complex and fascinating human being. He makes his own decisions and choices, and when he chooses badly, he suffers. His adventures are often strange, but they never seem contrived; instead, there is a perfect wedding of character and action. This combination of a heroic but still thoroughly human personality and a set of significant adventures is capable of generating tremendous interest. Indeed, as an adventure story, the *Odyssey* seems to require very little teaching. But the conscientious teacher will soon find that he can do much to help his students enjoy the *Odyssey* as an adventure story.

Whoever would read the *Odyssey* intelligently must know something of the Trojan War; for ninth graders, who have already studied Greek mythology, the teacher should be able to sketch in this part of the essential background in fifteen or twenty minutes. The teacher will also want to help his students keep a clear understanding of the passage of time in the *Odyssey*. The story actually begins about forty days from the end, despite the fact that Odysseus has been away from home for nearly twenty years. Students should be made to see that Books IX-XII, covering Odysseus' many years in "fableland," are told in flashback; they should also see that if the story were told in straightforward fashion, it would begin at Book IX, run through to the end of Book XII, and then pick up again at Book I. The teacher may ask his students to work out the time scheme; he will certainly want to ask them what difference it makes that the story is told in this manner. Another problem in time arises from the simultaneity of certain actions: for example, the action of Book XIII overlaps that of Book IV, and earlier, while Odysseus sits and weeps on Ogygia, Telemachus is beset at home in Ithaca with the mean band of suitors. The teacher will want his students to see the significance of the fact that the "awakening" of Telemachus and the "reawakening" of Odysseus occur at the same time.

Some insight into the structure of the *Odyssey* will also enhance the book for the student, even as an adventure story. The teacher will certainly not want to lecture on the structure separately, but rather point out the signs of it as he leads his students through the book. Thus, by the beginning of Book V students should be helped to see that they have come to a new part of the Odyssey: the action shifts here from Telemachus and his problems to Odysseus and his. And this observation should warn students to watch out for further evidence of four-book units. Do we find a corresponding shift between Books VIII and IX? And elsewhere? The major division in the *Odyssey* occurs between Books XII and XIII: Books I to XII, the first half of the *Odyssey*, set the scene for the joint action of Odysseus and Telemachus, in the remaining books, to accomplish Odysseus' restoration in Ithaca. Books I to XII complete the poet's treatment of the past; from Book XIII on the action moves swiftly without important breaks or flashbacks.

Student readers of the *Odyssey* will also profit by paying attention to certain recurrent ideas, themes, in the book. The major theme is, of course, the return of Odysseus from Troy to his homeland; but other themes should be noted. A second theme, also of great importance, is the relationship of man to the gods. We discover very early that the world of the *Odyssey* is a moral world, whatever characters in the story may think or assume to the contrary. There is abundant evidence throughout that bad deeds are found out and punished, and that those who persist in evil (e.g., the suitors) come to evil ends. A third theme, related to the second, is hospitality. It seems at first to have to do entirely with manners, with how one should treat visiting strangers in one's own home. But we soon see that it is closely related to the moral-world theme, for Zeus himself protects suppliants and beggars, and those hardy enough to mistreat strangers asking for hospitality draw upon themselves divine wrath. Note, for example, the courteous reception given Telemachus at Pylos and Sparta, and compare with it the suitors' cruel treatment of Odysseus when he comes home disguised as a beggar. A fourth theme that pervades the book is love of home. Telemachus loves his barren and rocky Ithaca, even though it cannot, like Sparta, supply grazing for horses. And

Odysseus' love of home is so strong that he is able to turn his back upon the tempting "paradises" that he visits in his travels. Somewhat similar themes are certain recurrent stories embedded in the *Odyssey*. The student should compare the several stories of returns—Nestor's, Menelaus', and Agamemnon's, several times told or referred to. The story of Orestes serves both as a reproach to Telemachus and as a model for his future behavior.

The teacher must also expect and try to answer a host of questions about customs and institutions in ancient Greece. For that purpose he might want to read *The World of Odysseus*, by M. I. Finley (Meridian paperback), *The Greek Experience*, by C. M. Bowra (Mentor paperback), and *The Greeks*, by H. D. F. Kitto (Penguin). These will not furnish answers to all of the students' questions—nothing will; but they will be of great help.

THE *ODYSSEY* AS A SYMBOLICAL NARRATIVE

Few readers of the *Odyssey* have been content to regard the book as nothing more than an adventure story. Even ninth graders can be expected to find symbolical import in certain episodes, e.g., Odysseus' experience in the land of the Lotus-eaters; and the plot itself—a journey home—has become an archetypal metaphor. The teacher should welcome these insights and explore them with his class, but he should, at the same time, resist the very strong temptation to read the *Odyssey* as an allegory. Although many of Odysseus' adventures lend themselves to symbolical reading, one does the book a disservice in attempting to force such interpretations upon every incident. It is enough to recognize the obvious symbolic import of certain episodes without feeling compelled to treat others in the same way—without wrenching the book to serve any single thesis or moral.

With this warning in mind, the teacher might point out to his students the possibility that the *Odyssey* is about more than one sort of return; in addition to the hero's physical restoration to his home and kingdom of Ithaca, there is his moral and spiritual return or regeneration. The remarks that follow are based mainly upon Denton J. Snider's perceptive reading (*Homer's Odyssey*, Saint

Louis: William Harvey Minor, 1895), with some help from George deF. Lord ("The Odyssey and the Western World," reprinted from *The Sewanee Review*, Summer, 1954, in Charles H. Taylor, ed., *Essays on the Odyssey*, Bloomington: Indiana University Press, 1963).

The *Odyssey* is the story of a man's return home from war—to the ways and institutions of peace and civilization from the brutalizing effects of war. From the beginning of the book we learn that this is a moral world. Zeus himself declares: "What a lamentable thing it is that men should regard *us* as the source of their troubles, when it is their own wickedness that bring them sufferings worse than any which Destiny allots them." This opening remark is particularly important because Odysseus suffers many troubles, and we are obliged from the outset to ask why.

At the beginning of the human action we see Telemachus awakened from childhood to manhood by Pallas Athene, goddess of wisdom. Telemachus soon declares to his shocked mother, who still thinks of him as a little boy, that he is "master in this house." But for all his newfound boldness, he still cannot cope with the horde of greedy suitors, who are eating up his patrimony while they urge Penelope to forget her lost husband and marry one of them. The situation on Ithaca, another direct consequence of war, has grown steadily worse while the rightful ruler has been absent. The deplorable state of things is made abundantly clear in Book II, where Telemachus gets no help from his apathetic countrymen.

Stirred by Athene, Telemachus addresses the assembly and then sails off to Pylos and Sparta in search of news about his father. One should compare the orderly and godfearing community of Pylos (to which Nestor has returned) with the degenerate Ithaca. Again, at Sparta we find a stable and peaceful land in which courtesy and decency are evident. Along with Telemachus, who was only a babe in arms when his father went to war, we learn from Nestor and Menelaus what sort of man Odysseus was. Menelaus is properly outraged over the disgusting behavior of the suitors, and pictures in his own mind Odysseus' vengeance upon them: "It's just as if a deer had put her little unweaned fawns to sleep in a mighty lion's den. . . . Back comes the lion to his lair and hideous carnage falls upon them all."

But Odysseus, when we first meet him, seems anything but a lion. He sits disconsolate on the seashore of Calypso's island, incapable of returning to his "lair." He has long since tired of Calypso and her lovely island and longs now for his own rocky Ithaca. Calypso has even offered him immortality, but Odysseus wants only to realize his potential as a mortal man and to recover his own kingdom. He is incapable of action until Athene intervenes in his behalf; then, at long last, he begins to build a raft on which to leave Ogygia. Note that nothing is new but the impulse: he has always known how to build a raft, and the tools and materials have been there since his first arrival at Ogygia. The point is that Odysseus has suddenly been reawakened, just as his son was awakened, and each by the same agent, the goddess of wisdom. Wisdom can, of course, be personified as a trait or quality, but it is also a mysterious thing within men. It is possible to say that Odysseus has for the past nine years been lacking in the best sort of wisdom (i.e., that he has been behaving foolishly) and that he has just now come back to his senses. From this point his "recovery" begins, but he still has a long way to go, literally and figuratively. He has been stripped of nearly everything: he left Troy with twelve ships and about six hundred men, as well as a great wealth of loot from the defeated city. Now he has no human companion, no ships (he soon loses even his raft to the angry Poseidon), and no wealth. In effect, he is reduced to minimum essentials; he has hit bottom in almost every way, as a pair of similes show us. Even ninth graders can feel the force of these similes of worthlessness—the first on page 96 ("a ball of thistles") and the second on page 97 ("a parched heap of chaff")—and they allow the teacher to show students how epic similes work in context. We cannot help feeling at this point that Odysseus is here passing his greatest trial, and his survival is further indicated by the simile on page 98: "He felt all the relief that a man's children feel when their father, wasted by long agonies abed in the malignant grip of some disease, passes the crisis by god's grace and they know that he will live." Athene is with him again (i.e., he has begun to behave again with his old wisdom), and if he can keep alive the spark of life, he will certainly manage to return home and set things right. The last simile in Book V completes a sort of chain: once ashore Odysseus covers his battered body "as carefully as a lonely crofter in the far corner of an estate buries a glowing brand under the black ashes to keep his fire alive . . ." (p. 101).

At the beginning of Book VI we see the old Odysseus again; he advances on Nausicaa and her maidens "like a mountain lion" (p. 105, and recall Menelaus' simile), and finds in the princess a charming and courageous young woman who knows what charity and hospitality mean. In the court of King Alcinous, in what is surely a symbolic act, Odysseus abases himself before Queen Arete (the Greek word *aretê* means inborn capacities, a man's potential for virtue or honor; see Bowra or Kitto) and begs to be taken home. Then, with the day of his departure appointed, Odysseus tells the story of his years of hardship, from the end of the Trojan War to his landing on Ogygia.

The Cicones, whose city Odysseus plundered, might well have asked him that familiar question put to visiting strangers: "Who are you, sirs? From what port have you sailed over the highways of the sea? Is yours a trading venture; or are you cruising the main on chance, like roving pirates, who risk their lives to ruin other people?" (p. 52, and elsewhere). And what might Odysseus' answer have been? At Ismarus he and his men are still warlike and destructive of peaceful human society. That their adventure was in every way ill-advised we see immediately from Zeus' treatment of Odysseus and his men, who are promptly struck by a storm and driven to the land of the Lotus-eaters. It might be added that they are driven right off the map: the adventures that follow have all the earmarks of a nightmare; they need not be set geographically, despite the efforts of retired British naval officers to map Homer's fableland in the Mediterranean basin. The Lotus proves a great temptation—it might be compared with narcotics which cause men to abandon reality willingly. But Odysseus manages to gather his men and escape.

Odysseus' next adventure, with the Cyclops Polyphemus, is one of his most terrible. Odysseus senses in advance that he is about to find himself "face to face with some being of colossal strength and ferocity, to whom the laws of man and god meant nothing" (p. 145). Actually, this description fits pretty well Odysseus himself, particularly if we see him as the Cicones saw him; it is not too farfetched to regard Polyphemus as a sort of mirror image of Odysseus—of what Odysseus has become after ten years of cruel war. If Odysseus' triumph over Polyphemus represents a triumph over a part of himself—that part which denies the laws of god and man—Odysseus still has a long way to go. His rash pride gets him into more trouble when he chooses to gloat over the blinded giant. Compare his behavior here with his wiser words later to Eurycleia: "Restrain yourself, old dame, and gloat in silence. I'll have no jubilation here. It is an impious thing to exult over the slain. These men [the suitors] fell victims to the hand of heaven and their own infamy. They paid respect to no one who came near them—good men and bad men were alike to them. And now their own insensate wickedness has brought them to this awful end" (p. 338). That sounds almost like the voice of Zeus, in Book I! But just after the defeat of the Cyclops, the will of Zeus and the will of Odysseus are still far apart. Again Odysseus finds that Zeus takes no notice of his sacrifice, and he takes this to mean that Zeus' "mind must already have been full of plans for the destruction of all my gallant ships and my trusty band" (p. 154). Note that Odysseus does not connect his own action and Zeus' as cause and effect, he does not moralize his own story; that task is left to us, who know from Zeus himself that men bring their troubles upon themselves.

Odysseus' experience with the winds given him by Aeolus is puzzling; when he is within sight of his homeland, he falls asleep and his men let the winds escape. It is clear, nonetheless, that Odysseus as leader is responsible for his men and must suffer from their "criminal folly." Aeolus, upon Odysseus' return, sees that Odysseus is a marked man: "Your very presence here is proof of [the god's] enmity," he says to Odysseus (p. 157). From here Odysseus travels to the land of the cannibal Laestrygonians, where, in an episode reminiscent of the visit to Polyphemus, he loses all but his own ship. Next he and his remaining men come to the island of the enchantress Circe, who turns men into swine. After a year Odysseus is ready once again to seek his homeland, but he has instead to visit the land of the dead. Here he gets news of home from the shade of his late mother and an important warning from the prophet Teiresias. The meeting with the other famous Greek heroes—Agamemnon and Achilles—teaches Odysseus two things: from Agamemnon he learns the importance of coming home cautiously; from Achilles he learns that death is no solution to a man's problems, no easy out.

After a return trip to Circe's island and more warnings, Odysseus successfully passes the temptation of the Sirens and steers his way between Scylla and Charybdis. Once again, however, on the island of the Sun God, Odysseus suffers from the folly of his men and learns another important lesson: see his speech to Amphinomus, in Book XVIII (pp. 279-80). When Zeus strikes the ship with a thunderbolt and breaks it to bits, Odysseus clings to a pair of timbers and makes his way as sole survivor to Ogygia.

It is certainly worth pausing at this point to ask what difference it makes that Odysseus' adventures (Books IX-XII) are told by himself. Note that the rest of the story is told by an outside, omniscient narrator.

Odysseus is now ready for the trip from Phaeacia to Ithaca. The Phaeacians' ships are as swift as thought itself and need no steering. Implicit in these remarkable facts is the notion that getting home is largely a matter of willing, not just wanting, to get home. It is also significant that Odysseus sleeps throughout the voyage and awakens on Ithaca, uncertain where he is. If we regard his adventures after Ismarus as a sort of nightmare, it is fitting that he should return from them, back into the charted world of reality, by awakening from sleep. When the disguised Athene meets Odysseus, he is as crafty as ever: indeed, his story is so very good that Athene herself has to admire his cunning. Nonetheless, she scolds Odysseus for failing to recognize her. His reply is particularly interesting: "Goddess," he said, "it is hard for a man to recognize you at sight, . . . for you have a way of donning all kinds of disguises. But this I know well, that you were gracious to me in the old days. . . . Yet when we had sacked Priam's lofty citadel and gone on board our ships, . . . I did not notice you then . . . nor see you set foot on my ship to save me from any of my ordeals. No; I was left to wander through the world with a stricken heart . . ." (p. 210). Shall we say that the goddess—the personification—of wisdom abandoned the man just after the sack of Troy and did not return to him until he came to Phaeacia? Or shall we say that Odysseus took leave of his good sense during the same period? Either way, we are saying the same thing.

Pallas Athene helps to plan the action of the second half of the *Odyssey* just as she did the first half. She also explains why she has sent Telemachus off to Pylos and Sparta. Now she gives Odysseus the appearance of a ragged beggar and sends him to the hut of his loyal swineherd, Eumaeus, where he begins sizing up the situation on Ithaca and making plans for routing his enemies. Odysseus tests Eumaeus with the story of the cloak (pp. 227-28), and Eumaeus passes the test handily; he knows and follows the laws of hospitality, and he is to be trusted as a valuable ally in the great effort before Odysseus.

In Book XV we turn back to Telemachus, who is just now departing from Sparta. With the help of the goddess (i.e., wisely) he escapes the suitors' trap, lands safely, and brings home with him a seer, Theoclymenus, who will later warn the suitors of the horror that awaits them. Odysseus reveals himself to his son, but very carefully: he must know first what sort of man this son is and whether he can be depended upon.

Students will appreciate Rieu's title for Book XVII, "Odysseus Goes to Town." But Odysseus has still more trials to suffer: perhaps nowhere else has he been required to put up with such indignities as here in his own home, where he is abused by his own goatherd and by the meanhearted suitors. It is the new Odysseus, the man recovered from his spiritual and moral weaknesses, who can take such insults quietly while he bides the time to strike. The suitors are nowhere shown in a worse light than when they set the two miserable beggars—Odysseus in disguise and the pathetic Irus—to fight for their food. The bullies laugh at the ignominious defeat of Irus, which prefigures their own (there is much irony here) and ignore a host of warnings. One such warning—Odysseus' speech to young Amphinomus (pp. 279-80)—will bear very close examination: it shows that Odysseus, once out of harmony with the gods, has now become virtually the instrument of Zeus' justice. He has also found the wisdom and the self-control with which to endure all sorts of vile treatment, including having things thrown at him in his own house.

Through these four books (XVII-XX) Odysseus is busy making ready. Along the way he welcomes signs of favor from Zeus (e.g., the thunder on p. 306). Continued provocations by the suitors show them as deserving the terrible fate in store for them and steel Odysseus to the task of slaughtering them. Warnings are there in plenty, but the suitors, hardened sinners, fail to heed them: perhaps none is more striking than their blood-spattered food, which Theoclymenus interprets for them (pp. 313-14).

Book XXI begins the last section of the *Odyssey*. Here again there is a rich strain of irony: little knowing how true his words will prove, Leodes, who tries and fails to string the great bow, says: "This bow will break the heart and be the death of many a champion here" (p. 320). At the same time, Odysseus reveals himself to his two faithful servants. When Odysseus, still in disguise, strings the great bow easily, the suitors are concerned only for their reputations; they continue their crude jesting at Odysseus' expense up to the moment when he signals Telemachus that the battle is to begin (p. 327). Even after he kills Antinous (and students may be asked why Antinous should be the first victim), the suitors remain ignorant of what is happening. But their fate is fixed, and not even the treachery of Melanthius can save them. Athene herself, in the guise of Mentor, is there to help Odysseus. Note that after the battle, when Eurycleia finds "Odysseus among the corpses of the fallen, spattered with blood and filth, like a lion when he comes from feeding on some farmer's bullock" (p. 338), he has to restrain her from gloating over the slain. Thus we have come back full circle, to the image, or prediction, of Menelaus early in the *Odyssey*.

Students might well be asked why Penelope is the last to learn that her husband is home. Like Odysseus, she is cautious: husband and wife are a perfect match. Students will also find valuable Odysseus' summary of his adventures on page 349.

Now, at last, justice has been done, but it is still a violent sort of justice, and the suitors' friends are already planning revenge. How is the bloodletting that began twenty years before at Troy to be stopped? Without courts of law there is little difference between justice and revenge. The answer is a divine act of oblivion. Zeus wipes the bitter enmity and its causes from the memory of men, and says: "Let the mutual goodwill of the old days be restored, and let peace and plenty prevail" (p. 363). Note also the last sentence in the *Odyssey*: "And presently Pallas Athene, . . . still using Mentor's form and voice for her disguise, established peace between the two contending forces." Odysseus is not only king again in Ithaca; he is also, once again, master of himself and therefore fit to rule his fellow men in peace.

THE *ODYSSEY* AS EPIC

When students have finished their reading of the *Odyssey*, the teacher will certainly want to tell them that it is an epic and, perhaps, point out some of its epic features. These are listed and defined in standard handbooks on literature (e.g., *The Study of Literature*, by Barnet, Berman, and Burto, Boston: Little, Brown, 1960), but the definitions will be meaningful only when the student has something to tie them to. Some such terms may, of course, have been introduced along the way; for example, students will already have seen the workings of *epic simile* in context, and there is no better way to become acquainted with such conventions. They will also have a very good idea of what *in medias res* means, whether they have heard that term or not. They can now be introduced to the terms *invocation* and *epic question* (or *argument*). *Epic formulas* should be easy to explain, for students will surely have noticed certain repeated elements as they went through the book. They are ready, too, to talk about *divine machinery*, the *visit to the underworld*, and the *epic action*. In Odysseus himself they have an *epic hero*, and if they know anything of other epics, they may want to compare him, as a sort of domestic epic hero, with the more familiar warlike hero, such as Achilles. How much of all this the teacher should introduce is up to the individual teacher, who knows his own class.

The following is a list of important gods and men in the *Odyssey* with pronunciation guide, identification, and, in the case of the gods, their Roman counterparts.

Gods

Zeus	(zoos)	Ruler of the gods on Mt. Olympus (Jupiter).
Poseidon	(po sy' don)	God of the sea (Neptune).
Athene	(ath ee' na)	Goddess of wisdom (Minerva).
Hermes	(her' meez)	Messenger of the gods (Mercury).
Aphrodite	(af ro dy' tee)	Goddess of love and beauty (Venus).
Hephaestus	(he fes' tus)	God of metalworking, Aphrodite's husband (Vulcan).
Ares	(a' reez)	God of war, Aphrodite's lover (Mars).
Artemis	(ar' te mis)	Goddess of hunting, chastity, sudden death (Diana).
Apollo	(a poll' o)	God of light, art, and medicine.

The household of Odysseus

Odysseus	(o diss' us)	King of Ithaca (Ulysses).
Penelope	(pe nel' o pee)	His wife.
Telemachus	(te lem' a kus)	His son.
Laertes	(lay air' teez)	His father.
Eurycleia	(you ree kly' a)	His old nurse.
Eumaeus	(you mee' us)	His faithful swineherd.
Philoetius	(fil ee' ti us)	His faithful cowherd.
Mentor	(men' tor)	His friend, an Ithacan noble.

The enemies of Odysseus

Antinous	(an tin′ o us)	Leader of Penelope's suitors.
Eury-machus	(you rim′ a kus)	Another leading suitor.
Melan-thius	(mel an′ thi us)	Disloyal goatherd of Odysseus.
Melantho	(mel an′ tho)	Disloyal maidservant of Penelope.

The journey of Telemachus (Books III, IV, XV)

Nestor	(nes′ tor)	King of Messenia (mes see′ ni a) living at Pylos.
Peisis-tratus	(py sis′ tra tus)	Nestor's son.
Menelaus	(men e lay′ us)	King of Lacedaemon (las e dee′-mon) living at Sparta.
Helene	(hel ēn′)	Wife of Menelaus, "Helen of Troy."
Theocly-menus	(thi o klee′men us)	Fugitive seer from Argos.

The wanderings of Odysseus (Books IX-XII)

1. The raid on the Cicones (sik o′ neez).
2. The adventure with the Lotus-eaters.
3. The adventure with Polyphemus (polly fee′ mus), a Cyclops (sy′ klops).
4. The visit with Aeolus (ee′ o lus), keeper of the winds.
5. The attack by the Laestrygonians (les tri go′ ni uns), giant cannibals.
6. The adventure with Circe (sir′ see), a nymph of the isle of Aeaea (ee ee′a).
7. The descent into the Underworld, the kingdom of Hades (hay′ deez):
    a. Elpenor (el pee′ nor), Odysseus' shipmate.
    b. Teiresias (ty ree′ si us), blind prophet of Thebes.

    c. Anticleia (an ti kly′ a), Odysseus' mother.

    d. Agamemnon (a ga mem′ non), king of Mycenae, Mene-
       laus' brother.

    e. Achilles (a kill′ eez), greatest of Greek warriors.

8. The adventure with the Sirens.

9. The voyage between Scylla (sill′ a) and Charybdis (ka rib′-
dis).

10. The island of the cattle of Hyperion (hy peer′ ion), the sun-
god.

11. The stay with Calypso (ka lip′ so), a nymph on the isle of
Ogygia (o jee′ ja).

12. The arrival of Phaeacia (fee a′ sha); the meeting with Nausicaa (naw sik′ a ya), daughter of King Alcinous (al sin′ o us) and
Queen Arete (a ree′ tee).

STUDY QUESTIONS

BOOKS I-IV

1. What great war has preceded the events of the *Odyssey?* Why
is it helpful to approach the story with some knowledge of this
war? (Students may want to consult Edith Hamilton's *Mythology*,
a Mentor paperback, pp. 178-201, for a brief account of the Trojan
War.)

2. How does the *Odyssey* begin? Does the discussion among the
gods serve to make us less interested in the human characters?
What are they discussing?

3. Which of the gods is trying to destroy Odysseus and which is
trying to help him? On the basis of what you already know about
Poseidon, how do you think he might be able to interfere with
Odysseus' journey? What qualities or attributes are associated with
Pallas Athene? Will Odysseus have need of these qualities on his
journey home?

4. Describe the situation that Odysseus may expect to find when
he returns to Ithaca. Why hasn't Telemachus tried to drive off the
suitors? Why hasn't Penelope married again?

5. What advice does Athene give Telemachus? Why does the
goddess appear in disguise? Is she, perhaps, testing Telemachus to

find out whether he is as good a man as his father? Have there been any indications that Telemachus could pass such a test?

6. How does Telemachus profit from his visits with Nestor and Menelaus? What does he learn about his father? What does he learn about the qualities which distinguish a true hero?

7. What plans do the suitors make for preventing Telemachus' journey home? What reason do they have for wishing him out of the way?

8. Odysseus has not yet appeared in these first four books of the *Odyssey,* but several characters have already spoken about his adventures. Which characters have a high opinion of him? What qualities are we prepared to recognize in Odysseus when he finally does appear? Write a paragraph describing Odysseus from the reactions of others. Remember that you have not yet met him; you must base your description solely on what other characters think.

BOOKS V-VIII

1. In Book V the scene and characters suddenly change. Is this change difficult or easy to follow? Why?

2. Describe Calypso's island. Who decides that Odysseus should be given his freedom? What does Calypso offer Odysseus in order to make him stay?

3. Comment upon Odysseus' reaction to the gift of immortality. Why does he refuse it? Is the refusal (a) because he wants to return to Penelope, or (b) because he has little respect for the gods, or (c) because human life, with all its dangers and disappointments, is still the most valuable kind of existence?

4. How does Odysseus leave Calypso's island? How is his voyage disturbed? Who comes to his rescue?

5. Comment upon the characterization of Nausicaa. In what respects does she resemble any other teen-age girl? What qualities set her apart from others?

6. Why does Nausicaa remain to talk with Odysseus after the other girls run away? How would you describe Odysseus' speech to Nausicaa? Is it sincere, cunning, flattering? Why doesn't Nausicaa bring Odysseus to the palace herself?

7. What was considered the proper way to receive guests in the ancient world? Do the Phaeacians demonstrate these principles of hospitality when they receive Odysseus? Why does Odysseus first approach the queen instead of the king?

8. What is a minstrel? Of what does the minstrel Demodocus sing? Does the song about Ares and Aphrodite imply a disrespectful attitude toward the gods, or is there simply enjoyment of the comic situation without disrespect?

9. When Demodocus sings about the fall of Troy, Odysseus immediately begins to weep. Why? Does such conduct fit your conception of a hero? Does Homer imply that this is a weakness, or would his conception of the hero include such behavior?

BOOKS IX-XII

1. Who were the Lotus-eaters? What happens to the men who are tempted to eat the Lotus? What do you think the Lotus is intended to symbolize?

2. Describe the Cyclops. In his encounter with Polyphemus, Odysseus demonstrates that he is daring, clever, and boastful. Note specific incidents which illustrate each of these qualities.

3. Who was Aeolus? What was his gift? Contrast the behavior of Odysseus to that of his crew with respect to the bag of winds. Can you justify the calamity which follows?

4. Describe the Laestrygonians. Is Odysseus cowardly when he does not return to fight these creatures? Or is he prudent?

5. Circe has the power to change young men into swine. Do you think that Homer intended us to find any symbolic meaning in this transformation? What is your interpretation? How did Odysseus manage to outwit Circe? Did he require any assistance?

6. Identify each of the following: Hades, Persephone, Teiresias, Agamemnon, Achilles, Elpenor, Tantalus, Sisyphus, and Heracles. How does Odysseus succeed in getting the spirits to gather about him?

7. Achilles, the most famous Greek hero, died gloriously on the field of battle. When Odysseus meets him in Hades, he tells Achilles that his fame still lives among men: "For you, Achilles, Death

should have lost its sting." But Achilles replies, "Spare me your praise of Death. Put me on earth again, and I would rather be a serf in the house of some landless man . . . than king of all these dead men that have done with life." Comment upon this exchange. Does Achilles still value heroism, or is he calling the whole concept of heroism into question?

8. When Odysseus' ship must pass by the alluring Sirens, he orders all his men to put wax in their ears. Why doesn't Odysseus put wax in his own ears?

9. Homer tells us practically nothing about the appearance of the Sirens or the source of their attraction. The reader is left to interpret. What do you think the Sirens are intended to symbolize?

10. The journey between Scylla and Charybdis puts Odysseus in a hopeless situation. He has been told by a goddess that it is not in his power to prevent the monster from destroying six of his men. Yet, when the time comes, he draws his sword anyway. Is this gesture admirable or merely foolish?

11. Has Odysseus learned anything from the adventures related in Books IX-XII? Is his character changed in any way as a result of these experiences? As you read on, try to decide whether any aspect of Odysseus' behavior in Phaeacia or Ithaca can be attributed to this past experience.

BOOKS XIII-XVI

1. Describe Odysseus' landing at Ithaca. Who brought him there? How do you explain the fact that Odysseus no longer recognizes his own kingdom?

2. Who was Eumaeus? Why does Odysseus tell him a long fictitious story about his origin and adventures? Why doesn't he tell the truth?

3. What does Odysseus learn about the fortunes of his wife and child during the twenty years that he has been away?

4. How does Telemachus escape the suitors' plot to murder him? Why does he visit Eumaeus as soon as he returns to Ithaca?

5. Some readers have felt that the reunion of Odysseus and Telemachus is lacking in warmth. Do you agree? Is the fact that

they had been separated since Telemachus was an infant sufficient explanation for the way that Homer treats this scene?

6. What plan does Odysseus devise for overthrowing the suitors?

BOOKS XVII-XX

1. What is the situation in the palace when Odysseus arrives there?

2. Odysseus assumes the disguise of a beggar so that he can test the loyalty of his subjects. How do each of the following meet this test: Melanthius, Antinous, Irus, Eurymachus?

3. What indignities must Odysseus suffer at the hands of the suitors? Is he wise to accept these meekly, or should he have fought back at the first provocation?

4. Who is Eurycleia? How does she discover Odysseus' true identity? Why does Odysseus insist that she remain silent?

5. What contest does Penelope propose in order to help her select a new husband? Does this indicate that she is no longer faithful to Odysseus? Or is she confident that none of the suitors will be able to meet her conditions?

BOOKS XX-XXIV

1. What is an *omen*? What omens indicate that disaster will befall the suitors?

2. What success do the suitors have with Odysseus' bow? What is their reaction when a mere beggar requests an opportunity to try his skill? How does he fare with the bow?

3. How does Odysseus announce his true identity to the suitors? Why did he wait this long before attempting to punish them?

4. Are the suitors all guilty of the crimes they are accused of? Does Homer present any of them sympathetically?

5. Describe the scene in the great banquet hall as Odysseus prepares to take his revenge. How many men take Odysseus' side? Who are they?

6. Which goddess appears to support Odysseus? Does she actually take part in the fighting? What is her disguise?

7. Whom among the suitors does Odysseus spare? Why? How are the servingwomen punished?

8. How does Penelope react to the news that Odysseus has arrived? Does her reaction surprise you? How does she outwit Odysseus in an effort to prove his identity? Has any other character in the *Odyssey* succeeded in outwitting Odysseus?

9. How do the families of the suitors react when they learn about the slaughter? What is the result of the battle between Odysseus and the suitors' families?

10. Who finally restores the peace in Ithaca?

Appendix:
A Note on Teaching
Slow-Learning Students

EDWARD B. JENKINSON

The majority of teachers who tested the units in this volume believe, with members of the state-appointed Committee on English for Slow-Learning Students and the staff of the English Curriculum Study Center, that slow learners should have the opportunity to read and discuss novels normally assigned only to their more academically talented classmates. Therefore, no separate literature sequence was designed for the slower students even though the staff of the Center originally planned, and at first attempted, to develop three distinct courses of study—for academically talented, average, and slow-learning students. The staff discontinued its search for novels that fit the familiar catch-phrase, "high in interest and low in reading level," when it learned from successful pilot-school teachers what slow-learning students could read and discuss.

By their responses to such novels as *The Light in the Forest*, *Shane*, and *The Pearl*, slow learners demonstrated that they need not be fed a steady diet of third-rate literature and watered-down classics, so typical of many existing programs for the slow track. Instead, slow learners have proved that they can read and discuss almost all of the novels in the suggested novel sequence (see page 145) and almost all of the novels on the additional reading list (see page 254). Slow learners do not progress through the sequence in the same time as their more talented classmates (some may take five school years to get as far as *To Kill a Mockingbird*), nor do they read all the suggested works. In instances in which they cannot read all of the novels by themselves, they have proved that they can participate intelligently in spirited discussions after the teacher reads particularly difficult passages of the novels to them.

Implicit in the reports from successful pilot-school teachers is a key word—*respect*. The successful teachers do not merely glance at a novel and discard it by sneering, "My slow kids could never read that." The successful teachers do not give their slow-learning students books labeled "reading" and filled with third- and fourth-rate short stories, humorous verse, and juvenile illustrations. Instead, the successful teachers approach their classes with respect for the minds of their students, and help develop those minds by giving the students a steady diet of respectable literature. The successful teachers know many novels, short stories, and plays and can choose work wisely for their classes. The successful teachers prepare their students to read a novel, help them hurdle the obstacles of difficult words, and select questions from the units that would stimulate lively discussion.

Looking upon most books with suspicion, most slow learners need to be prepared to read a book since they are convinced that lurking between the covers are hundreds of demons—difficult words. Most slow learners need to be "sold" on a book before they will even attempt to read it. Conditioned to advertising, most slow learners need a commercial that persuades them to buy the product.

Successful teachers of slow learners followed four major steps in teaching books like *The Light in the Forest*. (1) They prepared their students to read a novel by giving them an oral or written introduction like the one printed below. (2) They removed the obstacles —hard words—by writing the difficult words on the board before the assignment, by pronouncing them, and by giving students the contextual meanings of the words. (3) They guided students in their reading by giving them, in advance of the assignment, selected questions from the units. (4) They read difficult passages aloud.

Pilot-school teachers reported that slow students were eager to read *The Light in the Forest* after they were read an introduction like this:

The Lonely White Indian*

True Son has two families, but he belongs to neither. Thinking he is an Indian because he lived with the Delawares for eleven years, he tries to escape after he is returned to his white family. Disliking the ways of the white man, he is unhappy with his real parents and longs to return to his Indian family. But before he can escape from white captivity, the ways of the white man rub off on him. He is no longer the Indian he wants to be, nor is he the white man he needs to be to live in white civilization. True Son stands alone.

True Son has the strength of an Indian and the weakness of the white man. Taught to think like an Indian, he can until his white training interferes. Although he hates most white men, thoughts of one white boy make him temporarily forget his strong Indian ties long enough to betray his Indian friends and family.

True Son does find *The Light in the Forest,* but he must leave it behind. In finding it, he introduces you to a kind of Indian life that you do not see on television. In longing for his Indian family and the rich free life of the Delawares, he shows you why his tribe learned to hate white men and why it warred against white settlers.

The frustrated white Indian introduces you to the wonderful world of nature that he cannot long enjoy. In simple words he tells you why he thinks the white man is not always right and why the Indians whom he loves are sometimes wrong. He shares with you his love of freedom, his belief in a Great Being, and his hatred for the civilization that white men forced upon the Indian forest. He proves that white men could be as cruel as Indians in the 1760's, and he unwittingly demonstrates why he cannot belong to either his white or Indian family.

True Son is unforgettable. His troubles become your troubles; his joys become your joys; his friends become your friends. His ideas of Indian life may differ from yours, for he knows the Indians for what they are and for what they believe in. His idea of living with white men may differ from yours, for he sees white civilization from a different point of view. His failure results from his inability

* From "Study Aids for *The Light in the Forest*" by Edward B. Jenkinson. Copyright 1964 by L. W. Singer Company. Reprinted by permission of L. W. Singer Company and of the author.

to bring two different worlds together. But even in failure, he is a memorable character.

His is a confused—but sometimes happy—world. Filled with the talkative but purposeful Half Arrow, the stern but admirable Cuyloga ,the fierce but sensitive Thitpan, the bumbling but likable Gordie, and the cruel but helpless Uncle Wilse, the world of True Son rotates on twin axes--hate and love, misunderstanding and understanding.

True Son stands alone. But after you read about his fate, you will probably stand with him on the threshold of understanding why a boy of fifteen is torn between the carefree world of teen-age freedom and the troubling world of adult responsibility.

Successful pilot-school teachers reported that it takes a great deal of time to teach a book like *The Light in the Forest,* but the student's sense of accomplishment makes it well worth while.

Slow-learning students can, with help, profit from the units in this volume. They may never be able to read Shakespeare, but they should not be denied the privilege of trying. They may not respond to Shakespeare on the printed page, but they will respond to his language as they listen to records. They need not settle for less than good literature when they are given considerate instruction.